'FLASH…the HUMBLE HERO'

by

Lee Carey

'FLASH…the Humble Hero' is a work of fiction. Any references to real people, events, establishments, organizations, or locales are only intended to give the fiction a sense of reality and authenticity. *'Flash…the Humble Hero'* is the sequel to *'Gabby…All About Me'*.

Copyright 2013 by **Sandfiddler Publishing**

FIRST PAPERBACK EDITION

Lee's website: LeeCarey-author.com

*Also available in Ebook on Amazon.com

ABOUT THE AUTHOR

Lee Carey lives with his loving wife/editor, Kay, in Virginia Beach at Sandbridge Beach, a small coastal town. His writing career began in '99. To date, Lee has penned eight novels and two compilations of short stories. He enjoys writing, golf, surfing, and hanging out on the beach with Kay and friends.

Lee's attitude is: 'Paddle hard for every wave…it might be your best ride.' His sign-off slogan: 'Keep smilin…'

Other books by Lee Carey: 'Gabby…All About Me' – 'Pets in Paradise' – 'The Thin Line' – 'Dawn's Death' – 'Justice in Hollowell County' – 'If Bullfrogs Had Wings' – 'Out of the Rough' – 'Beach Shorts' – 'If You Dance…You Will Pay the Fiddler'. **All are available on Amazon.**

ACKNOWLEDGEMENTS

Any novel is comprised of multiple facets during the writing process. As expected, many months filled with long hours, together with numerous edits and changes, are the norm. And, I readily admit my works would be a pathetic mess if not for the dedication and invaluable assistance from my wonderful wife, Kay, who serves as my editor. (I should have applied myself better in school.) Her comments and suggestions benefit my stories almost as much as her tireless encouragement. "Thank you, Sweetheart, for all you do. I love you."

That said…an author would flounder like a fish on the beach if not for special friends/readers. Many people read the novels, period. They choose not to review for whatever reason, and move on. However, the truly blessed author has readers who write a review, become a friend through today's social media, and feel free to share valuable comments from their perspective. This author is blessed. "Thank you all, you know who you are." (You might even find you're a character.)

There is another step many of these friends/readers/and fellow authors take that greatly benefits this author. One is…they are willing to read my pre-published novel and post a review. And they share news or special offers about my works with their friends on social media. I recall from my days of owning a business, when it came to advertising – 'The best advertising is word of mouth.' "So, let me say to all of you who assist me in this manner, I appreciate you."

With the publication of 'Flash…the Humble Hero' I would be remiss not to mention my friends who have shared their time to read and review. So, to Larry, Joe, Patricia, Audrey, Beverly, Gene, Pauline, Mikki, Jennifer, Phyllis, Toni Lynn, Deb, and Kathy. 'Thank you!'

My sincere hope is that this novel is enjoyable and fun to all who read it. And I would be overjoyed if you felt led to write a review on Amazon, however, if not, I am still grateful you shared your time to read my scribblings. Keep smilin'… Lee

PROLOGUE

Wicked laughter erupted from the scraggly, forty-year-old man as he aimed the remote at the small TV and blackened the screen. "Yeah, those three are gonna have a New Year alright, 'cept it ain't gonna be 'happy'," David growled.

"Remember, honey, you're still on probation," replied his girlfriend. "Get nabbed, you're gone…for at least three years."

"Ain't no worry, Melody. I told ya this is our year." He scratched his four-day stubble and belched. "My mama always said, 'make hay while the sun shines', and that's what we're gonna do."

"You got a plan?" Melody asked, lighting the filter-less cigarette dangling from her thin, pale lips.

David shot her an icy stare. "Yeah, and you're in it, woman."

Melody sucked in a long drag and quickly blew white smoke from the corner of her mouth, her beady, grey eyes locked on his. "Fine." She pushed her boney frame from the rickety chair and stepped in front of David. "That means I have a say-so about the plan."

With a wave of his hand, David mumbled, "Get outta my face. Sure, it'll be *our* plan. Gonna take both of us to pull it off."

After a final pull on the cigarette, Melody stepped over and stubbed it out in the butt-filled ashtray on the small end table. "Okay. My first suggestion…we find out where this beach is. I ain't never heard of Sandbridge, and you ain't neither."

He pointed to the phone while a smile revealed crooked, yellowed teeth. "Think you could call information? Ask for a rental company at Sandbridge in Virginia Beach," David spoke as if talking to a six-year-old. "Then, you call them, and ask how to get there."

"Don't you dare talk down to me! I'll call, but first you'll tell me the plan." Melody sat beside him on the broken-down sofa and lit another cigarette.

Thirty minutes later, David stood. "What'cha think?"

Melody ran skinny fingers through her unkempt dark hair. "What's our back-up plan?"

David chuckled. "Back-up plan?"

"Yeah. In case something goes wrong."

"Make the phone call."

CHAPTER 1

Scooter turned his Datsun 240Z onto Sandfiddler Road and headed south. "Gabby, we're home!"

The mixed black lab sat up in the passenger seat and peered out of the window at the gently rolling Atlantic. *It's so good to be back, Scooter. Sandbridge is much better than New York City. I'll never get those kooky people in Central Park out of my head. Gee!*

"Whatever. Now don't bug me about taking little Flash for a walk on the beach without me."

Why not? I'll look after him. He needs to see our beach from a dog's viewpoint, Scoot. We won't go way down to the pier. I was thinking we'd hang around in front of the cottage. Okay?

"We'll discuss this later. Go ahead and wake up Flash. The little fellow has a home now. No more scrounging for food in the woods." Scooter turned into the sand-covered driveway. "I can't wait to get into my surf trunks and T-shirt. It's going to feel mighty fine walking barefoot in the sand."

Gabby leaned into the back and nuzzled Flash. The beagle slowly stood and yawned.

Scooter parked and hopped out. After he opened the hatchback, Gabby bailed out and yipped. Scooter lifted Flash and set him gently on the sand. "We're home, Flash. Gabby, take him over on the dune and you all tend to your business while I get the suitcase out."

Okay, Scooter.

Scooter smiled as he watched the beagle walk through sand for the first time. However, he had no problem sniffing around and cocking his leg. When the pups were done, they joined Scooter as he closed the hatchback. "Home again, home again, jiggety-jog," he cheered.

It's our home, Flash. Come on, let's go upstairs.

In ten minutes, Scooter walked out on the deck with a large glass of ice water. Both dogs were already stretched out, relaxing. He gazed across the ocean and inhaled the salty air. "This is paradise," he sang, off-key, into the Carolina blue sky. "Right, Gabby?"

You can say that again, Scooter, just don't sing it, please.

Scooter held his glass high. "Life is really, really good!"

This is better than living alone in the woods as a hungry, flea-bitten stray.

Scooter's glass almost slipped from his hand. He quickly looked at Gabby with puzzled eyes. She shook her head, snapping her gaze over to Flash. *Wow! That's so cool, Scoot!*

Scooter leaned over the deck and poured the cold water on his head. "I'm in really deep now."

The late October afternoon remained unseasonably warm as Scooter and Gabby slowly escorted a timid little beagle up and over the sand dune for his first visit to the coastline. At their backs, a descending sun cast a rosy hue around the edges of small puffy clouds floating lazily above the Atlantic. Sea-warmed wind currents carried hungry gulls low over the shallows, searching for baitfish to dine on as the day surrendered to sunset.

Twenty yards from the tide line, Gabby looked up at Scooter and released a pent-up sigh. *Scoot, I've gotta get in that water, cause I've been away too long. I'll see you slow-pokes later.* With a high-pitched yip, her pace shifted into a gallop, her big paws throwing sand in the air. Flash remained close beside Scooter's leg, shivering and looking back and forth from him to the ocean. Nervousness showed in the puppy's brown eyes. "Hey, little buddy, don't worry," whispered Scooter, stroking the trembling puppy's brown, white, and tan coat. "Won't take long and you'll be out there romping in the waves."

Flash pushed even tighter against Scooter's leg and gazed over the ocean, recalling his unbelievably good fortune of the past week and fully realizing Scooter and Gabby cared for him. He thought, ***I've been taken in by someone who really wants me. Miss Celie said she prayed every day for that to happen.***

The puppy's thoughts were suddenly interrupted when a loud splash sounded as Gabby plunged, belly first, into a cotton-topped wave. When Gabby popped up, she quickly paddled over knee-high swells and hollered, *Yippee! I'm back!*

Flash stepped forward two steps and plopped on his butt, shooting Scooter a wide-eyed stare.

Scooter knelt beside the big-eared pup and placed his tan arm over the panting beagle. "Listen, buddy. Don't worry. It takes some humans a while to get used to the ocean and the breaking waves on their first visit. Listen, here's a little secret about Gabby. You've got to promise not to say a word. Promise?" Scooter wondered if and when the pooch would speak again.

With a cold nose, Flash nuzzled Scooter's knee.

Scooter wasn't surprised Flash didn't speak, considering the awe of the new situation, and he knew it would be better to let everything unfold naturally. "I'll take the nudge to be a 'yes'." Scooter gently stroked Flash's head. "Okay, the day I brought Gabby down here from the shelter, she was excited and itching to hit the water. She raced down and jumped in and found herself suddenly swamped by a wave. After she rolled up onto the sand, she became afraid of the water. Anyway, one day a little girl got caught in a strong undertow and was being pulled out to sea. Gabby bravely dove into the water and rescued her. Now look how she enjoys the waves. She's realized there was nothing to fear except her own fear. So there's no rush. Take your time. You're got a permanent home with us whether you swim or not, Flash. I only want you to be happy."

Flash leaned against his new friend's leg and released a long, deep sigh. *This is not a dream*, he thought.

Scooter proudly watched Gabby paddling over the smaller breaking waves, pause and tread water, waiting for a small swell to ride into shore. Comparing her initial fear of the ocean to the present, he knew one day Flash would also hop the water-fear hurdle, becoming a wave-riding pooch. *I guess life is all about learning to overcome fears and pressing forward...no matter what age we are.*

A small, high-pitched whimper slipped from Flash when he observed Gabby bobbing on the ocean's surface and yipping with excitement. Scooter chuckled. "Waves are small today." However, before the next wave crashed on the shore, two large brown eyes met Scooter's as Flash wagged his brown and white tail at a high speed. "Come on, let's go get our feet wet. The water's still warm." Scooter stood and motioned to Flash. "I'll be right beside you."

Gabby continued doggie-paddling parallel to the shore, enjoying the ups and downs of the gentle swells. Once she spotted Scooter and Flash walking into the shallows, she hollered, *Come on in, the water's perfect.*

Scooter waved at Gabby.

Hey! Dolphins coming this way!

Flash looked up at Scooter as a wave broke, coming up to his close-to-the-ground belly. In a flash, the little beagle yipped, turned, and trotted back to dry sand.

Scooter laughed. "Hey, look out just beyond Gabby and watch the dolphins swimming past. They're really cool to watch."

Flash raised his head, gazing toward the horizon and slowly wagging his tail.

"They're very friendly and won't hurt you. In case you're wondering, they're not fish. They are mammals that live in the ocean and eat fish," said Scooter, watching Gabby ride a small wave onto shore.

When Gabby gracefully landed on the wet sand, she executed a full body shake. Droplets of water flew from her thick fur like a sprinkler. *Oh, it's so good to be home and back in the ocean. Why didn't you come out with me, Flash?*

Scooter said, "Flash is slowly getting used to the waves by watching you swim. I've explained to him about dolphins." Scooter looked down and smiled at his new puppy. "In fact, here comes another school of them, Flash. Look."

Gabby stood on her back legs for a better view. *Yeah, I saw them heading past. See 'em, Flash?*

Since Flash was built lower to the ground than Gabby, he sat on his haunches, raising his head high and peering over the breaking waves. He released two soft yips.

Scooter, I guess that means he sees them. I'm surprised he didn't speak.

"In time he will, Gabby. Remember, this is all brand new to him and much different than the woods." Scooter knelt beside Flash. "See the grey fin sticking out of the water? That's called a dorsal fin. Keep watching, and maybe the dolphins will jump all the way out of the water. That's how they play. Since they're mammals, they can't breathe underwater like fish, so they come up for air."

Scoot, you're getting a bit technical, don't you think?

"Not at all, Baboo. Like you, little Flash is a smart dude."

Flash returned to all four paws and stretched, staring at Gabby.

Scooter chuckled, wishing he knew what was going through the little beagle's mind. "Hey, it'll be dark in a while. Let's walk down the beach and stretch our legs after the long drive. Maybe we'll see a few sandfiddlers scrambling across the sand preparing for cold weather."

The trio headed south in a carefree stroll, with the pooches leading the way while they absorbed the sights and fragrances of the unoccupied coastline. Scooter observed Flash focusing his sensitive nose on various smells drifting in on a gentle southwest breeze. Gabby was prancing through the shallow water, eyeing anything that moved. She had always enjoyed watching shore birds, sea gulls, and breaking waves. For some reason, the solitude of the fall evening directed Scooter's thoughts to Miss Celie's genuine kindness toward all of them. He recalled her battle with cancer and whispered a prayer for her into the open sky.

After covering a quarter mile, Scooter noticed the sun touching down in the bay. "Okay, let's turn around and hit the cottage before it gets dark. Tonight we're having grilled burgers to welcome Flash to Sandbridge Beach. What'cha think, Gabby?"

Gabby's tail wagged so fast her butt wiggled. Her ears shot up, and she came to an abrupt stop. *You bet, Scoot-toot! That's what we had on my first night here.*

Scooter laughed, remembering the lucky day he rescued Gabby from the local SPCA. "Yes, we did, Gabby. Flash, are you up for one of my beach burgers?"

Flash looked up at Scooter with large brown eyes, licked his lips once, and yipped twice.

I'll bet he talks after tasting your awesome burgers, Scoot.

"Thanks for the compliment, Gabby. But don't fret, Flash will talk when he's ready. Maybe he's not as vocal as you are. Remember why I named you Gabby?"

Yeah.

Scooter broke into a quick jog, followed by his companions. "Last one to the cottage has to wash dishes," he hollered.

Gabby yipped loudly as she zipped by Scooter. *Won't be me!*

With stubby legs, Flash did his best to keep up with Gabby as he trudged past Scooter, throwing up puffs of sand behind him like dust. Scooter chuckled. "Life's good."

CHAPTER 2

Twinkling stars dotted the black sky like diamonds, appearing to be only inches above the dark, swelling waves. Scooter gazed, allowing this natural beauty to soothe his mind and help put his new life as an author in order. *It's gonna be a change.*

Scooter took a long pull on his sweet tea and looked at his two pooches. Gabby lay stretched out, deep in sleep on her back, four paws pointing toward the heavens. Flash was curled in a little ball, his head resting on big paws while his brown eyes watched Scooter's every move. His coal-black nose wiggled and twitched, inhaling the aroma of charcoal cubes getting hot in the grill.

Once the coals became white-hot, Scooter placed two large and two small hamburger patties on the grill's rack and slowly settled into his sun-bleached canvas beach chair. After releasing a long sigh of exhaustion, he sipped his tea. Flash pushed up to his feet and moved over beside the chair and whispered, *I'm glad you and Gabby found me, Scooter.*

Scooter felt a tender tug on his heart. He reached down and gently placed his hand on the young beagle's head and thought back to the day they found Flash in the woods beside the Pony Diner on the Eastern Shore. This little pup now sat calmly beside him, healthy and loved. Weeks of living unwanted in the woods had taken a severe physical toll on him. When Gabby had picked up his smell, she wisely used her instincts and patience to lure him out for small pieces of fried chicken. Within several minutes, Gabby had persuaded him to relax and not be afraid. Scooter knew it was not only a special day for Flash, but also for dear Miss Celie. Flash needed to know how she played a major role in his survival.

Scooter continued stroking Flash's head and nursed his tea. "Buddy, we're glad we found you, too. You know, Miss Celie was very important during the weeks you were trying to survive and stay alive. Every day she put out scraps and water for you. Remember how happy she was to see you today? She even cried happy tears to know you were healthy and clean. That kind-hearted lady deserves most of the credit for you being here with us, Flash. Next time we go to New York, we'll stop by and see her. Okay?"

Flash gave Scooter's hand a nose nudge. *She would sit on the steps and watch me eat. She said that one day someone would come along who loved me and would take me to a nice home. I didn't understand, but now I do, Scooter.*

Scooter wondered, besides Flash feeling more comfortable, what prompted him to speak. Maybe it was the perfect atmosphere of the night, knowing he was with them and this was now the new home promised by Miss Celie. Scooter nodded, stood, and flipped the burgers. "Gabby spent six weeks on her own before she was picked up and put in the dog pound. She's told me how hard those times were. I'm sure yours was no different."

Flash bowed his head. In a soft voice, he said, *My sister was with me when the people threw us in the ditch beside the road. At least we were together. But a few days later, she crossed the road because she smelled something to eat. We were starving. She found a box of chicken bones in the ditch. She was so excited to bring them back... she didn't see the big truck coming when she crossed the road.* Flash became silent.

Scooter sat and lightly rubbed the puppy's neck. "I'm so sorry, Flash."

The brown-eyed pup looked up at Scooter with glistening eyes. *Scooter, if my sister had been with me on the day you and Gabby found me, would you have brought her here, too?*

Swallowing quickly to keep his throat from closing, Scooter nodded. "Yes, Flash. We wouldn't have separated you two. It might not help much, but I know she's happy you found a good home."

Even though I can't see her, I still talk to her. Today when we were walking down the beach, I told her how much she would have liked you and Gabby. I'll always miss her. Right?

"Yes, but that's normal, Flash. Just remember, she's now in a very beautiful and extraordinary land, just for pets."

She is?

"Yep. It's called Paradise, and all kinds of different animals and birds live there and get along with each other. In fact, I believe it's even neater than here at the beach. So whenever you feel like talking to her, you do it."

Flash raised his head and gave Scooter's hand a gentle lick. *Thanks, Scooter.*

Scooter stood and placed the burgers on the plate. Gabby's snoot picked up the familiar smell, and she was on her feet faster than a lightning strike. *Oh, goodie! Time to eat. I'm starving.*

Holding the plate high over Gabby's head, Scooter replied, "Welcome back, sleepy head. Sure you wouldn't rather sleep through supper?"

Gabby gazed at the plate of her favorite goodies. *Heck, no! I want a beach burger. Oh, how about a slice of cheese...please?*

"Okay, let's eat and then turn in for a good night's rest. We're all hungry and pooped. Tomorrow's a new day."

Scooter broke each small patty into smaller pieces for the dogs' bowls, hoping Gabby would remember the improved manners he had taught her. No doubt little Flash would dive into his like a wild dog, but that was understandable, seeing he had spent weeks scavenging for survival. So if Gabby performed in orderly fashion, Flash might learn some manners. Feeling generous, Scooter split a slice of cheese and dropped pieces over their burgers. When he glanced down at his feet, there was Gabby, peering up, tongue out and tail fanning from side to side. The little beagle remained stretched out beside the computer desk, head on paws, big brown eyes observing. Scooter announced, "Okay, time to eat. Remember, no one will take it from you, so go easy. Come on, Flash, try my beach burger."

After he placed the feed bowls on opposite sides of their water bowls, Scooter straightened and watched the pooches approach. Instantly, Gabby's muzzle disappeared into her bowl. Flash eased up, sniffed the burger, and then looked up at Scooter with puzzled brown eyes.

"Go ahead, buddy. Help yourself. That's your burger," replied Scooter, taken aback by the pup's actions.

Gabby gobbled in an acceptable fashion, but still a mite fast. After her bowl was licked spotless, she hovered over her water bowl and slurped. Finished, she looked at Flash, paused, and settled on the floor, her twinkling eyes riveted on him.

Flash picked up a small piece of burger, held it gently between his front teeth, and looked at Scooter. "Eat it, Flash." In slow motion, the beagle chewed, gazing out the sliding glass door into darkness. After chewing to his satisfaction, he stepped over and politely lapped a little bit of water. He returned to the food bowl, repeated the same step, and again returned to his water dish. The slow, structured process continued.

Scooter's lips tightened into a smile while he finished preparing his burger and observing Gabby's shocked reaction. Her ears were up, and wide-open brown eyes watched Flash's unhurried, deliberate moves. Scooter decided to remain silent and see how long Gabby could remain quiet. Scooter opened a cold Coke and took a long sip. Gabby broke her silence. *What in the world are you doing, Flash?*

The contented beagle stopped chewing and turned toward Gabby. ***Eating.***

Scooter took a seat at the table to enjoy the preview of what was certain to be a rewarding treat in pooch behavior. Knowing Gabby was a pro with snappy comebacks, he wondered if this event might inspire Flash to utilize more of his verbal skills.

Gabby remained motionless, still amazed with Flash's composed routine. *No, you're not. You're playing with it. What's with the little nibbles? You're holding a normal-sized chunk between your teeth and then working it until little pieces fall back into the bowl. That's bad manners. If you're going to eat...EAT.*

Scooter swallowed a bite of burger and replied, "Looks like Miss Celie taught Flash some table manners, Baboo."

Gabby broke her stare from Flash and turned toward Scooter. *What he's doing is not polite manners, Scoot. It's silly.* She returned her gaze to Flash. *The size of the food is not important, as long as it fits in your mouth. And, besides, after he trims a piece to his satisfaction, it takes him a month of Sundays to chew it.*

Flash continued his technique of nibbling a nugget and sipping water as if he were dining alone.

Scooter chuckled, deciding to stoke the fire. "Gabby, maybe you could learn to chew slower and enjoy it more."

After crawling a few feet closer to Flash, she stopped. *I eat at a normal pace for dogs.* She pointed a paw at Flash. *What you're seeing is not normal. And what's with taking a little drink of water after each piece? You're supposed to finish eating and THEN wash it down. Flash, you beat all I've ever seen.*

The beagle finished another sip of water and returned to his bowl of burger. Before picking up another piece of grilled delight, he said, ***This is how our mammy taught us to eat, Gabby.***

Gabby pawed her muzzle, rolled her eyes, and released a deep sigh. *I'm pretty sure your mammy did not enjoy you and your siblings spending an hour pulling on her teats, Flash. I know mine didn't. No, admit it, you're a slowpoke. It's that simple.*

Scooter laughed so hard Coke trickled from his nostrils. Both pooches looked up at him. "I'm sorry," he said, wiping his face. "The teats thing caught me off guard."

Gabby yipped. *Well, it's true. My mammy gave us a certain amount of time, and then she cut off the milk and pawed us away. The purpose of eating is not to see how long we can drag it out; nope, we eat for out health and survival...period.* Gabby shook her head. *Eat any way you want, Flash. I'm guessing your burger is probably cold by now.* Her head settled on her large front paws.

After finishing off his burger, Scooter wiped his mouth and drained his Coke. "Well, even though I grilled those burgers, I can say they were delicious. I'm about to pop."

Gabby mumbled, *Yeah, it was good, Scoot-toot. Thanks.*

I like these, Scooter. Thank you.

"You're welcome. Glad you enjoyed them. It makes a cook proud to receive compliments." He leaned over, inspecting Flash's bowl and finding a few remaining pieces. "Are you finished, Flash?"

The floppy-eared pooch nodded. *I'm full.* He turned toward Gabby. *You want the rest, Gabby?*

Before his last word was out, the critical mixed lab was up with her muzzle buried in the bowl. With one gathering swipe of her tongue and a quick gobble, the bowl was spotless. *Thanks, Flash. You're all right, buddy. We're gonna get along just fine.*

Scooter picked up their food bowls and carried his plate into the kitchen. "Okay, Gabby, you and Flash go downstairs and do your math. And don't go roaming. Stay in the side yard. It's time we hit the sack."

Since sleeping ranked near the top of Gabby's favorite things, she hopped over in front of the sliding door. *No problem. I'm worn out. Come on, Flash, time to go to math class.*

Flash looked up from his water bowl, crystal droplets hanging from his white chin. *What's math class?*

Scooter placed his hand on the door handle but hesitated, anticipating Gabby's definition.

You know, Flash. We do number one...and then number two...and that's three. Got it?

Flash's head leaned to the side as he looked at her. *No.*

Scooter pulled the sliding door open. "Hurry back." As the two pooches stepped out onto the deck, he heard Gabby. *Just watch me, Flash. All animals do math.*

Scooter was brushing his teeth when he heard Gabby's bark at the door. He rinsed, spit, and hustled out and opened the sliding door. "Did everything come out okay?"

Finer than frog's hair.

"Good. Now let's get some shut-eye. Flash, you can sleep on the foot of the bed with Gabby. There's plenty of room, unless you'd rather sleep out here. Gabby prefers the bedroom because she's scared of the dark."

That's enough, Scoot. Anyway, it has nothing to do with the dark. The bed is more comfortable.

"Okay, whatever you say. BOO!" He laughed when Gabby jumped up and yipped.

Gabby trotted into the bedroom, shaking her head. *Sometimes you act like a child.*

Scooter chuckled and motioned to Flash. "Let's go. I'm sure you're pooped."

On the bed? You let dogs sleep on your bed...with you?

"Sure. No big deal. Lots of humans let their pooches and kitties sleep with them. I hope you don't mind me snoring, cause I do."

What's snoring?

They entered the room to find Gabby in the midst of making her three circles on top of the bed. When she was satisfied, she plopped down. Flash hopped up as high as his stubby legs would allow, then he frantically clawed until he made it up and on.

Gabby looked at her new companion. *Now, it's like this, Flash. You get that side of the bed. I get this side. And yes, Scoot snores. And before this night is over, you'll know what snoring is. Good night, Scoot and Flash.*

Scooter crawled beneath the cool sheets and shoved his feet between the pooches. "Sleep tight. It's been one fine day."

Thanks, Scooter and Gabby. I like it here.

Scooter turned off the lamp, fluffed his pillows, and gently settled his head on the pillow. "It's nice to be home," he whispered, suddenly feeling Gabby's paws twitching. "She's already out."

CHAPTER 3

A bright sun ascended from the Atlantic into a cloudless blue sky, kicking off a new day. Scooter stirred, shading his eyes from the light by rolling the pillow over his face. "Feels like I just got in bed," he mumbled. When he stretched out his legs, he felt a large lump. "Must be Gabby." He slid them to his left, feeling for Flash, but was surprised to come up empty-footed. "What?" he said, sitting up and forcing open his tired eyes. "No Flash?"

What're you kicking me for, Scooter?

As Scooter raked his blonde hair from his eyes, he leaned over and looked down at the floor. "Where's Flash?"

Gabby rolled onto her back and threw four paws in the air. *Probably in the kitchen, gently licking water from his bowl.*

Scooter pushed his legs over the side of the bed and scanned the room. "There he is, curled up in the chair."

Gabby scrambled up. *Yep, sleeping on top of your clothes. See, he's not right. That old chair is harder than a brickbat. I know, because one night when you were snoring real loud, I tried it out.*

Scooter's lips tightened as he smiled and gazed at their new addition sleeping soundly, his paws over his furry muzzle. "He's out like a light, Gabby. Probably the best night's sleep he's had since he left his mammy. Let's not wake him."

Good idea. I'm going back to sleep. Wake me when breakfast is ready. I'm thinking cheese toast.

Scooter entered the bathroom and then glanced back over his shoulder, watching Gabby roll into a tight ball. "I'm thinking Puppy Chow. Use your imagination to pretend it's cheese toast."

You're no fun.

Ten minutes later, Scooter stepped out and found both pooches sound asleep. He climbed into a clean pair of shorts and a T-shirt and walked into the small kitchen. While filling his antique percolator with water and coffee, he glanced out to the ocean, pleased to see glassy, waist-high waves rolling in. "Hang in there, waves. After breakfast, I'll be on ya."

He removed the bag of Puppy Chow from the pantry, unrolled the top, and filled the plastic cup. Stepping around the counter, he found Gabby and Flash in front of their prospective bowls. "Good morning, sleepyheads. Hungry?"

Morning, Scooter. I am.

We're getting dry dog food and you're having cheese toast, right? That's a bit one-sided.

Scooter divided the cup between their bowls. "Cheer up. These little nuggets guarantee you'll grow up to be healthy, wealthy, and wise." He chuckled and moved back into the kitchen and prepared two slices of cheese toast. "Today I'll call Darla Kay to confirm everything's on for the school kids to come down tomorrow. This is our final day to host the children until next spring. Flash, I'm sure you'll enjoy meeting the special needs children. They're so nice and always happy to visit the beach."

I agree with Scoot about that, Flash. Get ready to fetch Frisbees, cause most of the kids love tossing them.

Flash looked up, holding a nugget of food between his teeth. He chewed it slowly. ***I've never been around children.***

Scooter waved his hand in the air. "You'll do fine." Scooter pulled the pan of golden cheese toast from the oven. "Gabby will show you what to do. Oh, and for your info, Gabby, this is for both of you…"

Whoopee! You're gonna share your toast with us? Gabby bellowed.

"No, let me finish. I was saying, you *both* need to hold back the talking when our guests are here. We don't want to take the chance that someone else has the gift, like I do. So, no yakking, got it?"

Okay, Scooter.

I think Darla Kay's sweet on you, Scoot. Anyway, wouldn't it be funny if you pretended to be a ventriloquist and made me talk, but your lips wouldn't move? See, you ask a question and I'll answer it with my own funny answer. Wanna give it a try?

Scooter took a sip of coffee and shook his head. "No. We discussed that topic earlier this summer. And, for your information, Darla Kay is not sweet on me, we're good friends. Sometimes you can aggravate me like a sand-filled bathing suit."

Flash took in the conversation, looking from Scooter to Gabby, puzzled.

Hey! It'd be even neater to have both of us talking, Scoot. Darla Kay would think you were really talented.

Scooter gave Gabby a stern look. "Looks like you'll stay in the house while everyone's here. Flash can entertain the children. How's that sound? And you saw my lips moving, too."

Okay. I'll keep quiet, but I'll be watching Darla Kay flirt with you…lover boy. Gabby yipped twice and lapped water from her bowl.

With the last of his toast devoured, Scooter said, "Flash, I noticed you were sleeping on the chair this morning. Didn't you like the bed?"

The stubby-legged beagle turned toward Gabby. When he looked back at Scooter, he whispered, *It got crowded. Gabby stretched out, and her paws pushed me off. The chair is fine.*

No, I didn't. I always sleep curled up.

Scooter chuckled. "I understand, Flash. And, Gabby, to set the record straight, you always stretch out. If I snored, I hope it didn't keep you awake."

Flash glanced at Gabby, but remained quiet.

Gabby yipped. *Flash, your floppy ears are affecting your hearing. Scoot snores like a dog growling. That's probably what knocked you off the bed.*

"Okay, funny girl," Scooter said, sliding open the door, "go do your business while I straighten up the kitchen. The waves are good, so I'm going out to clear my head."

Business?

Another word for math class.

Oh. Okay.

Gabby looked up at Scooter. *While you surf, we'll walk the coastline. I'll be Flash's guide. The beach will mean more to him after he sees it from a dog's perspective.*

Scooter ran his hand through shaggy hair and sighed. "We'll talk about you giving a beach tour when you come back. *If* I agree, you will follow my rules to the letter. Now get." Gabby took off down the stairs, little Flash plodding behind.

After a hit and a miss to straighten the kitchen, Scooter switched from shorts to surf baggies and walked onto the deck, sipping coffee and admiring the waves. Tomorrow promised to be a good day, when one of the local schools would bring down a class of special needs children; sadly, this would be the final visit until next spring. Early this summer when Gabby was first introduced to them, she was an instant success. No doubt little Flash would follow suit.

Scooter leaned over the deck and saw his two pups behind the sand dune tending to business. They appeared to be getting along, and the word 'fortunate' came to mind. Friends had shared horror stories about bringing in a second pet, only to find themselves in the midst of turmoil due to jealousy and territorial battles. He believed his pooches' companionship stemmed from the fact that Gabby had played a key role in rescuing Flash. Gabby's compassion for others less fortunate, whether it was a child or an animal, was unique. Even though she didn't care to speak of it, Scooter knew the hard times Gabby spent while on the lam had made her more understanding of stray, unwanted animals. A tiny smile tightened his lips as his pooches raced up over the dune, heading for the deck stairs.

Scooter filled his lungs with salty air, knowing colder weather would soon be howling out of the north. Winter had a way of eliminating the gusto of living on the coast, so maybe by staying busy with final edits on his soon-to-be published debut novel, 'If Bullfrogs Had Wings', time would pass quickly. Also, the anticipation of hearing a positive response from Disney about a movie about Gabby also added fuel to fend off the dreary intrusion of winter. If that did not fill the bill, the sequel "Out of the Rough" would at least occupy his mind until spring arrived. As the excited canines climbed the steps, he whispered, "No matter. I doubt it will be a dull winter."

Gabby bounced onto the deck. *Okay, Scoot, we're ready. Flash doesn't understand what surfing is, so we'll sit on the beach while I explain how hard it is, but that you're really good.*

Scooter reached down and scratched her neck. "You rascal. Your flattery is exceptional. But I know how you operate, so I'm thinking you're just plain sneaky."

Gabby looked at him with golden brown eyes. *Wrong, pal. If I was sneaky, I'd already be on the beach. And surfing is very hard...and you're really good.*

"Okay. You two can go down on the coastline. Do not walk out of my eyesight in either direction. Understand?"

Flash nodded. Gabby replied, *Perfect. We'll behave and obey your rules.*

"Flash, don't let Gabby talk you into bending my rules. She has a silver tongue."

I won't. Flash shook his head, causing his floppy ears to slap his head. *Can I ask you something?*

"Sure," said Scooter.

How come Gabby calls you Scoot and Scoot-toot? Do you have more than one name?

Gabby rolled over on her back and yipped. *Yeah, they're his nicknames. You can call him those if you want. Right, Scooter-rooter?*

"Yeah. I don't mind. In fact, you can call Gabby by her nickname. You've probably heard me use it. Want to know what it is?"

Flash nodded.

Don't pay any attention to him, Flash. It's silly.

"Sometimes I call her Baboo. It sort of comes from her name like Gaboo, but, really, there was a character on the Seinfeld program called Baboo. For some reason, it's always stuck with me, so I tagged her with it. Right, Baboo?"

I don't answer to it, Flash.

Okay, I won't call you that if you don't want me to. Will I get a nickname someday?

Gabby yipped and Scooter laughed. "You bet. But nicknames don't wash up on high tides, they're special. We'll work on it, don't worry."

I've already got a couple. You want to hear 'em?

"Not now, Baboo. Let's go. I've missed the salt water and waves while we were gone." Scooter headed downstairs to the storage room to get his surfboard.

Two puppies sat on the sun-warmed sand, watching Scooter paddle his Dewey Weber longboard over the breakers and swells, then stop and spin around to face the shore. During Scooter's trip out, Flash emitted a few high-pitched yips. After the third one, Gabby asked what his problem was. *Scooter's going way out, and the waves are really big.*

Aw, I've seen him out with bigger ones than these. Wait until he catches one and stands up.

What?

Yeah, he'll paddle until the wave picks him up, and then he'll stand and ride it. It's cool. Maybe next summer when the waves are small, he'll teach me. Maybe you'd like to learn, too.

Flash looked at her, wide-eyed. ***I like dry land.***

I used to think that, too. But one day a little girl was sucked out by big waves. I jumped in and pulled her out. Since then, I love the water.

Gabby leaped from her seated position, sprinted straight out to the white-capped breaker, and jumped. Flash stood, tail curled over his back. ***Be careful, Gabby!***

Once she got past the breakers, Gabby doggie-paddled toward Scooter. Her black head was all Flash saw as he paced back and forth in the shallow water. She finally turned and paddled back. Suddenly a small swell lifted her and propelled her forward. *Yippee!* she hollered, rolling onto the damp sand. *Now that's fun, Flash!*

Flash trotted over to her. ***Wow! That was cool, Gabby. It didn't hurt?***

Gabby completed a full body shake. *Naw. The wave does all the work. Now, watch Scooter, he's getting ready to catch one.*

Both dogs stared toward the morning sun and watched their companion paddle. Scooter caught the wave, and then, in a fluid motion, stood up. Flash said, ***Wow! Look at him go.***

Now he will cut sideways. Then, he'll ride back and forth on the wave, and before it breaks, he'll kick out and go back for another one. I'll bet he doesn't even get his shaggy hair wet. Watch.

As Gabby predicted, Scooter milked the wave for all it had, foot-kicked the board over the back of the wave, and landed on his stomach and paddled back out. *See, told ya. Little dude, you're gonna learn so much living down here.* When Scooter looked toward them, Gabby jumped up. *Nice ride, Scoot-toot!* Scooter threw a hand in the air. "Thanks!"

Okay, you've seen how good he surfs, let's take a walk and check out our beach.

I like living here with you and Scooter. After my sister was hit by the truck, I was alone and scared, except when Miss Celie fed me. Many nights, I huddled in the woods, shaking and wondering what would happen to me. Flash paused and looked back at Scooter. **I never thought I would end up in a beautiful place like this.**

Gabby eased over close and nudged Flash with her nose. *I'm sorry about your sister. You're right about Scooter. He's one nice human. I give him a hard time and joke him a lot, but I really love him. And, I love you, too. We're going to have fun times together.*

Flash dropped his head. **I love you both, and Miss Celie, too.**

Straddling his board, Scooter watched his pups walking along the tide line. "It looks like they're bonding. They need their times together." He looked over his shoulder to see a nice swell growing from the blue-green water. "Let 'er rip, dude!"

Gabby playfully splashed along the edge of the tide line, scanning the ocean for dolphins and the sky for gulls, and shore birds. Little Flash plodded slowly through the fluffy sand, nose held high, sniffing, and his tail swished in quick fashion from side to side. Whenever he focused on a smell coming from the row of vacant cottages, his path veered toward them for a few yards.

Up ahead in front of Gabby, two gulls tucked their wings and headed straight down into the frothy white water and disappeared. Several seconds later, they popped out and slowly flapped, concentrating on swallowing their fishy treats. Gabby barked and took off after them. After twenty yards at breakneck speed, she pulled up and turned around, searching for Flash. She spotted his swaying tail halfway up to the cottages. She hollered, *Where do you think you're going, Flash?*

With assistance from the breeze, Scooter heard Gabby's question and looked in her direction. "Looks like Flash has a streak of adventure tucked away in his shy personality." He chuckled when Gabby trotted up the dune toward the beagle. "She'll keep him in line."

When Gabby pulled up beside her new roommate, his nose was only inches from the sand as he continued toward the grey cottage bordered with large clumps of sea grass. *Hey, you're not allowed to be nosing around cottages. That's one of Scooter's rules.*

Without missing a sniff or a step, Flash whispered, **Fox.** Then he yipped and hurried forward.

So? I know we have wild animals here. Come on, let's get back before Scooter puts us on restriction. We're out of his eyesight over here in the dunes. Gabby turned and took a couple of quick steps toward the ocean, then looked back, expecting to see Flash moseying along behind her. Instead, she saw his brown and white butt and waving tail through the sea oats, and then it disappeared. She spun around and bolted toward him. *Hey! You better get your mess back here!* Gabby emerged out of the sea oats and saw Flash drop to his belly and crawl under the slightly raised wood deck. *I don't believe this little weasel.* She eased up and peered beneath the deck into pitch black. *Flash? Come out right now or I'm going to rat you out to Scooter. You're not getting me put on restriction!*

Within thirty seconds, Flash's sand-covered muzzle appeared from under the deck. **The male fox lives under here, but he's not here now.**

Gabby released a soft growl. *You're skating on thin ice, buddy. Now let's go.* She turned and headed away. By the time she topped the dune, Flash had joined her. **I'm sorry, Gabby. I can't keep from sniffing.**

Ignoring his excuse, Gabby broke into a trot and noticed Scooter carrying his board out of the water. Flash followed, wondering what Scooter would say about his actions.

Scooter gently placed his board on the sand and ran his fingers through his wet hair. "Here come my companions. Did you have a fun walk?"

Gabby arrived beside Scooter and remained silent as she turned and watched Flash ease up slowly. She shook her head and stared at Scooter. Flash plopped down and pawed sand and spider webs off his snoot.

"Well?"

Gabby was not one to remain quiet for long. *Either Flash's floppy ears keep him from hearing, or he's hardheaded.*

"I saw you all going up to the cottage."

Not 'you all' Scoot...Flash. I had to go get him, since he totally ignored me when I called him to come back.

"Flash, it's not good to go snooping around other people's cottages, even if they're not there. Not everyone likes dogs. You understand?"

Told you.

Flash turned and looked at Scooter. **I'm sorry. I'll try not to do that again.**

"Good. I understand everything's still new and exciting for you."

Gabby recalled several scoldings she had received from Scooter for not obeying his rules. In her opinion, Flash's apology seemed nothing more than a casual statement. Not only that, the pup did not even come close to promising it would not happen again. So she decided to give

Scooter more information. *Scooter, when Flash finally slithered from under the deck, he blamed his disobedient act on his nose. Claimed he couldn't keep from sniffing. Even I wouldn't use something that silly for an excuse.*

Scooter realized this situation was about more than Gabby being upset with Flash running off to sniff out a smell, and it needed to be handled carefully. He knew this stemmed from jealousy, with Gabby thinking their new companion was receiving a pass. Scooter smiled. "I think Flash now understands I'm serious about you all staying on the beach and not snooping around other cottages, right, Flash?"

Yes, Scooter.

Well, maybe he does, but he didn't promise not to do it again. Besides, what's up with him not being able to keep from sniffing?

"Gabby, please listen to what I'm going to say. Every breed of dog is born with different traits."

I know that.

"Good. Now, beagles are known for their keen ability to smell. That's why they're used for tracking deer and rabbits. Just like labs, which you mostly are, are known for swimming and retrieving. This means natural traits are as normal to different species of dogs as, well, barking. Understand?"

Gabby released a long sigh. *I think I've got it.*

Scooter stood and brushed the sand from his wet baggies. "Glad we straightened that out. Let's get back to our cottage so I can shower and do some editing."

They walked across the vacant beach in silence until Gabby said, *So, since I'm a lab and naturally enjoy swimming, then it's fine and dandy for me to just hit the water anytime I feel the 'natural' urge, right?*

Scooter chuckled and looked down at his intelligent dog. "I knew something like that was coming, Gabby. That's one of the things I love about you."

Huh?

"You're always thinking how to turn things around for your advantage. Not that there's anything wrong with that. However, I never said a dog's natural traits should prevent them from obeying. So, Flash will not be allowed to go off hunting whenever he chooses. And that goes for you and swimming." Scooter reached down and gave her a gentle pat on the head.

I also figured you would say something like that, Scoot. Just checking. What if Flash does his sniffing thing again? Does he get on restriction?

Scooter chuckled. "Yes. And I'm sure you will tell him how much fun it is, right?"

Gabby yipped. *You bet!* She eased up beside Flash. *Take it from me. It's not fun to stay in the cottage and watch Scooter down here on the beach.*

I don't want to be put on restriction.

Scooter put away his prized surfboard. "All in all, we had a super-fine morning on the beach. You go do your business while I take a shower. Treats for my pooches when we go upstairs."

Oh, boy! Bet he gives us doggie jerky. I love that stuff.

I've never had it.

CHAPTER 4

Scooter knew that after a morning session on the waves followed by a refreshing outdoor shower, he would truly feel back home. Now comfortable in shorts and t-shirt, he towel-dried his mop of hair and punched out Darla Kay's office number at school. His exhausted, furry companions had gobbled up the jerky treats and were now stretched out on the deck, sound asleep, bathed by warm sunshine and a southerly breeze.

After several rings, Darla Kay's sweet voice answered, suddenly becoming even sweeter after Scooter identified himself. She confirmed the children's ten o'clock visit the following morning. She then inquired about Scooter's trip to New York. "I'm not busy, so give me a complete rundown of your novel's publication schedule."

Scooter proudly shared the news about his book, throwing in the possibility of a Disney movie featuring Gabby's life at the beach and her adventures in the ocean. Their trip to the Big Apple ended with their rescue of little a tossed-out beagle from the woods on the Eastern Shore. "Congratulations to both of you! I'm really looking forward to seeing you and the doggies tomorrow." Scooter hung up, a smile stretching across his tan face. *She's a real sweetie.*

Scooter filled a glass with ice and water; feeling energized, he opened his briefcase, removed a stack of manuscript pages that needed rewrites, and fired up his computer.

While his fingers danced across the keyboard, tid-bits of the many long, tedious months he had spent writing and editing his first Young Adult/Baby Boomer novel flashed through his head. An image of the day he adopted Gabby from the SPCA and her bold questions about his writing career suddenly popped pleasantly to mind. Ashamed, he admitted his three previous novels were not picked up by publishers, but he refused to give up. In all honesty, this novel would most likely not be in the publishing stage if not for Gabby's brave rescue of a little girl from the ocean's undertow. The pretty little girl happened to be the daughter of a big-time New York publisher. So, Scooter would always owe Gabby. She knew this, and at times played it to her advantage.

A couple of hours later, after completing a chunk of rewrites, Scooter stood and stretched. His four-legged friends were now awake, staring in silence toward the coastline. "They've been good this morning, allowing me to work in peace. I'll bet they would enjoy a surprise," he whispered, joining them on the deck.

Both of them turned, focusing four golden-brown eyes on him. *Are you done, Scoot?*

"Naw, just taking a break. You two had a nice little snooze, I see. Since you've been so quiet this morning while I worked, would you like to take a walk down the coast?"

Gabby bounced to her feet, tail flapping from left to right. *Okie-dokie! Let's go.*

"How about you, Flash? You want to cruise the beach?"

Sure, Scooter. Are you coming with us?

Scooter shook his head. "No. I have a little more work to do."

Gabby's ears perked up. *You're going to let us go alone? Really, Scoot?*

Scooter gave both a serious look. "Only if you promise to stay on the beach, no snooping around cottages, then turn around at the pier and come back. If you don't mess around, the trip takes one hour. Don't make me come looking for you. Do you both agree to my rules?"

Even Flash was up, wagging his tail. Gabby bounced on the deck like a rubber ball. *Yippee! We'll have fun, Flash. We're going cruising by ourselves. Come on.*

Scooter held his hand up. "Wait! Not so fast, young lady. I didn't hear you promise me."

Oh, sure, my favorite Scooter-tooter. I cross my furry heart and promise to be back here, with little Flash, in one hour…and we'll stay beside the water. She settled on her haunches at his feet, tongue dangling and eyes twinkling.

I promise.

"Okay. Gabby, you watch out for Flash. If you see any people, do not go up and bother them." Scooter looked at his watch. "It's eleven-thirty now. I'll expect you back by twelve-thirty. Have fun."

Thanks, Scoot-toot.

Yeah! Thanks!

As they bounced down the stairs, Scooter heard Flash say, **I called him Scoot-toot.**

Scooter chuckled and watched them sprinting toward the water. "A long walk, and they'll sleep the rest of the afternoon." He watched until they were out of sight, then returned to his computer and edits.

The two curious canines strolled down the vacant coastline as if it were their front yard, and, technically, it was. For a while, both walked in silence. *All joking aside, Flash. We are lucky. There are so many* unwanted and abused puppies out there who have no one to love and care for them.

I feel like all of this is one of my good dreams.

Gabby splashed through shallow water while Flash trekked across the damp sand, his nose poked high into the air and steadily sniffing, loud enough Gabby heard him. *There you go, smelling the air again. And, in case you didn't know, your big snoot whistles when you inhale. I now understand that you beagles have talented noses, but the tourists are gone, so forget trying to whiff burgers or grilled chicken.*

Flash looked at her and produced two quick nose whistles. **I'm searching for other animals. If there's food around, you'll smell it.**

Flash slowed his pace. *What is it now, Flash?*

Male fox.

Gabby walked on, shaking her head. *You're not in the wilderness, Flash. Let the fox be.*

Moving slowly, Flash started toward the same stilted grey cottage. **I better check this out.**

Remember, Scooter said, 'don't leave the beach'. No messing around the cottages.

Flash's tail shot up straight as he continued to inhale deep breaths, but he stopped his pursuit. **Okay. I promised Scooter.** He turned and followed Gabby.

Sandbridge Beach was home to various types of wild animals such as fox, possum, deer, wild horses, and feral cats. However, during Gabby's seven months of living there, this particular subject had never tickled her fancy. In her mind, Flash was enjoying his natural trait, so she decided to let him be as long as he behaved himself and obeyed Scooter's rule.

They neared the pier at Little Island and eased into the water up to their bellies. *See, there's nothing to be afraid of in the water.*

Scooter said I would get used to it.

Without a reply, Gabby jumped into the refreshing water, paddled out and then spent a few minutes riding some waves into shore. After her brief 'show off' swim, she and her stubby-legged companion headed back to their cottage for a snack and some cool, fresh water.

Scooter relaxed on the deck, sipping an icy Coke and checking his edits. He looked up to find two slow-moving doggies plodding along the tide line. "Here they come," he said, glancing at his watch. "They're pooped, but on time."

Gabby climbed the steps with Flash in tow. *Well, Scooter, that was fun.* She entered the cottage and could be heard lapping water from her bowl.

"Hey, Flash. Did you have a good time?"

Yes. Thanks for letting us go. I'm going to get some water.

Scooter watched him mosey inside as Gabby passed him coming out onto the deck and plopped down at his feet. "So, did you two follow my rules?"

Gabby stretched out and yawned. *Yes. But Mr. Nose got a whiff of the fox again. Scoot, he acts so weird when he's sniffing. Oh, and his nose whistles are annoying. But, according to Flash, his snoot says there's a fox living under a cottage not far from the pier. That beats all I've ever heard. Personally, I think the little guy spent too much time alone in the woods.*

Scooter chuckled as Flash returned to the deck. "Like I said earlier, don't be too quick to rule out a beagle's ability to smell and track, Gabby. They're known for having very sensitive noses."

Gabby yipped and rolled over, throwing her paws into the air. *Flash, you probably smelled a musty towel or bathing suit somebody left in the outdoor shower.*

I know what I smelled.

Scooter chuckled as both pooches traded verbal jabs. "Well, I'm proud of you for coming back on time. How about a little snack? I figure you're a bit peckish."

Peckish? What kind of foreign language is that? You know English is all I understand.

It has something to do with birds, right?

"Correct, Flash! It's an old country word meaning 'hungry'. See, when folks threw out corn for their chickens, the hungry ones ran up and pecked the corn."

If 'peckish' deals with eating, call me very peckish. Hey, I've got a great idea. How about getting us a plate with different treats? We'll close our eyes, smell each one, and tell you what it is. My snoot's pretty sharp when it comes to human food, which to me is more important than a stinky bathing suit or a nasty fox.

"Sounds good. You two wait out here, and we'll invent a new game. We'll call it 'Snoot Skill'". Scooter chuckled and hustled inside.

Gabby shook her head. *Don't encourage him, Flash. Sometimes he gets into these silly moods.*

Scooter rummaged around inside the almost-bare fridge for some goodies, hoping for something to confuse Gabby. "Yeah, that'll be the day," he whispered, removing a package that contained two slices of bologna. He also picked up a hunk of cheese wrapped in aluminum foil. "Both pooches will probably guess the cheese." Scooter pulled out a bag of doggie treats advertised to taste like real bacon from the pantry.

"Bingo. I'd forgotten about these. Gabby hasn't had one since I brought her here. Bet she's forgotten them." He removed a bag of Fritos and shook a few onto the napkin with the cheese, bologna, and fake bacon.

Two excited, determined doggies were waiting eagerly when Scooter stepped onto the deck. "Time to play 'Snoot Skill'. You ready?"

Let 'er rip, Scoot! I'll show this talented sniffer beagle what a dog's snoot is really for.

I'm ready.

Scooter placed the goodie-filled napkin on top of the grill. "Here are the rules. One of you goes over to one side of the deck, and one goes to the other side. Then close your eyes real tight, no peeking. I'll bring a treat over, hold it above your head, and you sniff. Now, do not say what you think it is after you smell. I'll do a countdown, and then you both answer at the same time. Keep your eyes closed the entire time. Got it?"

Bingo.

Got it.

The dogs perched against opposite railings. Obediently, they closed their eyes and tilted their noses high into the air. "Good. Since Flash is new, we'll let him go first." Scooter took a sliver of cheese in his fingers and stepped over to Flash. He held it six inches over the beagle's head. "Okay, Flash. Sniff. After you get a good whiff, say 'Done'."

The white muzzle stretched upward, and Flash's black nostrils quivered. The white-tipped, brown tail swished back and forth. ***Done.***

Scooter walked over and repeated the same presentation beside Gabby. Her smelling actions were identical to Flash's. *Done!*

"Now, I'll count to 'three'. Then, at the same time, both of you say what you believe it is. One – two – three."

Cheese! **Cheese!**

"Bingo!" said Scooter, giving a piece to each pup. "Well done. Now remember, keep your eyes shut. Here we go for the next test." He picked up two slabs of bologna. "Okay, Flash."

The multi-colored pup sniffed, slower this time. His swishing tail stilled while his floppy ears rose to their highest peaks. ***Done.***

Gabby sniffed once. *Done.*

Scooter counted, "One – two – three."

Bologna! **Possum!**

Scooter handed Gabby a piece. "Right, girl." He stepped over and gave Flash a piece. "It's bologna, little fellow. You've probably never smelled it before. Bet you won't forget it, either."

With her eyes still shut, Gabby said, *Where did that possum guess come from, Flash?*

That's what possum smells like. There were lots of them in the woods.

Scoot, this poor little puppy has so much to learn.

"Pay attention, Gabby. This next piece might be possum." Scooter laughed and picked up two Fritos.

You wouldn't know a possum if one crawled up in your lap, Scoot-toot. Gabby yipped.

Holding the crispy Fritos over Flash's head, Scooter said, "Try this one, Flash."

The beagle shook his head and raised his muzzle higher. After several very deep sniffs, nose whistles included, he said, **Done.**

There's the whistle, Scoot. Did you hear it?

"Yes. It's no big deal." Scooter chuckled as he moved beside Gabby and repeated the test. Instantly, Gabby replied, *Done!*

Scooter said, 'three'. *Corn chip!* **Corn!**

"Okay. Since it's made from corn…I'll call it a tie." He handed each pooch a chip. "Nice work."

Wait a minute, Scoot! That's no tie, because it's more than just corn. If I'm right, you call them Fritos. But they're not like the corn you eat on the cob.

"Baboo, they're made *from* the corn I eat off the cob. And, yes, they're called Fritos. Remember that, Flash. Okay, here's the final piece."

Flash, he only calls me Baboo when he's trying to pull something over on me.

Scooter chuckled, holding the fake bacon over Flash's head. "Okie-dokie, Flash."

One quick sniff and the beagle replied, **Done.**

That didn't take him long, Scoot. It must be a piece of fox. Gabby yipped twice.

"If it was a real fox, you'd be out of here like the wind. Okay, sniff."

Gabby stretched her head upward and snorted twice. Her ears shot straight up. After several seconds, she replied, *Done…I guess.*

"One – two – three."

Bacon! **Pork rind!**

Scooter laughed. "Close. At least you both know the smell of pork. But this is a doggie treat made to smell and taste like real bacon. It sure fooled Gabby. Okay, open your eyes." He tossed a piece to each of them.

That's sneaky, using fake stuff to fool us.

Scooter asked Flash, "Why did you guess pork rinds?"

When I lived in the woods, some of the men who came up to Miss Celie's diner would throw pieces to me. I heard one man say, 'Look, the

pup sure likes them pork rinds'. Besides, I don't think I've ever smelled bacon.

Gabby licked her chops. *Well, this little game proves my sniffer is a bit better than Flash's.*

"Well, you've been around human food longer than Flash. But concerning wild animal smells, little Flash would win by a 'nose'. Get it? A nose." Scooter chuckled and tossed them the remaining treats.

I told you, Flash, he's playing Mr. Funny Man. You'll get used to his not-so-funny jokes. Thanks for the goodies, Scoot. I'm pooped. Gabby yipped. *I smell a nap.*

Me, too. My legs are tired.

"That's fine. I noticed we're running low on vittles. While you rest, I'm going to the grocery store. There's more edits to do when I return, and then I'll fix supper and we'll hit the sack. Tomorrow will be a busy day with the children coming down. Sleep well, and I'll be back in an hour." Scooter walked inside and looked back to see his tired pups curled up in the shade.

CHAPTER 5

Scooter shoveled spoonfuls of milk-drenched Fruit Loops into his mouth between sips of black coffee and glanced at the wall clock with miniature surfboards as the hands. Gabby gobbled her Purina Puppy Chow, while Flash slowly chewed each nugget. Their energy and stamina were now fully recharged, thanks to the previous night's sleep.

What time will the special needs children be down, Scoot?

Scooter pawed a dribble of milk from his chin. "Ten o'clock. We have twenty minutes to get the utility cart on the beach, emptied, and everything set up."

No problem, unless we wait for slowpoke to finish eating. She cut her eyes at Flash. *They're nuggets of food, not little toys.*

"Cut him some slack, girl. His manners are fine," said Scooter, picking up the mug of coffee.

Ignoring Gabby's ridicule, Flash continued to nibble one nugget at a time, then dabbed his tongue into his water. "Okay, I'm finished eating. I'm going to pull the cart over to the beach and set up the chairs. Since it's not tourist season…no crowds."

Good. I'll wait here with Flash. We'll be down…if he ever finishes.

Scooter hit the deck steps. Over his shoulder, he hollered, "If he doesn't, Miss Mooch will gladly *gobble* up the rest."

Three years ago, Scooter started the Sandbridge Surfing School for special needs children. Schools in two nearby cities quickly signed up to bring their students to spend a day at the beach with a local surfer. After the first summer, Scooter was totally blown away with the success and growth of his endeavor, not to mention his growing heartfelt feelings toward these children, some of whom were unable to get out of their wheelchairs. Those on crutches enjoyed tossing them aside to play in the sand and shallow water. Scooter had taken out insurance and attended required classes to learn how to better assist the children with physical limitations. Of course, he also purchased the necessary licenses and insurance. He was now authorized to assist them, one at a time, into the water. Those with minor limitations were allowed, with Scooter's hands-on assistance, to ride small waves on either a boogie board or a foam surfboard.

Mid-way through the three-hour session, Scooter provided peanut butter and jelly sandwiches, potato chips, and lemonade for a relaxing lunch on the coast. At the conclusion of the gathering, Scooter presented each child with a T-shirt bearing a colorful picture of a child surfing down the face of a glassy wave. The words, 'Graduate of Sandbridge Surf School' were printed on the front.

Long ago, even before his novel was accepted for publication, Scooter had decided if school budgets became pinched to the point of not being able to pay, he would do his best to continue running the school. Now, with publication a reality, he contemplated giving the schools a fifty-percent reduction in fees. To him, the reward of bringing happiness to these challenged children was priceless.

While humming one of his favorite Motown songs, Scooter unloaded his homemade balloon-tired PVC cart that contained the essentials, such as chairs, Frisbees, balls, and several bright kites ready to be launched into the cloudless blue sky. "Okay, we're ready for the kids to have a fun beach day," he said to himself, in a pitiful attempt to squeeze his words into the music.

Scooter stepped back, taking in this small parcel of coastal paradise guaranteed to produce memories, laughter, and excitement. "Perfect. I'll go get the cooler of lemonade, sandwiches, and chips, and we're good to go." He moved barefoot through the warm, sun-kissed sand to the cottage.

His furry companions met him halfway. "Well, I see Flash finished his breakfast."

Gabby helped.

You gave me those last few nuggets.

"At least it wasn't wasted. Now, you two go down and hang around the site while I get our cooler and picnic basket. And," Scooter said, looking at both of them, "no talking around our guests. Got that?"

I do.

Me, too. But I'll have my eye on you and Darla Kay. Her sights are set on you.

Scooter waved his hand in the air and continued toward the cottage. "You're so wrong, Gabby," he yelled back.

The mixed black lab pranced into the water to cool her feet. *You're going to have fun playing with these children, Flash.*

I'm nervous.

Gabby turned toward the little beagle and noticed he was trembling. *No need to be. They love pups. Just be yourself, fetch whatever they toss, and take it back to them. If something goes in the water, I'll get it for you. Okay?*

I'll do my best, but I've never been around children.

Gabby yipped twice. *It's no different than being around Scooter.*

Scooter's not a child.

Ha! Wait until you know him better. He's always joking around, telling unfunny jokes and pulling little tricks. Once I realized that's how he was, it was easier just to go with the flow. You'll see. Gabby's ears perked and her tail whipped from side to side. *Hear that, Flash?*
   What?
   Gabby spun around and faced the cottage. *They're coming, Flash. Let's go greet them!*
   I don't hear anything.
   Gabby yipped as she walked from the shallow water. *I'm not surprised. You were given enough ear material to cover four ears. I can hear the children laughing and squealing, and they haven't even pulled into the driveway yet.*
   Flash trotted up beside her. **Wow! You hear as good as I can smell.**
   Guess we've got all of the major talents. Now remember to be yourself and prepare for lots of pats and strokes. Oh, and Scooter doesn't want us licking them. He claims our saliva makes sand stick to them. Suddenly, the quiet scene was interrupted with two loud beeps from a horn. *Told you, my beagle buddy.*
   By the time the pooches made their way to the cottage, they saw Scooter opening the passenger door for his friend, Darla Kay Williams, the teacher in charge. Gabby whispered as they trotted up. *That's the pretty lady who has eyes for our Scooter.*
   Oh. Okay.
   Darla Kay stepped out of the van, barefoot and wearing baggy white shorts topped with a pink T-shirt. Her shoulder-length blonde hair added to her natural beauty. She smiled as she greeted Scooter with a hug and gentle kiss on his tan cheek. "Good to see you again, Mr. Writer," she said, handing him a list with the children's names and physical disabilities. "We have four new children today. Sammy is the only one allowed to go into the water, *if* he agrees to wear a life vest. The little tike's a bit hardheaded, so we'll need your persuasive magic. As you can hear, they are wound tight with excitement." She giggled. "The trip down here had me feeling like I was trapped in a small cage with wild cats. Do I look as frazzled as I feel?"
   The squeals and chatter increased in volume as the two aides slid the van's side doors open. "You look fine, Darla Kay, like always. Don't worry about Sammy. After I explain the fun he'll have on the waves and what he'll learn, he'll beg to wear a life vest. You relax and let me and my cuddly canines take over." He nodded down toward Gabby and Flash, sitting calmly behind Darla Kay. Scooter noted the stare coming from Gabby's brown eyes and knew she was already into her role of Miss Spy.

Darla Kay turned and knelt. "Hey, Gabby. I hear they might make a movie about you saving the little girl? That's exciting." She stroked Gabby's back and leaned toward Flash. "And you're the new addition." She gently rubbed the beagle's head and floppy ears. "Nice to meet you, Flash. I'm Darla Kay."

Scooter stepped around the van and greeted the two aides, Barbara and Mary Beth, as they helped the excited children down the van steps. "Hey, girls. Good to see you again."

Barbara smiled, assisting one of the boys using aluminum crutches to the sandy ground. "Same here, Scooter. These little ones are about to explode with anticipation." She nodded toward Mary Beth, who was gently steering a wheelchair carrying an attractive little blonde haired girl down the ramp.

Scooter chuckled. "We'll exchange their pent-up energy for sun, fun, and a dose of first-class tired before this day is over."

"Hope you're right," replied Mary Beth, pushing the wheelchair toward the front of the van.

"Here, let me help this pretty little lady," Scooter said to Mary Beth, reaching out and gently giving a pat to the little girl's thin forearm. "Come with me, cutie. You sure have the prettiest blonde curls and blue eyes I've ever seen."

"Thank you," whispered the girl. "My name is Emmy. I'm named after my mother.

Scooter said, "Nice to meet you, Emmy. That's a pretty name, just like you. I'm Scooter." Stepping behind the wheelchair, Scooter said, "Hey, I have two cute puppies over here waiting to meet you. Do you like pups?" Scooter found her name on the list Darla Kay had given him and found Emmy suffered from spina bifida and was restricted to her wheelchair.

Emmy's smile slipped from her face. "I'm scared of dogs."

The young girl stiffened. Scooter replied, "Oh, I'm sorry to hear that, Emmy. My little doggies are real nice, and they love girls with golden hair." He slowly pushed her around the front of the van. "Here's one of my pooches. I'll make sure he doesn't jump on you. Okay?"

Emmy nodded.

Flash sat stoically on the sand. "This is little Flash. See, he's cute. Look at those floppy ears." The petite girl remained silent, keeping her blue eyes glued on Flash. "Hello, Flash. I'm Emmy. Dogs scare me because one time a big, mean dog tried to bite my mother while she was pushing me down the sidewalk."

Scooter felt the air rush from his lungs upon hearing the reason for Emmy's dislike for dogs. He knelt beside her wheelchair. "Oh, that's terrible, Emmy. I'd be scared of mean dogs like that, too, if one had tried to bite my mother."

"I was five when that happened. I'm seven now," she whispered, still staring at the floppy-eared beagle.

"Well, I promise you, little Flash is not mean. Watch." Scooter patted his thigh. "Come here, Flash. Show Emmy how kind and gentle you are." Flash put his tail in gear, swishing slowly from side to side. He moved very slowly several steps up to Scooter and placed his muzzle on his knee. Scooter rubbed his head and toyed with his ears. "See, Emmy?"

"Yes, sir. He seems nice."

"I bet he'll say 'hi' to you if I ask him, because he minds very well. Let's see. Flash say 'hi' to this cute little girl named Emmy." Flash released one soft yip and sat up on his haunches.

Emmy giggled. "He said it."

Scooter's chest expanded with pride as his heart tingled with joy as Flash continued to sit and wag his tail. "You know what Flash really likes, Emmy?"

Emmy looked up at Scooter with beautiful eyes. "What?"

"For little girls to rub his head. If you want to, clap your hands, and he'll come sit by you."

Emmy looked at Flash and then back up to Scooter. She glanced down to Flash and lifted her tiny hands and clapped once. As promised, Flash dropped to all fours, and, very slowly, tail still wagging, stepped up beside her wheelchair and sat. In slow motion, Emmy reached over the side of the chair and lightly placed one finger on his head, and quickly pulled it back. "I patted him and he didn't growl."

"That's because Flash is a nice doggie."

Gabby heard their conversation and eased up and settled beside Flash. Scooter introduced her to Emmy, and within a couple of minutes, Emmy was stroking both pups. Emmy's smile was now back in place. "I like your dogs," she said.

"And they like you, too. You relax a minute while I go see if I can help your teachers," said Scooter, heading around the van.

Scooter met Darla Kay at the van's door as she helped a rail-thin little boy on crutches. She winked. "Scooter, this is my friend Roland. Today is his first visit to a beach. Roland, meet Mr. Scooter." They shook hands.

A quick glance at the list revealed that young Roland battled cerebral palsy.

Big brown eyes peeked out beneath a thick wave of pitch-black hair. "Mr. Scooter, can we go down to the water? Will my crutches help me walk on the sand? Can I go in the water?"

Scooter chuckled at the rapid-fire questions. "You bet you can walk over the sand, buddy. And we'll have fun whether we go in the water or not." Over the past few years, Scooter had learned the hard way not to promise what he might not be permitted to deliver.

Darla Kay watched Roland maneuver smoothly in front of the van. Scooter noticed Emmy still talking to the pooches. Gabby looked over at little Roland, slipped away from Emmy, and headed toward them. Her ears perked and her tail wagged as she pulled up beside Scooter. Roland spotted the black pooch, and through a huge smile, said, "Look! This puppy looks exactly like my dog Blaze." The boy leaned forward and reached out a hand with wiggling fingers. "What's your name? Mine's Roland," he said as Gabby nuzzled the small hand. "Are you going to the beach with us? I hope so. Blaze has never been to the beach."

Once all six children were out of the van, Darla Kay released a long sigh. "Okay, kids. Whoever wants to go down on the beach, holler 'yeah'." The coastline exploded with thunderous 'yeahs' and whoops.

Scooter laughed. "Then let's get down there, beach bums!"

Darla Kay said, "After I get my beach bag and towel from the van, Emmy and I will come down."

"Okay. See ya on the beach, dear," replied Scooter, putting a hand on Roland's shoulder. "Let's get to the beach. Gabby will escort us."

The caravan trekked across the white sand toward the Atlantic Ocean. Scooter said to Gabby, "Girl, I think you've found a new friend." Gabby replied with a soft yip. "Good girl," said Scooter. "Thanks for remembering, no yakking, okay?"

"Are you talking to your puppy, Mr. Scooter?" Roland asked. "I always talk to Blaze, and you know what? He talks back to me. Did you know dogs could talk, Mr. Scooter? Blaze can."

Scooter almost tripped when he heard Roland's innocent announcement of conversing with his dog. He looked down at Gabby to find her staring back at him with wide open eyes and shaking her head. Scooter shrugged his shoulders, thankful Roland couldn't see his surprised reaction. Before Scooter put together a reply, Roland asked, "Did you know dogs could talk, Mr. Scooter?"

Scooter cleared his throat. "Sure. My pooches talk to me all the time."

"Do they talk like we talk?"

Gabby yipped. Scooter said, "Well, let's say I know what they're saying. Is that what you mean?" Scooter recalled the day he met Gabby and she first spoke to him. Naturally, he was thrown for a loop, afraid the lady at the SPCA could hear her. When he finally asked Gabby, she casually replied, *'Nobody can hear me except you, Scooter'*.

34

"Yeah, I guess so, Mr. Scooter," replied Roland, gazing into the sky at two gulls chasing each other. Thankfully, the little fellow dropped the discussion of talking dogs, his attention now focused on the acrobatic gulls.

Sweat beaded on Scooter's forehead. As they walked down to their coastline camp, Scooter said, "Okay, Roland, we're in Paradise. Let me go help the others. You and Gabby wait here, and I'll be right back."

"I think the beach is cool, Mr. Scooter. My parents take me to the park near my house, but this is better."

Scooter knelt beside Gabby. "Don't forget to remind Flash about not talking." Gabby nodded and nuzzled his arm.

Everyone was settled happily at the Sandbridge Surfing School when Darla Kay and Emmy joined them. The actions between Emmy and Flash proved they had already bonded. Scooter looked up when he heard Roland cheer. Gabby was in the water, showing off while body surfing the shorebreak waves. Cheers and claps encouraged her to dogpaddle out farther for a bigger wave. She successfully caught a nice swell, rode it in, and hit the beach. She pranced up and nuzzled her fans' extended hands.

Barbara spread out large towels printed with the surf school logo and helped the children with crutches sit down, and then she placed their crutches in a neat pile. Scooter launched a large, box-shaped red kite into the sky and tied the string to one of Roland's crutches. Scooter said, "Here, Roland. Keep an eye on this high-flying kite."

"I will, Mr. Scooter."

Darla Kay gently lifted another small, slender girl from her wheelchair and helped settle her on the blanket. She handed the blue-eyed, dark haired girl a green Nurf ball. "Marie, throw the ball toward the ocean and Gabby will go get it and bring it back to you." Gabby heard and rushed up and sat, her fluffy tail brooming the sand. Scooter checked his list to find Marie had cerebral palsy.

"Okay, Gabby. Ready, set, go!" Marie wound up and tossed the ball high. Gabby sprinted beneath it, splashed into the water, and waited. When the ball was within reach, she leaped, snatched it from mid-air, and plopped into the wave. Marie yelled, "Good girl!" Gabby splashed from the water back up to Marie, holding the ball high, and gently placed it on her lap.

While Scooter let out line to another brightly colored kite and allowed it to rise high above the beach, he kept one eye on Gabby's retrieval performance. "She's such a show-off, but a sweet one," he whispered to Darla Kay. "Looks like we have an excellent group today, Miss Teacher."

Darla Kay winked at him. "You know something, Scooter?"

Scooter tugged the kite string for more altitude. "Don't believe I've had the honor to meet Mr. Something." He chuckled.

Darla Kay bumped him lightly with her shoulder. "*Something* is not a person, it's a thing. Now listen. I'm being serious. I've been watching you interact with our children for three years. It's clear to me that you have the gift."

"The gift?"

She nodded. "Yes. It takes a unique gift to work with these children. The kids always unwind and relax when you're around. See, even little Roland is calm." She looked toward the boy as he tossed a Frisbee. Flash jumped up and plodded on big paws through shallow water and retrieved it. "On the drive down here, the little fellow was so wired up, if he wasn't wearing a seat belt, he would've been bouncing around the van like a rubber ball. Now look at him, enjoying a world of his own." Darla Kay lightly touched Scooter on his muscular arm. "If you ever decide to change professions, you could take a few advanced classes and work at the school." She stood on her toes and placed a light kiss on his cheek. "Anyway, I wanted to tell you what a superb job you do." She pointed. "There's Sammy playing contentedly in the sand. That outgoing, young fellow is in the early stages of muscular dystrophy, but he's still able to walk and still retains eighty-five percent use of his muscles. Water is excellent therapy."

Scooter stepped over and handed the kite string to Sammy as he constructed a sand castle. "Here, friend. Hold this for a minute while I fill the bucket with sand and tie the kite to it. Okay? Will you keep an eye on it while you build your castle?"

"Sure, Mr. Scooter. Would you fill my other bucket with water? Please."

"You bet, partner." Scooter looked at Darla Kay. "I'll be right back."

Scooter returned, toting a bucket of sea water. "If you need more, get my attention. Miss Williams said if you'd like to go in the water with me and learn to boogie board or surf, you can."

"Thank you, Mr. Scooter. I love the water, but I've never surfed."

Scooter chuckled. "Today's a great day to try. We'll go out a bit later, after you finish the castle."

"Okay, Mr. Scooter, I'll build real fast."

Stepping up beside Darla Kay, a black flash caught Scooter's eye. He turned to see Gabby carrying the green ball in her mouth, trotting up to Marie. Gabby's big brown eyes were locked on him and Darla Kay. "I see you, Baboo," he said. Thankfully, Gabby remained quiet, and Scooter knew his restriction on talking aggravated her worse than not getting a treat. However, he also knew what she was silently saying with her eyes – *I see you, Scoot-toot.*

"So, you were mentioning something about me becoming a teacher's assistant?" Scooter said to Darla Kay, keeping an eye on his nosey pooch.

Darla Kay giggled. "Well, yes, because you have a heart for these children. But I also know that's not likely to happen. However, we're all thrilled you started this school for special needs children to enjoy a slice of normal life. So, Scooter, in your own right, you are a teacher. I've always wanted to tell you how I felt about all that you do for us."

Scooter leaned close. "I don't know about the gift thing, but I know these children make me much happier than I could ever make them."

"Miss Williams! I need to go potty," announced Emmy, waving her little hands.

Darla Kay said, "Okay, sweetie, I'm coming."

"You know where the potty is, Miss Williams. I gave it a good scrubbing this morning. I'll see you later," said Scooter, watching Darla Kay trot toward Emmy.

Scooter gazed across the sea into the clear horizon where the sky kissed the ocean. He walked slowly into the water up to his waist and then turned back toward the children. A smile creased his face to see the contented young ones playing in the sand or tossing 'fetch toys' for his four-legged friends.

The touching scene stirred up a bittersweet memory from a time when he was much younger and was guilty of poking fun at unfortunate individuals with physical disabilities. He never made his cruel jokes where the subjects could hear, but his friends heard, and usually laughed at his heartless humor. After spending two years in the Army, which helped him mature, he enrolled in a small community college, and, for an unknown reason, decided to major in physical education and work with handicapped youth. A requisite of his college credits requirement was that he spend six hours a week volunteering at the nearby rehabilitation school for special needs children.

The afternoon before he was scheduled to begin his duties, he drove down the narrow country road and pulled up, stopping in front of the large, old brick building. Fear and doubt filled his entire being as he wondered what actually took place behind those walls and what he would be doing beginning the next day. The memory of his earlier cold, cruel jokes reared its ugly head. Determined to go forward with his decision, he took a deep breath, whispered a prayer of forgiveness, and drove off.

The following day, he reported with a stomach full of raging butterflies. What happened next gave a clear affirmation this was his true calling, and, more importantly, that he'd been forgiven. The kind teacher introduced herself and led him into a class filled with children ranging in age from six to ten. Many of the boys and girls wore white plastic helmets. Some were seated in wheelchairs, while others walked with crutches. However, when he knelt down to meet the little ones, every single child gathered around him as if he were a celebrity. Their smiles, high-fives, and innocent acceptance were the most sincere displays of affection he had ever experienced. In the midst of this youthful, unconditional love, his life was forever changed.

That afternoon on his way home he replayed the events of his first day and accepted the truth of why, in his earlier years, he had exhibited such a heartless attitude toward those less fortunate. It wasn't because he was a cold-hearted person. No, those unkind actions were rooted in fear, a fear that maybe he would be stricken with an illness and become like them. In his immature way, he fought that fear with irresponsible humor. Each of these terrible actions would always be his, but from that day until this very moment, these very special individuals had become a major part of his life. Today, and many others like it, were proof that long ago he made the right decision to put aside those fears and replace them with good.

As the refreshing water swished around his feet, he whispered, "Maybe on that day, I was entrusted with the gift Darla Kay mentioned. If so, I'll always treasure and share it," he said into the blue sky as salty tears burned his eyes.

Scooter returned from his inner reflections when he spotted Emmy and Darla Kay coming back from his cottage toward the group as brilliant sunshine reflected like heavenly rays off of the aluminum wheelchair. He hurried out of the water and met Emmy on the dry sand, watching Darla Kay trot back toward the cottage. "Hey, sweetie. Can I get anything for you?"

Little Emmy's beaming smile showed her joy at being on the beach. She said, "Miss Williams said to tell you she had to get something from the van and would be back in a minute."

"Thank you for delivering the message. Are you having a good time?"

She looked down and nodded. "Mr. Scooter, will you get Flash to come over and play with me? Roland's had him a long time. My mama said we should share. Right?"

Scooter knelt before her, his heart touched by her innocence. "Your mother is right, Emmy. I'll go right now and trade places with the floppy-eared puppy and send him to see you."

A light breeze ruffled the long blonde curls framing Emmy's angelic face. "Thank you, Mr. Scooter. I'll play real gentle with Flash. I like him." With skilled precision, she whipped her chair around and slowly rolled back to her area.

Scooter stood. "I'm sure you will, Emmy. Flash *and* Gabby love cute little girls."

Scooter's replacement for Flash was smoother than a bullfrog's skin as far as Roland was concerned. Watching the big-pawed beagle trot over to Emmy, Scooter untied the kite string from Roland's crutch. Once the kite was higher in the cloudless sky, he handed it to Roland. "Fly this, dude," said Scooter.

They laughed and talked about beach stuff like sandfiddlers, sharks, and dolphins. During the question-and-answer session, Scooter realized this young boy was not only inquisitive, but very intelligent. Thankfully, the topic of talking dogs did not return.

About eleven-thirty, Darla Kay joined Scooter and Gabby as they entertained Marie. With Gabby at the 'ready', Scooter would sail the Frisbee out and over the breakers. After he yelled 'fetch', Gabby would plow through the white water, retrieve it, and catch a wave to shore. She would gently place it on little Marie's knee, sit back, and soak up the praise. "Marie, when Gabby came to live here she couldn't swim. Now look at her, I think she's part fish."

"I wish I lived here, Mr. Scooter," replied Marie. "It's so wide open and pretty."

Darla Kay tapped Scooter on the shoulder. "We've got thirty or forty minutes before lunch. Why don't you take Sammy out now? That way, he won't have to wait the required thirty minutes after he eats to go in the water."

"Good idea, Teach. You take my place and fling the Frisbee for Gabby while I go explain to Sammy what we'll do. Oh, I hope you're hungry for my famous PB&J sandwiches and chips."

Marie blared, "Oh, I love peanut butter and jelly sandwiches!"

"Me, too, Mr. Scooter," cooed Darla Kay.

Scooter gave her a gentle nudge and walked over to Sammy and his sandcastle. "Dude, that's cool," said Scooter, kneeling beside the large, fancy creation from an artistic mind.

Sammy swiped a sandy hand across his sweaty forehead, replacing sweat with sparkling sand. "You really like it, Mr. Scooter?"

"You bet. Are you finished?"

The boy paused, giving his structure a careful 'once-over'. "Yes, sir. All I need to do is fill the ditch around it with water. Will you get me some water?"

Scooter nodded and reeled in the kite and untied it from the bucket. He took the two large buckets and trotted down to the water. "Gonna take a lot to fill that moat."

Sammy was still admiring his handiwork when Scooter returned. "This is the first castle I've built since I got sick, Mr. Scooter."

"Well, you sure didn't forget how to construct a fine one. It's certainly better than I could do." Slowly, Sammy emptied both buckets into the trench. "Perfect. The moat is now filled to the rim. But I'll bet when we get back from surfing it will be empty."

"Yes, sir. The sand sucks it up." Evidently the word 'surfing' was slow to register because a few seconds elapsed before Sammy's eyes lit up, and he grinned. "That's right! You're going to teach me to surf. Cool beans! I'm ready, Mr. Scooter."

"Bingo! Let me go get your life vest and surfboard. Oh, all first-time surfers wear the vest. It's no big deal."

"Sure, I don't mind as long as I can go out on a surfboard. Wait until my friends hear about this."

Scooter lifted the wide foam surfboard and orange life vest from the cart. The sound of a panting dog caught his attention. *Scooter, can I go out in the water with you? I need a break. These little ones are running my legs off.*

Quickly looking around for the possibility of someone within earshot, and not seeing anyone, Scooter leaned down. "Easy, girl. Be careful with the talking. But, in answer to your question, sure you can."

In a lower voice, Gabby said, *I looked before I spoke, Scoot-toot.*

"Okay. Here, take the vest over to Sammy. I'll be there as soon as I attach the leash to the surfboard." He handed the vest to his talented mixed black lab and watched her bounce over to a super-excited boy.

While Scooter tied the leash, he eyed the low tide waves rolling into shore. "Perfect for a beginner. Thanks, God."

Sammy listened carefully to Scooter's instructions and details about how the board would be picked up and carried by the wave. After receiving answers to a couple of basic questions, Sammy slipped into the vest and buckled it tight. "I think I'm ready."

The boy's wide eyes and grin warmed Scooter's heart. "You'll do fine. Don't worry about standing up at first. Ride it in on your belly or knees to get the feel. Remember, you and the board are one with the wave. Gabby and I will be out there with you. Ready?"

Sammy nodded and stroked Gabby's head. "Mr. Scooter?"

"Yes."

The little boy raked his foot back and forth over the sand and gazed at the ocean. His eyes became moist. In a soft voice, he said, "Mr. Scooter, I really want to go out, but I feel sad for my friends who can't. I know they would, if they could."

Scooter felt a tug on his heart. This boy suffered from muscular dystrophy, a disease that would eventually deteriorate his muscles. The odds were, in a year or two Sammy would be unable to accomplish what he was about to do, and yet he was concerned about his friends. Scooter knelt beside the compassionate young man and swallowed a growing lump in his throat. "I understand, Sammy. We always have some kids down here that are not physically able to go into the water. If it makes you feel any better, I always encourage them to join in the fun and excitement of watching their friend attempt to surf. Please understand this, buddy," he placed his hand on the boy's shoulder, "in every case, the other children always cheer and clap for their brave classmate. It's sort of like they'll be out there with you mentally. Okay?"

Sammy looked into Scooter's eyes and nodded.

"Good." Scooter stood the red and white board upright beside Sammy. "Boys and girls," he announced loudly. When they looked his way, he said, "Sammy, is going out to try and ride a few waves. He said he's doing this for each of you, too. So, help him with your support by clapping and cheering!"

Scooter's eyes blurred with stinging tears when smiles instantly appeared on everyone's faces and the beach exploded with loud claps and rhythmic chants of "Sammy! Sammy!" Both pups added barks and high-pitched yips.

"Okay, dude! Let's hit the aqua!"

Two guys, plus one paddling pooch, waded through the white water up to their waists. Scooter set the board on the water's surface. "Pull yourself up and lay on your belly like I explained."

While the teachers and kids continued yelling Sammy's name, the boy worked himself up on the soft foam longboard and squiggled his lanky body into position. "Like this?"

"Perfect." Scooter shot a thumb up to the spectators, and then pushed the board forward. "Sammy, can you feel the motion of the ocean beneath the board?"

"Yes, sir. It's really neat."

Once they were out past the small breakers, Scooter turned the board around to face the shore. "Wave to your classmates." The boy gripped the board with his left hand and raised his right. The volume of the cheers increased. "See, they're having fun, too. Wait until you ride one into shore. They'll go bonkers."

"I hope I don't fall off."

Scooter chuckled. "If you do, it's no big deal because all surfers wipe out. Plus, you can swim, and you're wearing a life vest. No fear – no foul." Scooter watched Gabby paddle up and place her front paws on the board. Sammy laughed. "Hey, Gabby!" She yipped once.

Scooter gazed toward the horizon, searching and praying for a perfect swell. Gabby kept Sammy occupied and relaxed. The crowd's noise dimmed a bit, anticipating the show. Suddenly, Scooter said, "I see one with your name on it, Sammy. Here it comes. Get ready. Ride the first one in on your belly."

Sammy nodded. Gabby smoothly pushed off the board and doggie-paddled to the side. As the swell approached, Scooter placed his hand on the tail of the board and slowly pushed it enough to gather speed so the wave could pick it up. "Perfect! Here you go, Sambo!" The beautiful glassy water lifted the board and boy, propelling them smoothly and gently toward the shore. The kids screamed 'Sammy' over and over as they witnessed their friend's first ride. Gabby yipped, answered by a loud bark from Flash. Scooter swallowed another lump and moseyed forward, watching every moment of Sammy's ride. "Thank you, God."

The long board remained straight and steady as it entered the shallow water. Sammy yelled and shot both fists into the sky. "I did it! I surfed!" He slithered off of the board into ankle-deep water and waved. Suddenly, he stood straight up. "Mama! Daddy!"

Scooter pulled up beside the new surfer to see a woman waving to Sammy while the man snapped pictures. Sammy hurried from the shorebreak and made his way onto the beach, arms wide, preparing for a victory hug. Darla Kay walked up slowly behind Sammy's parents and waved to Scooter. "Got ya!"

Scooter returned the wave. "A priceless surprise!" After meeting Sammy's parents, Scooter asked his excited surf student if he wanted to ride some more. The answer was a quick, "Let 'er rip, Mr. Scooter! Watch me, Mom and Dad."

Everyone lined up along the damp sand, rooting for their surfing buddy. Waves sent from above continued to roll in, setting the stage for Sammy to hone his surfing skills. On his third ride, he 'officially' entered the 'wipe out' category. When he popped up on the surface, his smile was bright enough to light a dark night. "Mr. Scooter! I wiped out! Does that mean I'm a surfer?"

Scooter helped him back on the board and gave him a high-five. "You bet, dude!" On his following ride, Sammy struggled to his knees and rode in, arms waving. "Look!"

It took some verbal doing for Scooter to convince Sammy they needed to go in for lunch. "We don't want your friends and parents to starve. They're waiting on us before they dive into my famous peanut butter and jelly sandwiches." Scooter chuckled. "And you're gonna be sore tomorrow. But it's a good sore." He pushed Sammy out for his final wave. "Make this one your best. You've ridden 'em well."

Sammy looked at his surf instructor with twinkling eyes. "Thank you, Mr. Scooter. I love surfing."

The final wave proved to be the best. Its height was almost waist-high, and it rolled slowly, perfect for a solid ride. "Here it comes, Sambo Surfer. Let it rip!" Scooter lightly pushed the board, allowing the wave to lift and propel Sammy. As the wave supplied the power, the crowd exploded with cheers. Scooter watched the young boy quickly struggle up on his knees. Holding his breath, Scooter whispered, "Stand." As if Sammy heard, he pushed up on one foot…then the other. With arms outstretched like a scarecrow, Sammy maintained his delicate balance. The board and wave cooperated. The young surfer remained standing all the way in to the shallows. Sammy shouted, "Yeah!" as he hopped off and splashed through the water toward the crowd, but this time, he went directly to his classmates. High-fives, cheers, and laughter greeted him. Then, after his friends had their moment with the brave surfer, Sammy strutted over to his parents, smiling and pumping his fists.

Scooter paused in waist-deep water and pulled a pooped-out Gabby into his arms as he shed several happy tears. "Baboo, today's been very exceptional, for many reasons."

Life is better when we help others, Scoot. She laid her wet head against his chest and released a deep sigh.

CHAPTER 6

Beneath large, colorful umbrellas, a cluster of happy humans enjoyed a beach picnic. Conversations mostly centered on Sammy and his successful ventures on the waves and the playful puppies. Pride radiated from Sammy's parents like the warmth on the sun-kissed sand. Darla Kay, Barbara, and Mary Beth listened intently, absorbing as much of their students' excitement as possible, knowing today was their final class trip to Sandbridge Beach until next summer. Scooter tossed pieces of his sandwich and chips to the pooches stretched out at his feet, totally exhausted.

As lunch wound down, Sammy's father stood and excused himself, saying he would return with a surprise. This announcement created a buzz among the kids. Darla Kay slipped over beside Scooter. He whispered, "Now it's clear why you wanted me to take Sammy in the water before lunch. You got me good, girl."

Darla Kay leaned close, their bare arms touching. "When his mother called and asked if they could come watch their son attempt to surf, I readily agreed, especially considering Sammy's deteriorating condition. At this point, his muscle loss has been slower than expected, but I'm a believer in taking advantage of opportunity while physical conditions allow." A sweet smile appeared as she looked into Scooter's blue eyes. "I couldn't guarantee her that Sammy would try, but I did convey my confidence in your ability to encourage kids. And again I was right."

"You made the right decision. But I really didn't have to coax him. The boy didn't hesitate, except he felt bad because his friends were unable to go out. After I explained they would be happy cheering him on, he agreed." Scooter took a pull of his lemonade. "The touching part was that, after his last wave, he went to his friends before going to his parents. He's one special boy, Darla Kay. But, honestly, they're all exceptional."

"Yep, and you have the gift." She leaned back and looked him directly in the eyes. "I'm sorry this is our last class this year. I'll certainly miss this place…and you."

Scooter placed his tan hand on hers. "Ditto. Remember, you have an open invitation to come visit."

Darla Kay smiled. "You always say that, but it seems my schedule stays so full." She gazed across the ocean, deeply drawing in the salt air. "Maybe I'll set aside a day before winter arrives."

Sammy's father trotted up, carrying a large blue and white Igloo cooler. "Who wants homemade strawberry ice cream and vanilla wafers for dessert?"

The group, including Scooter, loudly voiced their positive reply with 'I do!' Two pooches signaled their approval with several high-pitched barks. "Good," replied the kind man, "because we've got plenty." He placed the cooler down and lifted the top. Sammy pushed up and joined his father. "Dad, you scoop, and I'll serve."

While everyone held plastic bowls full of cold, pink delight, dotted with sweet brown cookies, Scooter raised his hand. "I'd like to thank the Dowdys for supplying this delicious ending to my bland lunch." This produced several chuckles. "But I also want to thank each of our first-time students for coming today." Scooter paused and made eye contact with the four new kids. "It's been a real pleasure to have you here. As always, we love having all of you. My furry friends and I hope you will come back next summer." He looked at Darla Kay and the aides. "And, I thank you dedicated and nice girls for making this possible." Scooter shoved a spoonful of ice cream in his mouth.

The applause began with Sammy, quickly joined by everyone else. Even Gabby yipped twice. "Thank you, friends," said Scooter.

While Gabby and Flash licked Scooter's bowl, he gathered the others' bowls and deposited them in a garbage bag attached to his cart. He picked up an armful of t-shirts and knelt in front of the children. "This gift comes from me and Gabby and Flash. You can tell your friends you've graduated from the Sandbridge Surfing School. Even though all of you didn't actually surf, your cheering and encouragement gave Sammy the Surfer Dude the desire to go for the big one and ride it standing up." The group cheered and clapped.

Scooter presented the little girls their shirts first, then the boys. "Wear 'em with pride, little beach bums."

In unison, they yelled, "Thank you, Mr. Scooter and Gabby and Flash!" Roland added, "We had a cool time at the beach!"

As the yellow van backed out and pulled away, Scooter waved. He looked down at the tired pups beside his feet. "Well, did you two have a fun day?"

I did. It'd be neat to do this every day.

Scooter, I had lots of fun. And I like the children. They were friendly, and now Emmy's not scared of dogs.

Scooter knelt and rubbed their heads. "And I'm very proud of you. I watched how you both played with everyone and fetched the toys they tossed. I know it was a long day, but together we made them laugh and showed them a good time. Oh, and thanks for not talking around them."

You're welcome, Scoot. In case you're wondering, it's very difficult for me not to talk. So, now I will ask, what are we having for supper?

"Is food all you think about?"

No. I also like afternoon naps, playing in the water, and talking.

"Good. You've played in the water and you're talking, so now go take a nap while I bring the stuff from the beach. Then I'll shower and relax on the deck and decide what we'll have for supper."

That's a great idea, Scoot-toot.

I'm going to sleep, too. My legs feel heavy.

A distant rumble of thunder rattled Scooter from a peaceful, dreamless sleep. An exhausting, yet enjoyable, day had drained his energy, and the outdoor shower readied him for a nap. He slowly opened his eyes and sat up in his reclining beach chair. Dark clouds roiled over the Atlantic, moving south toward Sandbridge Beach. "Looks like we're in for a thunder boomer," he whispered, not wanting to wake the pups who were stretched out, side by side, in the far corner of the deck. Standing, he looked at his watch. "Better get supper on the grill before we're treated to a shower from above."

While washing off two large chicken breasts in the sink, Scooter decided to work on novel edits after supper. Thunderstorms always put him in a creative writing mood. After placing the breasts on a plate and dosing them with salt and pepper, he stepped outside in the waning light and quietly lit the gas grill. Suddenly, the phone threw its shrill ring through the screen door and into the calm evening. "Wonder who that is?" He stepped inside.

"Yel-low," Scooter said cheerfully.

"Hey, Scooter, it's Darla Kay. I hope I'm not interrupting your supper."

"Nope, and if you had, I wouldn't give a hoot. What's up?"

A deep sigh preceded, "I think I've lost my charm bracelet down there. I have scoured every inch of my beach bag and the school van until I'm seeing double. That bracelet means so much to me."

The sound of her voice cracking alerted Scooter to the fact this was not just *any* bracelet. "Settle down and let's take this one step at a time. Did you wear it on the beach?"

"I'm not sure, Scooter. My head was so scrambled from trying to keep the kids quiet on the drive down. Normally I never wear jewelry on the beach; at least, I try not to. And this bracelet was given to me by my mother when I turned thirteen. May I come down and look for it?"

Gabby and Flash entered the small living room and settled at his feet. "Don't you worry, dear. A friend of mine has a metal detector. First thing tomorrow morning, I'll borrow it, search where you parked and then over on the beach in case you forgot to take it off. We'll find your bracelet." Her light sniffles filled his ear.

"Oh, Scooter, I feel so bad. Only last week I had the jeweler clean it and put on a new clasp. It's silver and packed full of charms. Every birthday and Christmas until Mom passed away, she gave me a different charm. It breaks my heart to think I lost it."

Scooter pursed his lips and looked out the picture window in time to see a bolt of cloud-to-ground lightning dive into the ocean. "With a metal detector, Darla Kay, I can find it. We know where our camp was set up, and since you didn't go into the water, if it did come off down there, it's findable. I'll call Mike tonight and tell him I'll be by in the morning to borrow the detector. I'd do it tonight, but a thunderstorm is preparing to visit. Promise me you'll not worry."

Her sniffles ceased. "Okay, Scooter, I'll try."

"You get some rest. It's been a long day. I'll get on it at daybreak. As soon as I'm holding it in my hand, I'll call you."

"Thank you, Scooter. If anyone can find it, you can. Call me at home or leave a message for me at school. Give the pups a hug from me. Good night."

"I will. Sleep well." He placed the receiver in the cradle and took a deep breath. "We've got a little problem to solve," he said to his now-standing companions.

What kind of problem?

"Darla Kay thinks she lost her silver charm bracelet somewhere down here. Her mother gave it to her when she was a teenager. It means a lot to her because it holds many memories."

What's a bracelet?

Scooter chuckled and picked up a fork and the plate of chicken. "Let me put the chicken on the grill and I'll explain, Flash."

Yeah, Scoot-toot, don't forget our supper. I'm starving.

Scooter slapped the breasts on the hot grill and paused, gazing down to the dimpled sand where their camp had been. The wind had increased as low pressure and dark clouds approached. A downpour would compact the sand, leveling out the footprints, and pushing the light-weight bracelet a few inches deeper. "I'd better call Mike. Without his metal detector, we don't stand much chance of finding it."

Scooter entered the cottage and went over to the phone. While dialing Mike's number, he heard Gabby attempting to explain to Flash what a bracelet was. *Look at it this way, Flash. It's like a dog collar, but for* humans. *Some wear them around their neck like dogs, but others wear them on their arms. I don't know why, since they don't need a license like we do.*

Scooter listened to several rings, and then Mike's answering machine clicked on. While the machine was telling him to leave a message, he said to Gabby, "That's pretty good, Baboo."

I still don't understand, Scooter.

When Scooter finds it, I'll show you how they work. Like I say, you've got a lot to learn.

Scooter left a brief message and placed the receiver down. "Well, he'll call back. I'd better tend to the chicken." He moved outside, wondering if Mike was out of town on business. "If so, I'll rent one," he whispered, picking up the long, two-pronged fork.

Gabby and Flash took their position beside the grill. *Scooter, can I help you look for Darla Kay's bracelet tomorrow?*

"Sure, you both can. We're gonna need help *and* luck. Darla Kay's a sweet person, and I'd really like to find her bracelet." Scooter forked the breasts and flipped them.

I was wondering. Since Darla Kay's got eyes for you...if you find this bracelet... you will move up a couple of notches in her 'like' column. Right?

"Will you lose the idea of Darla Kay having eyes for me? We're good friends, Gabby. If I didn't know better, I'd think you were jealous of her. Is that it? You don't want anyone sharing my time?"

Don't be silly. I'm only telling you what I see and feel. Females have unique instincts. But, to ease your mind, I know you'd never neglect tending to me.

"Exactly. So drop the subject. I want to find her bracelet because it means a lot to her. End of story."

Good. I'm happy now. How much longer before we eat?

"Thirty minutes."

Flash hopped up and paced the east railing of the deck. His tail wagged as he jammed his snoot into the darkening sky. Scooter asked, "What is it, Flash? Do you smell something?"

The floppy-eared pooch shuffled up beside Scooter. ***While you cook, I'd like to walk down to the beach and look for Darla Kay's bracelet.***

"I appreciate that, little dude, but it's getting dark, and these clouds are gonna dump a load of water in a little while. Let's wait until morning. Her bracelet isn't going anywhere."

But I need to go now.

"Oh, you gotta do your math?"

Scoot, he prefers 'do your business'. The 'math thing' goes right over his head.

No, not my business. But if I go now, maybe I can find it.

"How are you going to find something when you're not sure exactly what it is?"

I know, Scoot-toot. He probably wants to stroll the beach and sniff out the fox.

Flash looked at Gabby and then back to Scooter. **If it rains tonight, I won't be much help tomorrow.**

Maybe his nose doesn't work if the ground is wet.

Come on, Scooter, let me go. It won't take long.

Scooter spotted the angst building in the bewildered beagle's eyes. He glanced out and noticed the lightning had moved farther out over the ocean, leaving only dark clouds. "Okay, Flash. You can go sniff the area where we were today. If the bracelet slipped off of her wrist or fell out of her bag, it should be down there. Where? I have no idea. I'll call you when it's time to eat."

Flash broke into a trot, heading down the stairs. **Thanks, Scooter...I want to help Darla Kay cause she's real nice.**

Gabby shook her head as she moved to the railing and watched the beagle plow through the sand toward the angry ocean. *Poor little fellow, he means well. I told you, he has so much to learn about the beach and humans.*

Scooter flipped the chicken and chuckled. "I'm sure you'll teach him. But I liked the comparison you used about the human bracelet and a dog's collar. I hope Flash got the picture."

Look at him. He's down there sniffing for something with no smell, that he can't eat, while missing this wonderful aroma of chicken grilling. One of these days, I'll teach him how to put the important things in the correct order.

"You do that, Baboo." Scooter stepped over beside Gabby. "He looks pretty serious about his search. Look, he's using his nose like a plow, digging a couple of inches below the surface. And it appears there's a particular method to his hunting technique. See, he started down at the north boundary of our camp and is moving east and west in a straight line? That's amazing."

That's silly. If his nose is so sensitive, why doesn't he stand in the middle and take big sniffs? Gabby yipped. *Bet we would hear his nose whistling from here. Once he...wait, what am I saying? Now I'm thinking like him. Darla Kay's bracelet doesn't smell like a fox or a wild animal.*

"Well, at least he's happy doing what he can. Darla Kay will appreciate that."

Darla Kay will appreciate having the bracelet in her hand. Hey, when you find it tomorrow, will you get on one knee and give it to her? I've seen humans do that on TV.

"No, Gabby. Where do you come up with this crazy nonsense?" Scooter kept his eyes on Flash's flapping tail and precise movements. His back-and-forth actions reminded Scooter of cutting grass. Flash wasn't overlooking an inch, coming or going. However, the amount of time it appeared to take to cover the narrow area from the west boundary to the tide line could take hours. Scooter knew the little fellow was exhausted from a busy day, but there he was, nose down, tail wagging, plodding along at a snail's pace.

Scooter, my nose tells me our chicken is ready. I'd like mine cut into medium-sized pieces, please.

"Right. Everything is almost ready. Go tell Flash it's time to eat. We'll continue the search in the morning."

Okay. Don't start without us.

Scooter chuckled, forked the chicken onto the plate, and turned off the grill as the fragrance of rain replaced the aroma of grilled chicken. "I hope Mike gets my message," he mumbled, walking inside.

By the time Scooter had sliced the chicken and prepared the doggies' bowls, Gabby rushed inside, out of breath. Scooter watched as she poked her muzzle into the water bowl and slurped wildly. "Where's Flash?" Scooter asked, peering onto the deck.

With beads of water dripping from her chin, Gabby looked at him and plopped on her haunches. *That dog is not right, Scoot. Just not right. I told him our chicken was ready, but he ignored me and kept pushing his big snoot through the sand. So, to get his attention, I stood in front of him. Want to know what he did?*

"Yep."

Scooter, the nit-wit growled at me. His back fur even stood up. In case you didn't know, that's a serious warning to humans and dogs. This bracelet hunt has taken control of our little Flash. I'd hate to see him after a rabbit. You better go talk to him.

Stifling a chuckle, Scooter placed her bowl of Puppy Chow and chunks of chicken on the floor. "You eat while I check on him." He picked up a small piece of moist, grilled chicken. "Maybe a whiff of this will convince him to take a break and come eat."

Gabby nodded, preferring to eat over providing a reply.

Several large drops of rain pelted Scooter as he moved across the beach, the typical beginning to a coastal gully-washer. Aided by heavy, water-logged clouds, darkness hovered only minutes away. Scooter reached the west border of their camp and paused, watching the beagle's tan and white butt and swishing tail moving toward the ocean. "That's one focused, determined dog."

When Flash reached the eastern border, he used his paw to dig a small hole. Then he stepped south twelve to fifteen inches, dropped his nose, and resumed his search, heading back toward Scooter. After taking a nibble of the warm chicken, Scooter said, "If this won't tempt him to take a break, nothing will." The rain increased.

Finally, fifteen minutes later, Flash reached Scooter. "Hey, buddy. You've almost covered a third of our area. How about taking a break until tomorrow morning? Your supper is ready, and a heavy rainstorm is looming." Flash paused, looked up at Scooter, and remained quiet. Kneeling, Scooter said, "Taste this chicken." Scooter extended the chicken to Flash.

Flash quickly turned his sand-covered muzzle away from the offering. *No, Scooter. If I smell it, my focus will be messed up. I'll be up after I find the bracelet.*

The seriousness of his statement stunned Scooter. "Before you finish, Flash, we'll be in the midst of a downpour. Come inside, eat, get a good night's sleep. Tomorrow I'll use a metal detector to help *you* find Darla Kay's bracelet."

Flash slowly dug the small hole and turned around, nose to the ground. With no reply to Scooter's suggestion, the pup headed east. "Okay, buddy, it's your call. When you come up on the deck, bark, and I'll open the door." Scooter turned, popped the chicken in his mouth, and returned to his cottage. "Wait until Gabby hears this," he said as the rain fell faster.

Gabby had finished eating and was stretched out on the hardwood floor when Scooter entered. Without lifting her head, she said, *He didn't come with you, did he?*

Scooter put a chicken breast and several slices of iceberg lettuce smothered with Italian dressing on the plate. "Nope. Our little pal's fueled by a huge dose of dogged-determination, so strong he refused to even smell the piece of chicken. He claimed it would mess up what he was sniffing for." Scooter shook his head and filled a glass with sweet tea. "Since it's no longer lightning, I figure it's best to let him continue." He glanced at his answering machine, and seeing no red light blinking, took a seat at the table, and released a sigh of worry and exhaustion.

Gabby pushed into the upright position and pawed her muzzle. *Scoot, in my opinion, Flash is wound too tight. I came to this conclusion the first night I watched him eat. I've never seen any dog take little nibbles at food and then touch his tongue to his water. Don't forget, I witnessed him going bonkers sniffing out the 'invisible' fox, too. Let's hope he outgrows this weird disorder.*

"It's not a disorder, Baboo. I've told you that beagles are born with an exceptional ability to smell, and with that comes a driving desire to hunt. I consider that a trait, not a disorder. Concerning his eating manners, I'm guessing since he's a new member of our family, he's being overly careful to make a good impression." Scooter forked a leaf of lettuce.

Okay, I'll buy the hunting thing. But if you remember when I came here seven months ago, I didn't worry about my manners until you mentioned them. See, I'm normal.

Scooter laughed and wiped his mouth with the napkin. "So, are we to use you as the model of normal dog behavior?"

You won't go wrong, Scoot-toot.

"By chance, while I was out with Flash, did the phone ring?"

Nope. Hey, that reminds me. What are you going to do if you don't get the metal detector?

Cutting another slice of tender chicken, Scooter replied, "Guess I'll rent one. It'd be worth it to find Darla Kay's bracelet."

Yeah. And that would up you on her list of nice guys.

Scooter ignored her remark.

The rain and wind had increased, just shy of becoming a first-class storm. A pitch-black sky added to the already dreary conditions. Scooter finished his supper and quickly washed the dishes. Standing in front of the glass doors, he saw absolutely nothing except white water riding atop waves just before they crashed onto the shoreline. He glanced at the wall clock, which read quarter past eight. He calculated how much ground Flash might have covered by now; his estimation – maybe half of the camp area.

Gabby broke the solemn silence. *Do you think Flash will come in later? I know he's soaked.* The unmistakable sound of worry was evident in her every word.

"Not until he finds the bracelet, Gabby."

You're kidding, right?

"No. There's no doubt he's on a mission. He barely paid me any mind."

Well, what happens if he doesn't find it, Scoot?

Scooter stroked her head. "I don't know. When I was younger, a friend of mine used to deer hunt with his Bluetick hound. That dog would rather run a deer than eat, exactly like Flash is doing. Anyway, one very cold day, they went hunting in the Dismal Swamp. That place is like 'no man's land'. Old Blue got on a scent and off he went. No matter how much Wayne called and blew his cow horn, Old Blue continued running. Eventually, the hound was out of ear-shot. Wayne, on the verge of freezing, finally returned to his truck and waited, hoping Blue would give up and find his way back." Scooter stood and returned to the window.

Well? Did he? Don't leave me hanging, Scooter.

"Wayne never found him. He figured Blue may have dropped dead or had a fatal run-in with a bear. My friend gave up hunting and became a veterinarian."

That's a sad story. I guess you're right about some hunting dogs not wanting to quit. Well, at least we know where Flash is, and we don't have bears at the beach. Do we?

Scooter laughed and took a seat at his computer, needing to get his mind off of little Flash. "No bears. At least I've never heard of any down here. Anyway, while we're waiting, I'll do a few edits."

Good. I'll take a nap.

Scooter fought fatigue and trudged through edits on three chapters, and then shut down the computer. He pushed up from the chair and stretched his tired muscles. The clock said it was after eleven o'clock. Gabby remained in a tight ball, sound asleep. "Oh, man." He opened the sliding door, relieved to see the rain had become drizzle. "Okay, Flash, I'm coming to check on you. It's late and we all need sleep."

The clouds drifted slowly across the sky and revealed a sliver of a pale crescent moon. When Scooter neared the camp, he saw a dark figure, low to the ground, moving slowly on the southern end. Wet sand stuck to his bare feet as he hurried over to Flash. "Hey, dude. How're you holding up?"

Flash refused to halt his hunt. ***Pretty good. The hard rain stopped. Nothing so far, but I'm not finished. If I don't find it here, I'll sniff the path everyone took on their way down here.***

"Flash, I know you're tuckered out, like Gabby and me. We all need our rest so when sunrise comes, we can start refreshed, hopefully using the metal detector. Mark your place and let's go in. You've done well."

You go sleep, Scooter. If the bracelet is down here, I'll find it before daybreak.

"Aw, come on, Flash. I can't sleep soundly knowing you're out here alone sucking sand up your nose. It'll be so much easier with the detector."

Silence.

Scooter felt a twinge of anger rising. Holding it at bay, he said, "Okay. Have it your way. Since the rain has almost stopped, I'll leave the sliding door open enough for you to squeeze in whenever you're ready. I'll leave a dry towel on your sleeping chair. Good luck." Scooter turned and headed back, looking forward to crawling between the cool sheets.

Okay, Scooter.

A sleepy-eyed Gabby greeted Scooter at the door. *Well?*

"I'm going to bed. That little hardheaded hound is determined to scour every inch of our camp area, and then he's planning to search the path we walked down there. The boy is in a zone, Gabby. I sure hope he finds it, but the chances are slim to none, and Slim just left." Scooter closed the door, leaving enough room for Flash to enter. "You coming to bed?"

Yep. Going to do my math, and I'll be right there. I need my beauty rest.

Before crawling into the soft bed, Scooter folded a thick towel and placed it on the bedroom chair where Flash preferred to sleep. By the time Scooter had brushed his teeth, Gabby was back and curled up on the foot of the bed. *Nite, Scoot-toot. It's been one exciting day, full of surprises.*

Scooter fluffed his pillows, slipped beneath the sheets like an exhausted eel and turned off the light. "Right you are, Baboo. See ya in the morning," he said as his head hit the pillow.

CHAPTER 7

One of the best benefits of coastal thunderstorms, besides delivering water, comes when their visit occurs during the late evening and night. Usually, the result is a magnificent sunrise popping from a glassy ocean and a cloudless blue sky. This proved true the following morning at Sandbridge Beach.

A red-orange glow slowly lured Scooter from a restful sleep. After gathering his mental bearings, the first item on his agenda was to check on Flash. After palming his eyes, he gazed over to Flash's chair. Scooter was thrilled to find it now held a motley-looking beagle with a sand-covered muzzle. A fresh grin tightened Scooter's lips. As he looked at the little beagle, a ray of sunlight twinkled on something shiny lying across the white paws. Scooter squinted and leaned forward. "Oh, my goodness! You found it, Flash!" The loud announcement filled the silent room, quickly upping both pooches' heads as if they were yanked up by strings.

What's going on, Scoot? Gabby hopped to her feet, glaring at him with puzzled eyes.

Flash sighed and aimed his snoot in their direction. ***I found Darla Kay's bracelet.***

Gabby snapped around and yipped. *Great, Flash. Where was it?*

Scooter quickly slid from bed and knelt beside the chair and hugged the still-damp, sand-covered puppy, carefully lifting the silver, charm-filled bracelet. "I'm proud of you, boy. Your dogged-determination and expert sniffing paid off."

Gabby repeated her question. *I asked where you found it.*

The last place I looked, Gabby.

Gabby moved forward and propped her head on the footboard. *Does that mean if you'd looked there 'first' you would've found it?*

Yeah.

A flood of happiness shot through Scooter while he ran the sand-encrusted bracelet through his fingers. "Gabby, he means the search ended once he found it. Get it? The last place he looked."

Gabby pawed her eyes. *It's too early for you both to be talking weird.* After a long yarn, she said, *I knew he would stop looking when he found it, as long as the fox didn't come around.* Gabby yipped twice. *Anyway, nice work, Flash. I'm proud of you, too.*

"Where was it, Flash?"

On the path we took to the beach, between our camp and their van. It was down pretty deep because the sand's fluffy there. And I think people had stepped on it.

I've got a question, little buddy. Scooter said you refused the piece of chicken. I'd like to know why.

To smell it, which I always do before eating anything, would have messed up the scent I was sniffing for. Scooter, did you save my chicken? I'm real hungry.

Wait just a minute! Eating would mess up a what? Scent? I think all that sand went up your nose to your brain.

When Darla Kay left, she hugged and stroked us, right?

Yeah. Don't forget, she kissed Scoot-toot on the cheek. If you needed a reminder of her fragrance, you could have sniffed his cheek. Gabby yipped three times.

Whatever. Anyway, I remembered her scent. Since she wore the bracelet, it would also smell like her. You with me so far?

"I am, Flash. It makes sense."

Yeah.

But, unlike an animal that leaves a fresh scent with each step, the bracelet wouldn't hold her scent for very long. That's why I wanted to search for it quickly, especially before it rained. Her fragrance remained on it longer because it was fairly deep in the sand. Anyway, now Darla Kay will be happy.

Scooter placed the bracelet in front of Gabby. "Can you smell Darla Kay's sweet fragrance?"

Gabby sniffed it up and down. *No, I can't, Scooter, but there's no missing Flash's wet-fur stink. Not much smells worse than wet fur...PU!*

"Flash, you are King for a Day! And yes, I saved the chicken for you. Let me get dressed, and you can have it for breakfast. Then, I'll call Darla Kay. She's gonna be thrilled."

I'm hungry, too, Scoot. You have any chicken for me?

"Nope, but I do have a cup of Puppy Chow with your name on it."

Gabby shook her head and hopped from the bed. *That's okay, Flash won't eat all of his.*

After Scooter placed their breakfast bowls on the floor, he poured a steaming cup of hot, liquid caffeine and dialed Darla Kay's home number. She answered, fatigue accenting her words. Scooter quickly delivered the good news, using his most cheerful voice. After hearing his announcement, her emotions took over. While Scooter waited patiently for her to regain her composure, he glanced at the little hero and watched him devouring the hunks of grilled chicken. Today, slow nibbles were absent, and Flash did not stop until the bowl was bare. Then he went over and slurped his water. Gabby was already finished and watched her little buddy's new eating technique in amazement as her anticipated chicken hand-out disappeared. She looked up at Scooter. *Well, our little dude's eating habits have certainly changed all of a sudden.*

Scooter smiled and replied to Darla Kay's question, "Okay. That would be fine. I'm sure we'll enjoy whatever you prepare. Yes, I'll tell them. See you around six. He's right here." He held the receiver a foot from the floor. "Flash, someone wants to speak to you."

Flash pawed drops of water from his muzzle and approached the receiver. As Scooter put it to his ear, he said, "Okay, Darla Kay, Flash is listening."

Scooter was unable to hear her words, but in thirty seconds, Flash yipped twice and looked at Scooter. Returning the receiver to his ear, Scooter said, "Whatever you said made him yip and wag his tail, so that means he's happy. Yeah, he refused to quit searching until he found it. No, I'm not sure what time he came in. Gabby and I were sound asleep. Good, we'll see you this evening. Have a great day. Bye."

No sooner than Scooter put the receiver down, the phone rang. Mike's familiar voice said, "Sorry I missed your call, Scooter. My flight was delayed in Chicago, which caused me to miss my connecting flight. I just walked in the house. You want me to bring my metal detector down?"

"Glad you finally made it back. It looks like I won't need the detector. We found the bracelet...well, my new beagle sniffed it out. Thanks, Mike. I'll talk to you later. See ya."

Darla Kay's coming over tonight, Scooter.

"Yep. I'll bet you'll get a surprise meal for your hard work and determination. By the way, since you're the King today, what would you like to do, Flash?"

Yeah, Flash, make it real cool. Try something brand new.

Suddenly, Flash sneezed so hard he scooted back a couple of inches on the hardwood floor. He shook his head and pawed his muzzle. Gabby yipped. *I'll bet your snoot's packed full of sand.*

I want to learn to swim. Gabby makes it look like fun.

Scooter nodded. "Okie-dokie. You've picked a perfect day because the waves are small. Gabby, will you help teach him?"

Sure, Scoot. With those big paws, he won't have trouble paddling.

Thanks, Gabby. And whenever you're ready, I'll teach you to track scents.

"Now, that's a fair trade," said Scooter. "Before long, I'll be surrounded by multi-talented pooches."

The October sun deposited pleasant warmth over the coast. Scooter relaxed in his canvas beach chair and watched Gabby finally coax Flash out over his head and instruct him, visually and verbally, on the art of dog paddling. After only a couple of attempts, the young beagle was splashing alongside Gabby. They moved slowly, parallel to the beach. Scooter cheered them on, feeling another jolt of pride as he hustled down the steps and across the beach. Walking out waist-deep, Scooter hollered, "You've got it, Flash! Nice work, Gabby!"

It's fun, Scooter!

Several dolphins lazily worked the area fifty yards out past them, and Scooter pointed them out. Both pooches turned, facing the horizon. Suddenly, Flash worked himself around and headed to shore. Gabby bellowed, *Hey! Where're you going?*

To shore! They're big!

Scooter chuckled, understanding it would take time for the new pooch to become totally comfortable with the 'things' that lived in the ocean. When Flash's paws touched bottom, he trotted through the white water and performed a full body shake. "Well, buddy, you can add swimming to your list of new accomplishments," said Scooter in an encouraging voice.

Scooter, I know you said those dolphins won't hurt us, but my legs were getting tired.

"I'm sure you washed off a lot of last night's sand."

Flash shook again, sprinkling Scooter with fine droplets, and then he plopped down and released a sigh.

Gabby skillfully rode a small wave into the shallows. *What a great way to start a day. Flash, not bad for your first time out in the ocean.*

Thanks. You're a good teacher.

Don't worry about the dolphins. They're gentle…unless you're a small fish, right, Scoot?

"Right," he replied, standing. "I need to go up and finish my edits and write a biography page for the book. What are you gonna do?"

Take a nap.

Me too.

The trio crossed the warm sand toward the cottage. When they came upon the area Flash had scoured only hours earlier in search of the bracelet, Gabby stopped and looked it over. *I've never seen so many paw prints in one area, Flash. But I'd like to know why there are little holes at the top and bottom edges.*

Oh, that's where I stopped and turned around. Digging the hole let me know I'd covered that area. It was dark out here.

"That's pretty creative, Flash," said Scooter.

I think this 'hole' thing is overkill, Scoot. Gabby yipped once.

Well, that's the point, Gabby. I wanted to cover the whole thing.

"I get it, Flash," replied Scooter, chuckling.

That's what I meant, guys.

Gabby resumed her walk to the cottage, shaking her head. *He's hopeless, Scooter. I never thought these words would come from my mouth, but here I go: Scoot, it's time you told a few of your lame jokes to begin teaching our up-tight beagle about humor.*

"Great idea, Gabby. Maybe I'll throw out a couple while Darla Kay is here tonight."

Gabby broke into a trot, puffs of sand flying from her hind feet. *Ah, I should've kept my mouth shut!*

Flash walked silently beside Scooter.

"She's joking. That's her way of saying digging the holes was a good idea. You'll get used to Gabby's ways. It certainly took me a while."

It's no big deal. I would've done anything to find Darla Kay's bracelet.

Scooter reached down and gave Flash a couple of soft pats on the head. "You succeeded. Tonight you'll see one happy woman."

After returning to the cottage, both pooches hit the deck and sprawled out in the sun. Scooter filled a glass with ice and sweet tea and settled behind his computer to begin his bio page. "One small paragraph will hold my skimpy history." He chuckled. "Life is still good at Sandbridge Beach."

CHAPTER 8

The afternoon could have been considered dull, except for one fantastic bit of news. The phone call came at four o'clock as Scooter was heading down the stairs for an outdoor shower in preparation for Darla Kay's visit. When Scooter answered, he figured it was Darla Kay with additions to the evening's celebratory festivities. However, when a young woman identified herself as Jan Robbins, a director's assistant with Disney Productions in Burbank, California, Scooter thought he would explode. However, he kept the lid on his excitement by recalling the instant jubilation he felt upon seeing an envelope in the mailbox containing a response from a literary agent to his first query letter. In a rush, he ripped it open, only to find a rejection letter.

With a sweaty hand, Scooter kept the receiver tight against his ear and his exhilaration down while listening intently to the young woman's introduction and reason for her call. As she spoke, Gabby and Flash entered and plopped at his feet, heads tilted upward like they knew what was happening. Scooter covered the mouthpiece and whispered to Gabby, "It's the movie people." Instantly, Gabby yipped, bounced a couple of times, and then rolled onto her back and wiggled her paws in the air. Scooter stifled a grin and aimed his gaze to the blue-green ocean as he replied, "Yes, I have a pen and paper right here."

Flash remained motionless and wide-eyed, taken aback by Gabby's actions. Scooter's hand flew across the page as he scribbled notes, nodding like a blonde bobble-head doll with bulging peepers. Every detail of Disney's plans for Scooter and Gabby's first tasks was clearly and efficiently covered by the professional assistant.

"Yes, indeed. We would be thrilled to come to California and meet with you, Ms. Robbins," Scooter said, feeling his heart rate increase.

The next tidbit of information was revealed and turned Scooter's legs into rubber, causing him to lean against the counter for support. His writing hand tensed. With his mouth dry as sand, his reply came out in a whimper. "Ah, yes. Sure, we can fly. No, Gabby's not afraid. Ah, well, no, ma'am, she's never been on a plane before." He glanced down at the now still Gabby, her ears perked and eyes opened wide. Nodding, he said to the lady, as calmly as possible, "A private jet? Oh, sure, that would be neat, I mean, fine. Ah, I also have a newly rescued beagle pup. Would you mind if he came along? I'd hate to put him in a kennel." Scooter glanced at Flash. "Oh, thank you, ma'am. Yes, he's very well-behaved."

Back into the note-taking mode, sweat beaded on Scooter's forehead. "Yes, ma'am. That's fine, we'll be there. Thank you so much." Slowly, Scooter placed the receiver in the cradle and took a deep breath, swiping the puddle of moisture off his brow.

Gabby hopped to her feet and raised her tail. *What, Scooter? Did I hear you say something about flying? You remember how I hated crossing the bridge tunnel over the Chesapeake Bay, so forget about me getting in a plane. Are they going to make the movie about me?*

Suddenly the small, hot kitchen was void of air. Scooter said weakly, "I need fresh air." Slowly, as if walking on tacks, he made his way onto the deck and inhaled several gulps of salt air. Gripping the deck railing hard with white knuckles, he gazed over the calm ocean. Gabby nuzzled up against his bare leg. *You feel all right, Scoot?*

"Yes. Disney wants to make the movie," he whispered, afraid to announce the news too loudly in case this whole scene was a dream and he would wake.

About me?

"Yep, all about you."

What's a movie?

Scooter felt a grin forming, but tight nerves prevented it from appearing.

It's like a real long television program with no interruptions.

What's a television program?

I'll show you later. Anyway, Scoot, you'd better sit down. You look pale.

Taking Gabby's advice, Scooter backed up like a mummy and fell into his canvas beach chair. Gabby eased up and gently placed her chin on his leg. Scratching her ear, he said, "They want us to be in California on Friday and stay until Sunday afternoon. They will put us up in a fancy, pet-friendly hotel."

I know I might sound like Flash by asking this question, but...where is California?

"The West Coast, Baboo. We're sitting on the East Coast now, so the West Coast is behind us."

Is it a long way from here?

Scooter nodded. "Yes. But Disney is sending one of their private jets to pick us up Friday morning at six o'clock at the Norfolk International Airport. Oh, and the nice screenwriters we met in New York will meet us at the studio."

Gabby lifted her head from his leg and backed up. *That's nice, Scoot, but I'm not sure I will be at the studio.*

"What do you mean, you might not be there?"

You have a short memory, but I don't. See, I've not forgotten the long, high bridge and dark tunnel we crossed going to New York. Well, imagine how I'd handle being way, way up in the air. I've seen the jets flying fast out here over the ocean.

"Okay. Your decision not to fly takes a load off of my mind. I'll call the nice lady back and tell her we're going to pass on being considered for their movie. I'm sure they can get another dog that looks like you. Well, guess I'll go down and take my shower and get dressed before Darla Kay arrives." He stood and stretched.

Gabby yipped. *Hold on, Scooter-tooter. I said 'no' to flying, but not 'no' to the movie. Listen, let's look at this situation logically. Since this movie is about me doing things here at my beach, then it makes perfect sense to make it at Sandbridge. I suggest they get on the plane and come to us, not the other way around. Now, call her and tell her.*

Scooter discharged a deep sigh. "The movie business doesn't work that way, Gabby. They call the shots, period. Remember, I told you they have an ocean in California."

You also said their water is colder. So if I'm going to be swimming around, I prefer to swim in our water…it's warmer.

Scooter knew Gabby well enough to know she would not miss the opportunity to be in a movie featuring her – either because of the flight or the temperature of the ocean. He realized the best way to handle this situation was to let the details rest and allow her time to mull on it. In a short while, she would change her mind. "Baboo, I'm only telling you what the lady told me. She did not ask me what we preferred to do." He headed toward the stairs. "I'll be in the shower."

Wait, Scoot!

Scooter threw up his hand, disappearing down the steps, whistling the song "What a Difference a Day Makes".

Scooter moved around the kitchen as smoothly as riding a glassy wave, wiping the counter with a towel in one hand and skillfully tossing two bright orange placemats onto the table. "Bingo," he said when they landed and stayed. Glancing at the wall clock, the surfboard hands showed six o'clock. "Any time now," he said, stepping onto the deck just as Gabby and Flash made their way over the sandy dune coming toward the cottage. Gabby's head was down, her gait slow. "I'll bet Flash got an earful about the trip." No sooner than he threw up his hand to them, the doorbell chimed. "Darla Kay's here," he hollered, then turned and hurried inside to open the front door.

"Hey, Darla Kay." Scooter took the large picnic basket from her as she kissed his cheek. The fragrance of perfume filled him with pleasant, warm sensations. "We have a lot to celebrate tonight."

She fingered a strand of long blonde hair behind her ear. "You bet we do. Where are my favorite furry friends?"

Scooter closed the door with his bare foot and followed her into the small living room. "They're coming up from a stroll on the beach." He set the large basket on the kitchen counter. "How about a glass of sweet tea?"

Darla Kay looked at him with twinkling azure eyes and smiled. "Sounds perfect."

While he filled two tropically decorated glasses with ice cubes and poured the tea, the sound of paws tromping up the steps slipped through the open sliding door. "Here come King Flash and the Queen."

"Oh, good!"

Flash lagged several steps behind Gabby as they entered the kitchen. Scooter suddenly remembered he had forgotten to remind them about not talking. He knelt beside Gabby and whispered, "No talking." She nodded once and walked over beside Darla Kay with little Flash in tow.

Darla Kay sat, lotus style, on the floor and pulled them close. "It's so nice to see you both again. Without having little children to look after, I can spend more time with you." After giving each one a hug, she looked into the beagle's big brown eyes. "Flash, you'll never know how happy I am that you found my bracelet. Thank you." She gave him another hug.

Scooter handed Darla Kay the tea, along with a long, slender package wrapped in silver paper. "This belongs to you. Flash worked like crazy to find it."

Darla Kay looked up and gently took the package. A lone tear trickled down her tan cheek. "To have lost this bracelet my mother gave me would have broken my heart." She followed a sip of tea with a deep breath and corralled her emotions.

Flash instantly sensed her tender feelings and snuggled closer to her, resting his head on her bare leg. Gabby leaned gently against Darla Kay's arm. Darla Kay removed the silver paper and opened the narrow box. "Thank you all." Scooter knelt and fastened the silver charm bracelet around her wrist.

Darla Kay hugged the puppies again and flashed Scooter a bright smile, her eyes still moist.

Scooter stood and said to his four-legged companions, "Did you two have a relaxing beach walk?"

Gabby released a low yip. Flash followed suit.

Darla Kay giggled. "Sounds like a 'yes', Scooter. You certainly have two very intelligent pooches."

The butterflies fluttered wildly inside his stomach. "If you only knew, dear." He stepped over and opened the picnic basket. "Let's see what Darla Kay brought for our supper. Ooh, lookie here." Scooter removed a shiny insulated bag and unzipped it. "Wow! Three thick steaks." He shot Darla Kay a grin. "Yummy."

The attractive blonde hopped to her feet and joined Scooter at the counter, snuggling close. "We'll split one for the little ones. If you'll perform your magic on the grill, I'll handle everything else. Remember, this supper is to show my appreciation to Flash…and, of course, I'm pleased you and Gabby will join us." She hugged Scooter and pecked his cheek.

Gabby yipped. Scooter knew exactly what she was thinking. He winked at Miss Spy.

"We're honored to be a part of this celebration, Darla Kay."

"Okie-dokie, you start the grill while I make the salad." She pulled out two large baking potatoes wrapped in aluminum foil. "I started these at home in the oven, but they're much better when finished on the grill."

Scooter stepped out onto the deck and fired up the grill. "Darla Kay, this is 'high on the hog' compared to our normal suppers." Gabby eased up and nudged his leg. "Are you hungry, Baboo?"

Gabby glanced back into the kitchen as Darla Kay chopped lettuce and talked to Flash. *Hey, Scoot, I don't know what to do about this movie thing. I'm really mixed up.*

Scooter motioned to her, and they headed downstairs. Standing in the cool sand below the deck, he knelt and stroked her head. "The decision is yours, Gabby. I understand how you might feel uneasy about flying, but, really, there's nothing to it. No matter what you decide, I'll back you."

You know how I'm always acting tough and brave? Well, I'm really not. Those jets that fly overhead are going really fast, Scoot.

Scooter smiled. "Would you believe me if I said flying is safer than riding in a car?"

Well, so far you've never steered me wrong. But, at least in a car…we're on the ground.

"Right. But according to statistics, flying is safer. That's just a little nugget of information for you to think on as you make this important decision. Until you've made up your mind, I won't say anything about the movie to Darla Kay. Now, let's go help her with supper. You always think better with a full belly."

Okay, Scooter. Thanks for understanding.

"You're welcome. All that matters to me is that you're happy."

I'm hungry, Scoot.

As they climbed the steps, Scooter chuckled. "That doesn't surprise me."

Scooter placed the potatoes and steaks on the grill and closed the lid. "Supper's on the grill, friends. It won't be long."

Dusk placed a golden canopy over the coastline. Darla Kay pulled up beside Scooter as he manned the grill. "If they taste half as good as they smell, we're in for a treat."

Scooter carefully forked the smaller steak and placed it on the plate. "This one's for our carnivore canines...just a tad past rare." He gently flipped the other two slabs of beef and rolled the potatoes. "I strive for perfection on the grill."

Darla Kay giggled. "I'm sure they'll be wonderful."

"Speaking of perfection, you should've seen Flash hunting for your bracelet. Beagles have a talent for working scents, but this little fellow was so focused. There was no deterring him."

Darla Kay looked at Scooter. "Do you mind if I ask you a question that's been nagging me?"

Scooter brought the top down on the grill. *Oh, I hope this isn't what I think it might be.* "Sure, ask away."

Darla Kay slipped her perfect figure into the sun-bleached recliner. "Well, I call and tell you about my bracelet. You say you'll borrow a metal detector and search for it. To me that made sense. But early the next day, you call and inform me Flash sniffed all night and found it in the sand. Right?"

Scooter thought, *Yep, I know where this is going.* Since Scooter had no prepared answer, he replied, "Yeah."

"So, I'm puzzled how Flash knew what I'd lost and what he was looking for. How did you get that across to him?"

If there was ever a time to get creative, it was now. Maybe it would be best to pretend he was creating a story. Scooter lifted the top on the grill, pushing the steaks around with the tongs. "I understand your curiosity, dear." He shrugged his shoulders. "All I can figure is Flash sensed my anxiety after talking to you. Then, he followed me outside when I walked around the area where we were set up. Guess he was sniffing for your scent. Like you said earlier, those are two very intelligent pooches." *I hope that reply works because it's the best I've got...besides the unbelievable truth.*

Darla Kay nodded. "Well, dogs do possess a finely-tuned sense of smell," she said, gazing across the ocean.

Scooter chuckled and placed the remaining steaks and potatoes on the plate, then turned off the grill. "That they do. Okay, it's time to devour these delicious-smelling steaks. This will be the first steak little Flash has ever tasted."

While Darla Kay put the tea and salads on the table, Scooter, surrounded by his pooches, divided the steak and cut each half into small cubes. After adding a little Puppy Chow, he scraped the steak into the bowls and mixed it up. "Y'all will love Darla Kay's special treat. Don't get too used to this type of fancy eating; we can't do this every night." Scooter waited for the pups to sit and relax before placing their bowls on the floor. "Remember your manners. We have company."

Darla Kay sidled up to Scooter. "I think close friends supersede 'company', Scooter. You agree?"

Before he could answer, Gabby paused and looked up at them with twinkling eyes. Scooter quickly picked up on her thoughts, knowing he would hear her opinion later. "Yes, I do, Darla Kay. You're considered 'home folk'." He placed his arm around her shoulders and gently kissed her cheek. "Now it's official."

She laid her head on his shoulder and smiled up at him. Gabby cocked her head in that quizzical manner dogs often do and yipped, then returned to her steak supper.

"Now it's time for us to dine." Priding himself on being a Southern gentleman, he pulled out the chair for her to sit. "I think good music will set the atmosphere. I hope you like smooth jazz."

"I love it."

Scooter stepped over to his small CD player on the end table, selected 'Greatest Smooth Hits', and hit the 'play' button. "This one has all the best songs," he said, taking his seat.

A tenor sax kicked off the song, quickly followed by a perky drum and bass beat. "That's it. Now, add a delicious steak, baked potato, and salad, and we're dining in a five-star restaurant on the beach," Scooter whispered.

Darla Kay extended her glass of sweet tea toward Scooter, and they clinked. "Here's to all of my beach friends, and to Flash for finding my special bracelet. Thank you."

As expected, the meal was first class, as was the conversation. Scooter was happy Darla Kay did not mention the Disney movie; instead, she asked for a detailed account of how they found little Flash. Scooter gave most of the credit to Gabby for her compassion in dealing with a very scared stray pup. "The vet in Salisbury, Maryland, did a fantastic job taping Flash's hind leg and treating him for worms, ticks, and fleas. We almost didn't recognize the little fellow when we picked him up."

Darla Kay looked over at Flash, who was stretched out on the floor with his head on his big paws, dozing. "He was one lucky puppy to be found by you two. I'll bet he will never forget that day."

"Just think, if we hadn't gotten Flash, your bracelet might still be somewhere out there in the sand."

Darla Kay nodded. "Since you said he found it halfway between the van and our spot on the beach, I've been thinking. I'll bet when I took it off and went to put it in my tote bag, I missed the opening. See, Emmy was with me, and I was probably talking and not paying attention. Anyway," she held up her arm and smiled, "I got it back and promise to be more careful from now on."

Scooter returned her smile. "The other good news is we found a perfect reason to dine together. I also promise it won't be our last dinner."

Darla Kay placed her soft, delicate hand on his. "You have no idea how glad I am to hear that."

Gabby yipped once and rolled over on her back with all four paws in the air. Scooter and Darla Kay laughed. As Peter White's guitar kicked off 'Kinda Sweet', Scooter tapped his fingers on the table. "Now here's one of my favorites."

Darla Kay nodded. "Mine, too. Hey, do you dance?"

"I've been known to cut a few rugs with dull scissors." He chuckled. "You want to dance with a barefooted guy?"

Darla Kay hopped up from the chair. "I sure do." She reached over and took his hand.

They moved into the living room and eased, with perfect rhythm, into a slow jitterbug. Both pooches sat quietly on their haunches, taking in a sight neither had ever witnessed. Scooter was stunned that Gabby remained silent, but not as stunned as he was at how well Darla Kay could move. She smiled when he slowly spun her, brought her back, and they finished the song in close contact. After the song ended, he bowed. "You are very good. Thank you."

"Thank you, sir. You have excellent timing and rhythm."

The next song began as they continued gazing into each other's eyes. Richard Elliot's sax kicked out a remake of The Stylistics 'You Make Me Feel Brand New'. Darla Kay nodded and held him close. "This is one of my favorites." They danced as if they'd been partners for years.

When the song came to an end, Scooter said, "Now it's one of mine. Thank you."

"You're welcome," Darla Kay whispered, before giving him a hug and a soft kiss on his lips.

After the table was cleared and the dishes were washed and dried, the four of them settled on the deck, listening to the music. As the waves slapped the shore, they gazed up at the stars punching through a pitch black sky. Scooter leaned against Darla Kay's shoulder. "Life's good at the beach."

She gently took his hand and laid her head on his chest. "Very, very good."

An hour later, Darla Kay said she needed to get home and hit the sack since tomorrow's schedule was packed. Scooter replied in a whisper, "Time goes way too fast when you're having fun."

They stood, taking one last look at the white-capped waves rolling into shore. "I hope we do this again, Scooter."

"I'll make sure we do," he said as they walked inside. He paused and turned, looking back at his relaxed puppies. "You go out and do your business while I carry Darla Kay's basket and escort her to the car." The pups pushed up on their paws. Gabby slowly led the way toward the stairs, and her deep brown eyes remained locked on Scooter's.

Scooter opened the door on Darla Kay's yellow VW convertible 'Bug' and set her picnic basket in the passenger seat. For the first time in three years, their parting gave him a twinge of nervousness as Darla Kay's smile lit up the night as she stepped up close. Scooter wrapped his arms around her. "It's funny. Flash found your bracelet, and you've found my heart." Then he kissed her on the lips.

When the kiss ended, she looked up into his eyes. "Now, I'm doubly happy."

As Darla Kay slipped into the seat, Scooter said, "Good. I'll be in touch. Drive safely, and have a great day with the little ones." He leaned in the open window and kissed her again. In the darkness behind them, a familiar yip sliced the silence.

Scooter watched her back out of his sand-covered driveway and waved. As he climbed the front steps, Gabby and Flash joined him. "Well, did you two enjoy your supper?"

It was good.

You can tell me now, Scooter.

Opening the door, Scooter replied, "Tell you what?"

That I was right about Darla Kay having eyes for you.

Scooter pushed the door closed and knelt beside Gabby. "You're half right, Baboo. For a while, I've had eyes for her, too."

I knew it!

"Flash, now you've seen how happy you made Darla Kay by finding her bracelet. I'm proud of you."

Thanks, Scoot-toot.

Two pooches and one tired but happy man entered the bedroom. Flash curled up in his favorite chair. Gabby leaped up on the foot of the bed, turned around three times, and plopped. Scooter slipped between the sheets and turned off the light. "Sleep well. I'm very proud of how you both behaved tonight. Thank you."

I've decided your delicious cheese toast will be the perfect breakfast reward. Thank you, Scoot. Good night, and go easy on the snoring.

In a quick minute, Scooter fell asleep wearing a smile.

CHAPTER 10

The past two days could not have been any more frantic as Scooter scrambled to finish final edits and polish his minuscule bio for the back flap on his novel and promos. Then, to kick Scooter's already pressing agenda into high gear, Gabby announced she would board the Disney jet and fly to California.

Gabby's decision had come in the middle of the night after Flash's honorary supper with Darla Kay. The announcement was preceded by two loud barks. *I'll do it, Scooter!* Once Scooter had calmed his nerves from her startling, eye-opening, ear-splitting barks, they had discussed aspects of the matter for two hours. Gabby asked many questions Scooter was unable to answer. Finally, the black pooch yawned, circled three times, and plopped, quickly returning to a deep sleep. Unfortunately, Scooter spent another hour of restlessness before slumber finally claimed him.

Over the next two days, Scooter completed the final tasks on his novel and 'overnight' expressed it to New York, one day before the deadline. He also made time to squeeze in a very enjoyable lunch at a popular boardwalk restaurant in Virginia Beach with Darla Kay. He proudly shared details about the trip and Gabby's possible future in Disney movies. Naturally, the charming Darla Kay was ecstatic and offered well wishes to all. Scooter promised to keep her informed while he was away, along with a fancy dinner when he returned.

Scooter and pooches entered Friday morning's pre-dawn with a serenade of waves crashing onto the Sandbridge shore, easing them from a deep slumber. After showering, dressing, and loading two battered suitcases in the red Datsun 240Z, Scooter hurried inside and emptied his old percolator of its caffeine-loaded liquid into his mug. When he stepped out onto the deck, both pups lifted their heads and looked, but remained silent. Scooter settled into his favorite canvas recliner and gazed into the raspberry hue filling the horizon. He inhaled a lung full of ocean air and quickly released a tension-filled sigh, realizing today's flight to the California coast could possibly open a new door to their future.

Scooter and his furry friends' day would be filled with sunshine. Scooter glanced over at Gabby, noticing her muzzle resting between the wooden deck rails, staring across the blue-green ocean. Over the past two days, her lack of conversation told him she was committed to the trip, but not fully at ease with getting on an airplane and venturing into the skies. However, being the brave dog she was, he knew she would stick by her decision to prevent losing face. Little Flash took everything in stride, doing a fine job of remaining composed. Scooter understood that, in Flash's case, everything was still new.

Several minutes later, Scooter drained his coffee and stretched. "Okay, it's time to hit the road. Look out California…here come the Sandbridge beach bums." He knelt and motioned the dogs over and placed his arms around them. "We're gonna have a blast. In a few days, we'll know if Gabby will become a movie star."

I hope it's worth it, Scoot.

"Baboo, your name will be right there with Rin-Tin-Tin and Lassie."

Gabby backed up and looked at him with questioning brown eyes. *Who?*

Scooter chuckled. "Only two very famous movie dogs."

Oh. Okay, let's get rolling before I change my mind and let one of them do the movie.

Thanks for taking me, Scooter. I'm excited. This beats living alone in the woods.

Scooter stood. "You're welcome, Flash. We're happy you're going with us."

Traffic increased as the trio wormed its way into the city limits of Norfolk. Scooter weaved his sports car through the tangle of vehicles and finally, white-knuckled, pulled into the 'long-term' parking lot. "We've arrived!"

Gabby groaned as Flash yipped. Their quick replies reflected their thoughts at this juncture of the trip. Had Scooter voiced a similar sentiment, it would have been a whimper.

"Okay, I'll need to put your leashes on. Do me a favor and please walk calmly beside me nice and slow, and remember to place your yakking in the silent mode. The airport will be crowded."

If I see something or someone weird, I'm speaking up.

Scooter paused and gave Gabby the 'look'. "Keep your opinions to yourself, girl."

I'll be quiet.

Scooter shut off the engine and hopped out. After leashing his pooches, he finagled a leash and suitcase in each hand. "Lead the way."

Gabby paused. Her head turned from side to side. *This is a big place.*

"Move along, Gabby. We need to find the private jet information booth. After we're told where to board, everything else should be a piece of cake."

Even if it is cake, I'm not in the eating mood this morning.

"Well, that's a first."

The trio maneuvered between the maze of parked cars. When the double-glass doors automatically opened, they entered a crowd of people emitting bland stares while dragging luggage across shiny floors. "We go left here. Normally dogs are not allowed in here, so just ignore the folks looking at you. Disney got us special permission."

Gabby's head swiveled from left to right. *And I thought Central Park was filled with kooks.*

"Hush."

Scooter spotted the small red booth set back in the corner beyond the major airlines' booths. "Private Flights." He guided the pooches up and planted a nervous smile on his face. He placed the suitcases on the tile floor, then pulled out the paper containing his flight information.

"May I help you, sir?" asked the middle-aged lady with small, gold-framed glasses dangerously perched on the tip of her nose. With beautiful hazel eyes, she slowly checked out the trio and removed a ballpoint pen from a grayish bun on the back of her head.

"Yes, ma'am. We're here for a flight from Disney," replied Scooter, stunned by how official and important his statement sounded. He handed the nodding woman the piece of paper with the plane number, departure time, and the Disney representative's name and phone number.

The petite lady's delicate fingers danced over the keyboard, each touch accented with soft clicks and beeps. After a loud double beep, she looked up and smiled. "Yes, Mr. Bissell. Your plane is waiting outside in the private lot. Boarding will be in approximately twenty minutes. You'll have no problem finding the plane once you're outside…just look for the Gulfstream 5 with Mickey Mouse ears on the tail." She giggled.

"Thank you. I'll take my two pooches, and we'll have a seat until it's time to board."

The clerk moved out from behind the counter. With a sweet Southern accent, she said, "May I pat your doggies, please? If Disney sent a plane for them, they must be famous."

Scooter chuckled. "Yes, it's here for Gabby, the black one. She's not famous yet, but she might be selected to play the main character in a movie about her. The beagle's name is Flash, and, like me, he's along for the ride."

The lady knelt beside the pooches and cooed, "Well, in my opinion, all cute puppies should be famous, so both of you qualify." She gently stroked them.

Scooter, this is nice, but I'm over it.

Scooter cleared his throat. When Gabby's eyes met his, he shook his head.

"Oh, I can't wait to tell my scrapbooking friends about meeting a future movie star. I think they both should be in the movie," she said.

"If that happened, I'd be boarding the next plane to Nutville. But, if everything goes as we hope, Gabby will be in at least some parts of it." Scooter tugged on the leashes. "We'd better go relax a bit before we board. They've never flown before."

"Thank you for allowing me to meet them. I'll never wash my hands again." She giggled and moved behind the counter.

Scooter led the pooches over to a vacant row of colorful plastic chairs against the wall. "Sit. We've got a few minutes to wait, so it's a good time for us to unwind."

She better wash her hands, Scoot-toot.

"Why?"

I smelled soap and perfume, and it was strong. I'll bet you caught a whiff, didn't you, Flash?

Yeah, even before she touched me. I'll bet her paws smell like salt water now. Flash yipped.

Gabby settled gently on the black and white tile floor. *He's learning. I'm a good teacher, Scoot.*

"Relax and hush, Baboo." Scooter sighed deeply and leaned to his left, gazing out the large, tinted window in hopes of seeing the shiny private jet with black mouse ears on the tail. "It must be parked around the corner."

Fifteen minutes had passed when the lady approached, a tiny smile on her face. "Sir, the plane is ready to board. I hope you all have a great time."

Scooter stood and lifted his two bags, then situated the leashes in his hands. "Thank you. We'll do our best, ma'am."

"Follow me," she replied, eyeing both dogs with twinkling, captivating eyes.

The foursome moved quickly across the floor and out the door and turned right. "Your chariot awaits," she announced, pointing with her pen.

Scooter gazed ahead at the huge plane. He shook his head. "I can't believe this is happening to us."

Gabby yipped. *Imagine how I feel.*

A tall, thin man sporting a bushy white moustache glided down the royal blue carpeted stairway from the sparkling, silver plane. He wore black pants and a starched white shirt beneath a maroon sport coat, a small Disney logo embroidered on the pocket. As he strolled briskly toward the trio, he smiled and saluted. "Greetings! My name is Lt. Jim

Wilson. I'll be your personal attendant and co-pilot on today's flight. Prepare to fly on one of the finest planes in the blue skies."

I sure hope it flies.

Scooter nodded, lightly tugging Gabby's leash. "Easy, girl. Nice to meet you, Lt. Wilson. This is some plane, sir." The men shook hands.

Wilson reached for Scooter's bags. "You'll be our special passengers on our G5. This baby zips through the skies so smoothly you'll feel like you're sitting comfortably in your own living room. I'll take your luggage and let you lead these two beautiful puppies up the stairs and board. My instructions are to provide you with Disney's first-class treatment. Follow me, please." Wilson picked up his pace and hopped up the stairs.

Sitting in our living room. Ha! That's a stretch.

Little Flash paused. ***Scooter?***

"Yes?"

This plane is big.

"That it is, little buddy. Like the man said, big planes fly much smoother. You'll like it. Let's move along." As they reached the steps, Scooter said to Gabby, "I've heard these private jets are extraordinary. We're going to have a great time. Remember, stifle the talking until we're alone. Okie-dokie…up the blue stairs on our way into the blue sky."

You go first, Flash.

Nope. I'll follow you.

Scooter nodded toward the stairs. "Get moving. They have a scheduled takeoff time, and we're not going to make them late." Excitement tingled Scooter's nerves like a blast of winter wind. "This is so cool…flying from one coast to the other coast."

Gabby paused in mid-step and looked up at Scooter. Even though she remained quiet, her brown eyes implied, *Enough, Scoot.*

Wilson was waiting for them when they reached the doorway. "Come right in and settle wherever you'd like. As you see, we have several chairs and sofas for your comfort. Once we get up to cruising altitude, I'll serve you a light breakfast." He pointed to the well-furnished, roomy area. "Make yourself at home."

Scooter stopped to eye the state-of-the-art gallery and fancy furnishings. Both dogs nuzzled tight against his bare legs. "Magnificent."

After Wilson slipped the two suitcases into a hidden compartment under a large, leather sofa, he stood and straightened his sports jacket. "Disney believes in doing everything first-class. Our pilot, Captain Blow, will come meet you in a few minutes. We're scheduled to leave for the runway in approximately ten minutes. If you need anything, let me know."

"Thank you, sir. We'll kick back and prepare for the flight of our lives," said Scooter.

Wilson disappeared into a small room and closed the door, Gabby said, *I hope it's not the last flight of our lives. Anyway, we're now locked into this silver bullet.* Her eyes darted around, taking in the spacious area and classy furnishings. *Scooter, the sofa sure looks more comfortable than yours.* She pointed with her paw. *See, the cushions aren't flat, they're fluffy, and they smell better, too.* Gabby gently climbed up onto the slick brown cushion and plopped. *Oh, yeah! Wake me when we get there.*

"I'll remember what you said the next time I see you snuggled down on my stinky couch with squished cushions. And by the way, the smell is leather. It's made from cow hides."

Gabby's head shot up. *Yew...that's nasty.*

Before Scooter put together a snappy reply, the cockpit door opened. A fit, thirty-something man wearing a starched white shirt sporting gold epaulets on the shoulders, a narrow red tie, navy blue slacks and shiny black shoes, approached. He extended a hand to Scooter. "I'm Captain Brian Blow. It's nice to meet you all." They shook. "You've already met my co-pilot Lt. Wilson. He enjoys tending to our passengers, so he probably played down the fact that he's a very qualified pilot. We're all in good hands."

Scooter nodded, realizing the mens' professionalism originated from Disney. "We're glad to hear that, Captain. I'm Scooter, ah, I mean, Dooley Bissell. Scooter's my nickname." Pointing to the pooches, he introduced each one as he stroked their heads. "They're a bit nervous, but we're looking forward to the flight."

Captain Blow knelt in front of the sofa and gave each pup a gentle head pat. "It's an honor to fly you all to the beautiful state of California. And, Gabby, I've already heard you might become a Disney movie star. My ten-year-old daughter will be excited when I tell her about meeting you. She's wild over Disney's animal movies." The pilot stood and glanced at his watch. "So, since you're ready to climb into the blue skies, we'll be flying in fifteen minutes. Once we're cruising, you'll be served a delicious 'Wilson Breakfast'. That man can outcook my wife, and she's a chef." Blow chuckled. "Also, Wilson will bring out special harnesses for the pups to wear during takeoff and landing and will instruct you on how to use them. Oh, Scooter, wherever you choose to sit, you'll find a seat belt beneath the cushion."

"Thank you, Captain. About how long does it take to go from coast to coast in this jet?"

Captain Blow smiled. "We'll be traveling around six hundred miles per hour, so we should cover the twenty-four hundred air miles in about four hours. And don't forget to set your watch back three hours."

Wide-eyed, Scooter nodded. "Thank you. I'll set it now. And only four hours, that's amazing."

Captain Blow saluted them. "Good. I'll come back and check on you later." He pivoted on the heel of his shiny shoe and returned to the cockpit and closed the oblong door.

Scooter reached under the sofa cushion and located the seat belt. "I bet we'll barely feel the takeoff or landing. When Wilson brings your harnesses, we'll hook them up here on the sofa so we can sit together. Are you getting excited?"

Flash shook his head so hard, his floppy ears slapped his neck. Gabby aimed her muzzle at Scooter as if it were a rifle. *Why did you ask how long the trip would take?*

Scooter reached over and rubbed Gabby's ear. "I wanted to know. Why?"

Well, think about it. Up to that point everything was going fine. The delicious breakfast filled my thoughts, and then your curiosity switches the subject. Dogs don't understand speed, but we know how long four hours is. So, I figure it this way....we're going to be flying very fast, right?

Scooter nodded. "Yep. And we won't even feel it."

Gabby's head flopped onto her paws. *It doesn't matter if we 'feel' it, Scoot, because now I know it's fast. Not knowing that little tid-bit of information would have been better for my nerves. But it's too late now.*

"Sorry. Go back to thinking about breakfast."

I have one more question.

"Okay."

What's with all these pictures of a mouse with big ears? There's even one on this plane.

Scooter laughed. "That mouse is famous. His name's Mickey. Walt Disney began this company by doing cartoons about Mickey and his girlfriend, Minnie. You're going to see a lot more of them when we visit the studio."

This trip is getting wackier by the minute.

Suddenly, a loud whirring sounded from the back of the plane. Gabby jumped to her feet as her black tail swished from side to side. Flash covered his ears with his big paws. Scooter chuckled. "That's only Captain Blow starting the engines."

The door to the gallery opened, and Lt. Wilson emerged holding two red nylon harnesses. "Time to buckle up, friends. You won't have to wear them very long since this baby climbs quicker than a hungry monkey up a banana tree. Are you all going to remain on the sofa during takeoff?"

Scooter replied, "Yes, sir. We'll sit together. I've already found my belt. Show me how to hook up my furry companions."

Wilson handed one to Scooter. "Nothing to it. Just follow me, sir." He gave Flash a pat on the head. "I'll put this section around his chest, pull his front legs out, and click it under his belly. Then, this clasp will fasten to the hook beneath the cushion." Scooter watched him quickly strap in the cooperative little beagle. "That's it! Now you're ready," he said, scratching Flash's back.

Scooter followed suit with Gabby, who turned out to be not quite as easy to work with, due to her nervousness. A questioning stare filled her deep brown eyes, but she remained silent as she squirmed. Once she was hooked up, Scooter said, "Now you're ready, Baboo." She yipped twice as the G5 began to roll forward.

Wilson nodded. "I'll go take my seat up front with Captain Blow. Relax and enjoy the takeoff."

The plane picked up speed as it turned. Gabby said, *I'd be happier if we went to the other coast on the ground.*

Scooter laughed and reached over and gave her a hug. "You're a mess, girl."

Can I ask you another question, Scoot-toot?

"Sure. Fire away."

Gabby pushed up and leaned against him. *All of these round holes on both sides are windows, right?*

"Yep."

Why do we need windows? Who wants to look out from up here?

A chuckle escaped Scooter, rewarded by a cold glare from Gabby. "Windows allow light to come in."

Gabby shook her head, refusing to break her stare. *Don't toy with me, Scoot. The main reason.*

"Okay. Many people enjoy looking out and down at cities and bodies of water, and when the plane descends for landing, they can see roads, cars, and buildings. In fact, everything looks very small, like tiny toys. Before we get above the clouds, I'll show you."

Gabby leaned away from him and slowly shook her head. *You won't be showing me. The only reason I'm in this metal seagull is to get to California. I did not, let me repeat, I did not come on this trip to look down and see everything looking small. See, if big buildings and water and roads look tiny, that means we're very high in the air. I prefer to forget that. So, pretend I never asked the question.*

Scooter nodded, feeling the plane come to a stop. Knowing they were sitting on the runway ready for takeoff, he decided to withhold this piece of info. The faint 'ding' in the gallery drew their attention up to the small flashing sign to 'Fasten Seat Belt'. Settled between his cuddly canines, he placed his arms around them and pulled them tight. "Everything will be just fine. We're in this together."

Gabby placed her head on the cushion and covered her eyes with her paws. Flash sat straight up and looked at Scooter. *I want to look out the window, Scoot.*

"Good. As soon as we unfasten the seat belts, we'll look out together."

There was no comment or movement from Gabby.

Suddenly the two tail-mounted engines revved, reaching a high pitch. A few seconds passed before the plane moved forward, quickly gathering speed. Scooter whispered, "Here we go." They had only covered a short distance when Scooter felt the front end rise, upping the angle of the nose. The powerful engines revved higher as more fuel was supplied, and instantly the G5 left the grey concrete runway. "We're up."

Nuzzling against Scooter's thigh, Flash looked at him with large brown eyes. *Off the ground?*

"Yep. You've seen seagulls running along the beach and flapping their wings, and then suddenly they're in the air. Well, that's what we did. Cool, right?"

Un-huh.

Gabby remained silent and motionless.

Scooter glanced out the far window as the plane peaked upward and banked left, entering the morning sky. Reaching the first stage of altitude, the plane leveled off a bit and settled into a less angled climb as wisps of clouds zipped past the oval windows like white smoke. Suddenly the 'ding' alerted them that the seat belts could be removed. Scooter looked up and saw the small, red rectangle sign go black. "Okay, belts off," he said, clicking the release on his lap belt. "Want me to take your harness off, Flash?"

Yes.

"Gabby?"

Not yet. I feel safer with it on.

Scooter freed the beagle from his harness. "Just let me know when you're ready, Gabby." Flash hopped from the sofa onto the carpeted floor and completed a full body shake. Satisfied, he leaped up into the captain's chair closest to the window, placed his paws on the padded arm, and peered out with his black nose pressed against the thick, Plexiglas window.

Scooter gave Gabby a soft stroke on her paw-covered head and then stepped over and knelt beside the chair. "Beautiful isn't it?"

The white stuff is the same clouds we have over our beach?

"Yes. We're going through them now. Soon we'll be above them, and they'll look like big cotton balls beneath us. We won't be able to see any water or buildings until we get ready to land. It's a smooth ride, right?"

Yes. Smoother than your car, Scoot.

Scooter chuckled and rubbed the beagle's back. The door to the cockpit opened, and Lt. Wilson entered the gallery. "Did you all enjoy the takeoff?"

"Smooth as silk."

Wilson rubbed his hands together and smiled. "Great. Now, are you ready for some breakfast?"

Gabby's head popped up as if yanked by an invisible string. Scooter nodded. "I am. Captain Blow told us you make a mean breakfast."

Wilson grinned. "Do you prefer your eggs fried or scrambled?"

"Scrambled is fine."

"The sides are bacon, grits, and buttered biscuits. Coffee or milk?"

"Coffee will be perfect, black, please."

Wilson looked at the pooches. "For you, I have Purina Puppy Chow and a couple of sticks of Pupperoni for dessert. Of course, that will be served with two bowls of cool water. I'm betting your throats are a mite dry. We take pride in catering to our clients' needs. Relax. I'll be back with your vittles in a few minutes."

Scooter moved over beside Gabby. "I'm glad to see you are back with us, girl. Your sudden return wouldn't have anything to do with food being mentioned, would it?"

Being nervous makes me hungry.

Scooter talked around a slight smile. "Sounds reasonable, Baboo. Not only do you get Puppy Chow, but your favorite Pupperoni treats, too. We're flying first-class."

Gabby attempted to scratch her ear, but the harness impeded her movement. *I've got an itch. Get me out of this contraption.*

Unhooking the webbing, Scooter knew this was only an excuse to keep Gabby from admitting she now wanted out to be brave like Flash. He gently slipped the harness from her. "Now you can go over and look out the window with Flash."

The look Scooter received let him know she would not be joining her buddy. She scratched her neck. *It seems Puppy Chow follows me from the ground up into the sky. You will share some of your breakfast with us, right?*

"Yes, but you must eat your PC first. We wouldn't want Lt. Wilson to think you didn't like his offering. I selected scrambled eggs so I could put some in your bowl."

Gabby nuzzled against his chest. *Thanks, Scoot-toot.* She pointed a paw at Flash. *What's he doing? Trying to smell a wild animal? Maybe he's looking for the mouse.* She yipped twice.

Flash turned and looked at her. **There's no wild animals way up here, Gabby. All I see is fluffy clouds under us.**

Thanks for that little piece of 'how high up we are' info, Flash. I plan to hunker right here to eat.

Fifteen minutes had passed when the door in the rear of the gallery opened, drawing the trio's attention. Lt. Wilson pushed a chrome cart covered with a white linen cloth down the wide aisle. "Breakfast is served."

Gabby yipped twice.

"Sure smells delicious," added Scooter.

Wilson stopped the cart beside a large, shiny mahogany table surrounded by four high-backed leather chairs. "Allow me one minute to set the table."

The swishing of Gabby's tail against Scooter's leg prompted him to rub her head and calm her. "Be easy. It's worth waiting for."

Flash hopped from his perch beside the window and sidled up to Scooter's other leg. Wilson said, "Ready. Scooter, come on back here and have a seat at the table. I'll set the dogs' goodies on the floor. If you need anything else, just let me know." He backed the cart out of the way.

Scooter took a seat in the comfortable chair and instantly noted the quality piece of furniture. "Thank you, sir. This looks and smells fantastic."

Gabby and Flash dropped to their haunches, eyeing Scooter's every move for a few seconds before diving into their Puppy Chow.

After the first mouthful of eggs, Scooter realized just how hungry he was. He scooped up a load of grits, yellow with melted butter. "If Disney feeds us like this, we'll all get fat."

Gabby downed the last few nuggets of her food and lapped from her water bowl. *I'm ready, Scoot-toot. How about a few eggs and some bacon?*

Scooter reached down and picked up her bowl. "Okay. This is your portion. No more mooching. Remember, I have four small sticks of Pupperoni for you and Flash." After placing a few clumps of cheese-coated eggs and crumbled pieces of bacon in the bowl, he set it on the floor. "Enjoy."

Gabby took a lengthy whiff of the offering. *Wow! This sure beats a few pieces of your cheese toast, Scoot.*

Scooter looked at Flash, finding him chewing slowly between laps of water. The pup was certainly set in his fine-mannered ways. Devouring his delicious meal, Scooter took in the majestic sight of cotton clouds floating across the vast horizon of blue sky. He recalled how this all came about. *This mind-blowing trip and special treatment is all due to the unique and talented pooch I adopted from the shelter. I must be dreaming.* He took a sip of the aromatic, flavorful coffee as the cockpit door opened. Captain Blow approached to check on them. "What do you think of Wilson's breakfast?"

Scooter nodded, swiping his mouth with the linen napkin. "It's definitely a ten, Captain Blow. You were certainly correct."

Blow looked down at the pups as they worked on their dessert. "I'll bet you shared some of it with our friends, right?"

"You bet. I prefer to touch down in California without teeth marks on my ankles."

Lt. Wilson came forward carrying a steaming cup of coffee. "Sorry for the delay, Captain, needed to grind more beans."

Blow took the cup and inhaled a deep whiff. "You'll hear no complaint from me, partner. Smells delicious, as always."

Suddenly, Gabby pushed against Scooter's leg. The prickliness of her normally soft fur grabbed his attention. He leaned over and noticed her back hair standing on end like porcupine quills. Her head swiveled from Captain Blow to Lt. Wilson. With no warning, she bolted under the table toward the captain's chair beside the window and leaped up into it. Amazed and wide-eyed, Scooter watched her peer out of the oval window, her nose leaving moisture trails. Then, as quickly as she entered the chair, she bounded out and again nuzzled against Scooter's leg. Before he spoke, she dropped to her haunches and released the loudest, deepest wail he had 'never' heard. Everyone looked at her, including Flash, but Scooter sensed there was a definite meaning to this new-fangled sound. Within seconds, another wail filled the gallery. This time, it reached a higher pitch, then slowly slipped into a long, low moan.

"Gabby, what's the problem?" Scooter asked, bending over and stroking her perked ears.

Captain Blow said, "Might've been the little air pocket we just passed through. Animals sense even the smallest of them."

Knowing Gabby, Scooter pursed his lips and leaned closer. He whispered, "What it is? You can tell me quietly."

Gabby shoved her icy nose against his cheek. *Who's driving?*

"What?"

Gabby nudged him on the neck with her muzzle. *The two pilots are standing here, Scoot. Who is driving?*

Knowing this was a serious inquiry, Scooter's answer needed to instantly settle Gabby's fear. He gently pulled her head against his. "Everything's fine. We're flying on automatic pilot. Relax."

Gabby leaned back and glared into Scooter's eyes. *Don't toy with me, Scoot.*

Thankfully, Lt. Wilson broke their private discussion. "Captain Blow, I'm going to fix us a couple of fried egg and bacon sandwiches on toast."

"Great. I'm starving. After a bathroom break, I'll be in the cockpit." Blow looked at Scooter. "I'm glad you enjoyed your breakfast. We should be landing in a little over two hours. Relax and enjoy the flight. Take a nap if you choose."

Scooter and Gabby watched the two men leave. As soon as they were out of sight, Gabby leaped up, front paws on the leather seat of the captain's chair. *Scooter, no funnies, okay? I'm not in the mood.*

"Okay."

I understand nothing about 'flying' except we're high in the air. For a while, I felt comfortable while there was someone driving this thing you call a plane. And then I see the man who is supposed to be flying it standing here talking to us and sipping coffee. And the other man, who can also fly it, is here, too. So, tell me...who is flying this plane? We're not in a car where I can see what's happening. I'm really confused and scared, and getting very upset. Do you understand?

Scooter knelt on the tightly knit carpet. He wrapped a comforting arm around Gabby. "The plane is flying on automatic pilot." Knowing this explanation would do nothing to soothe her anxiety, so he placed both hands gently around her muzzle. "Before you ask what that is, I'll tell you. See, they have buttons and other devices that I don't understand that keep the plane on a straight course, without a human steering it. I know this is hard for you to understand, too. But everything is very safe. If not, Captain Blow would not have been back here."

Shaking her head, Gabby turned and walked down to the comfortable sofa and hopped up. After three turns, she plopped down and covered her head with her paws. Scooter looked over at a clueless Flash. "Are you okay, buddy?"

I guess so, Scoot. After eating, I'm getting sleepy.

Scooter picked up the last piece of crispy bacon, broke it in half, and gave Flash a piece. Scooter gobbled his bacon. "Let's go relax on the sofa. We had an early start this morning. My eyes are a bit heavy, too."

With a pooch on each side, Scooter laid his head back and closed his eyes. He placed a hand on each puppy and sighed deeply. "Better get some rest. We're going to have a busy day at the Disney studio."

By the time Captain Blow and Lt. Wilson quietly passed them on their way to the cockpit, Scooter was drifting off, feeling Gabby twitching and hearing Flash snoring lightly.

After a long nap, Scooter stirred, slowly returning from a dream where he was flying the G5. Gabby and Flash shared the co-pilot seat, focused on his every move while glancing from time to time out the windshield. As he stretched, Scooter glanced at his watch. After a big yawn, he said, "Time to rise, sleepy heads. We'll be landing in a few minutes."

Gabby pawed her big brown eyes and looked around. *I can't wait to get my four paws on the ground.*

Me, too.

Lt. Wilson joined them. "I think our passengers were a little pooped. Did you recharge your batteries?"

After clicking the clasp on Gabby's seatbelt, Scooter nodded. "I sure did. Your delicious breakfast had something to do with that. How long before we touch down?"

"Twenty minutes. Feel free to look out the window as we begin our descent. Captain Blow will turn on the sign when it's time to buckle up." Wilson headed to the back to prepare for the landing.

"Who is interested in seeing California come into view as we approach? Flash? Gabby?"

With his hind leg, Flash scratched his floppy ear. *I would, Scoot.*

"Okay. How about you, Gabby?"

Slowly sitting up, the lab looked into Scooter's eyes. *What do you think?*

"Well, earlier you hopped in the chair and looked out."

That was out of desperation...had to see if we were still in the air. I found no delight in peeking out, believe me. So, in answer to your silly question...I'll sit right here until I can get off of this thing and lick the ground.

"And I respect your decision, Baboo. You know, if Disney chooses you to play in the movie, you'll be flying a lot."

Gabby's unblinking stare remained stern. *If they want me, maybe I'll stay here until the movie is finished, and then fly home.*

Scooter hoped she would decide against that, since it could take a month or more to film her parts. They had never been separated, so this would prove difficult. He knew she must really detest flying to be thinking about such a serious measure. "We'd sure miss you, Gabby. But it's your choice."

They felt the plane gently descending and banking left as the dual engines cut back. When the seatbelt sign lit up, Scooter took a seat and hooked Flash into his harness in the big chair beside the window so they could see the landing. "Okay, you're both hooked up. Flash, this is the best part of flying. Whenever I fly, I sit beside the window. It's so cool to see a big city from above."

Flash put his black nose against the Plexiglas oval as his tail waved from side to side. *This is exciting, Scoot.*

Captain Blow's voice came over the speaker. "I just received special permission from the tower to head out over the ocean and come in from the West to land at the Bob Hope Airport. Keep your eyes open, friends. The Pacific Ocean is awesome from up here."

"That's cool," said Scooter. "Gabby, are you sure you don't want to see the Pacific Ocean? You might be filming parts of the movie there."

No, thank you, Scooter. If I see it, I'll be standing in the sand, not up in the clouds.

The G5 dropped in altitude, slipping through the puffy clouds like a sharp knife. "Hey, Flash, now you'll be able to say you've seen both oceans."

That's neat.

Captain Blow banked sharply, bringing the large buildings into view, then leveled out and descended. Off in the distance, the blue Pacific appeared. "There's the ocean way out there, Flash. It's beautiful."

I see it, Scoot.

The gentle descent brought the coast of California into a much clearer view. Wilson appeared beside the chair. "That's some sight, isn't it?"

"You bet. The ocean looks so majestic from here. How far is Disney's studio from the coastline?"

"About fifteen miles down I-10, and when traffic isn't congested, it only takes thirty minutes. You will enjoy spending time on the studio lot. Everything is first-class. And wait until you eat in the cafeteria. I guarantee it will be some of the best food you've ever tasted. Their food makes my breakfast seem like stale bread. Oh, and your little pals will be amazed at all of the squirrels who reside on the studio's property."

Scooter replied, "Oh, and the airport is named after Bob Hope. I never knew that."

Wilson nodded. "Yes, it is. And we also have our own hangars there. A limo will be waiting to take you to your hotel and then be available to you later. Disney's a stickler for keeping to appointments and schedules.

Okay, I'm going up to the cockpit for the landing. Enjoy the view and the smooth-as-glass landing by Captain Blow."

Scooter scratched Flash's ear. "There goes one nice man." Breaking his gaze on Los Angeles, Scooter turned to find Gabby in her same position, paws over eyes. "It won't be long before we're on the ground, Gabby."

In a muffled voice, she said, *That's the best news I've heard since breakfast.*

Scooter, is our ocean this big?

Turning back, Scooter replied, "Sure is." He spotted the glassy blue waves peeling from left to right, topped with white water. Captain Blow banked to their right and headed inland, cutting back the engines to accelerate the descent. "Get ready, we're close to touch down," Scooter announced.

I can't wait.

Flash and Scooter watched the buildings, roads, and tiny cars and trucks fill the window as they increased in size. Scooter loved landings. He enjoyed rating the smoothness of the plane connecting with the runway. Scooter watched in silence as the surrounding area slowly came nearer, and then the grey concrete runway appeared beneath them. "Here we go."

Closing his eyes to concentrate solely on the landing, Scooter held his breath and waited. Within a few seconds, the wheels touched the runway like a butterfly with sore feet. "Wow! A definite 'ten'."

Are we down, Scoot?

"Bingo!"

That was smooth, Scooter.

Captain Blow reversed the powerful engines, slowing the jet. The main terminal zipped past as Blow steered the G5 down the runway and turned left. Scooter spotted a shiny, black limo sporting a small Disney logo on the door across the tarmac. "We're certainly going in style."

I don't care about style; I just want to get off of this plane.

After they pulled up beside a big hangar, the cockpit door opened, and Lt. Wilson emerged. "We're here, friends. It's been a real pleasure to serve you. And, Captain Blow has requested and received approval to fly you back to Norfolk." Wilson extended his hand to Scooter. As they shook, Wilson gave Flash a gentle stroke. "I wish all of our passengers were as pleasant to travel with as you two nice pups."

"Thank you, sir. This has been an outstanding flight with outstanding service." Scooter unbuckled Flash and then himself. Wilson released Gabby from her harness. "Gabby, have a great visit to the studios. I wish you the best in trying out for the movie. You'll make a fine actress." Gabby yipped.

Wilson handed Scooter the two leashes and removed their luggage from beneath the sofa as Captain Blow joined them. Scooter shook his hand and said, "Great landing, Captain. A perfect 'ten'."

"Thank you, Scooter. Wilson and I rated all three of you even higher." He pointed out the window as the limo pulled up beside the plane. "There's your ride. You'll be taken to the Coast Anabelle Hotel so you can freshen up and relax for a couple of hours. Then you'll be driven to the studio. Enjoy your stay, and we'll see you on the return flight."

Scooter said, "Okay, let's go." Gabby pulled him forward into the open door and down the steps like a bouncing ball. As soon as she hit the sun-kissed asphalt, she rolled over on her back, wiggled her paws in the air, and yipped several times. Flash paused to observe her antics. The pudgy, tuxedo-clad limo driver laughed out loud. Scooter said, "I'd say she's glad to be on the ground." Leaning down to Gabby, he whispered, "Let's walk over to the grassy area beside the hangar. I'm sure you both need to take care of business." As they headed off, Scooter nodded to the driver. "We'll be right back."

"Take all the time you need, sir. I'll load your luggage."

The trio returned to find the driver perched beside the open rear door waiting for Scooter and his companions. Flash and Gabby trotted forward and hopped right into the huge backseat. Scooter thanked the driver and slid in across the slick leather seat, inhaling the new car fragrance. The driver gently closed the door and climbed behind the wheel. "We only have a ten-minute ride to our favorite, pet-friendly hotel. Sit back and enjoy the scenery." The tinted window silently moved up, separating the driver from the weary travelers.

CHAPTER 11

Scooter leaned back and allowed the soft leather seat to swallow his tense body. He gazed out the window as the limo slipped into traffic behind a new maroon Mercedes convertible on North Buena Vista Street. His thoughts continued to spin inside his head, fueled by the sheer reality of the situation and its prospects. Gabby and Flash, heads touching, peeked out the other window in silence.

The screenwriters for the movie, a husband and wife team, was solely responsible for writing Gabby's story and submitting it to Disney. Paul and Ruthie Sizemore were close friends of Scooter's New York publisher, Jason Goldberg. Through Jason, they heard about Gabby's rescue and adoption from the SPCA and her brave actions that saved Jason's little daughter, Kay, from drowning. They believed the story would be right up Disney's alley. It didn't hurt that several of their previous submissions had been picked up by Disney, which gave them the proverbial foot in the door. So, technically, Scooter's brave puppy was solely responsible for this trip and movie. *Who would've ever thought it?*

Gabby backed away from the window and crawled into Scooter's lap. *I thought my nervousness would go away once we were on the ground. It didn't, Scoot.*

"Join the crowd, Baboo. I'm nervous, too."

Little Flash is as calm as if we were walking on our beach. What's with him?

Scooter stroked her back. "Guess he's still trying to get used to having a home where he's loved and cared for. With you and me, we were already comfortable in our laid-back lifestyle." Scooter looked at her and smiled with tight lips. "Don't worry. In time we'll get used to these changes. But, the truth is, as long as we're all together, we'll be fine."

Gabby propped her chin on the window sill and took in the surroundings. *Scoot, if I get the part, I will have to stay here by myself for a while, right?*

Those words pinched Scooter's dry throat like iron fingers. If there were any other way, he and Flash would gladly remain here with her, since the school children's outings were finished for the winter. But with his debut novel due out shortly, he would be required to travel to various cities for book signings, so the option to stay was no longer viable. "Let's not put the cart before the horse, Gabby. We'll deal with whatever needs to be done." He wrapped his arm around her and pulled her tight. He heard her soft sigh.

Flash slipped down to the seat and up against Scooter. ***Where are we going now?***

"To our hotel," replied Scooter, pleased to have the subject changed.

What's a hotel?

That's where we spend the nights while we're here, Flash. I'll bet our room will be fancier than Scooter's cottage. Gabby yipped.

"I'll remember you said that, Baboo."

Just teasing, Scooter-rooter.

The light turned green, and the limo moved forward. Once they were through the small intersection, the driver slowed and made a left turn onto West Olive Avenue for a short distance and then turned left into the hotel parking lot. Scooter leaned across the seat and peered out the window. "Looks like we're here." The pooches scooted across the seat and jammed their noses to the tinted window. *Wow! Look at this place.*

"I see it."

When the limo came to a stop in front of the large sandstone building trimmed in a rust color, the driver jumped out and opened the rear passenger door. "Welcome to the Coast Anabelle Hotel. I'll get your luggage from the trunk and escort you inside."

Scooter thanked him as he leashed Gabby and Flash. Leaning down to his pups, he whispered, "Now, please be calm and stay quiet until we're in our room."

Gabby waited until she heard the trunk pop open. *No worries, Scoot. We'll behave, right, Flash?*

Yep.

The trio followed the driver up the brick steps under a red and tan awning and into a spacious, beautifully decorated lobby. Scooter's eyes darted from side to side as they made their way up to the polished redwood counter. When the driver placed their luggage on the red carpet, a white-haired gentleman wearing a starched, light tan shirt with a thin maroon bow tie greeted them. "Welcome, Mr. Bissell." He leaned forward and looked down at Gabby and Flash. "And we welcome you both. We love pets here, so make yourselves at home."

Scooter was stunned the gentleman knew his name. "Thank you, sir."

The man nodded and offered a slight smile as he double-tapped the chrome bell on the counter. "Your room is ready, sir," he said, handing Scooter the gold key. "Disney prefers our Deluxe Studio Suite for their guests. If you need anything, please call me. We're here to serve."

A young man wearing the shirt and tie like the clerk's, along with black trousers and shoes, nodded and picked up the suitcases. Scooter stepped over and tipped their limo driver. "Thank you."

"Thank you." The pudgy driver glanced at his watch. "I'll return in two hours to drive you over to Disney studios."

The clerk said, "Mr. Bissell, please follow Robert. He'll show you to your room. Enjoy your stay with us."

Robert crossed the huge lobby with Scooter and the pooches close behind. "Sir, you are on the second floor. We can take the elevator or the stairs." He glanced down at the dogs. "Some pets aren't too fond of the elevator."

Scooter chuckled. "Good suggestion. Let's not experiment. We'll take the stairs."

When they reached their floor, Robert turned and headed down a long hallway. They passed several rooms before the bellhop stopped in front of a door with 213 in gold-plated numbers. Using a master key, he opened the door and stepped aside. "These are our first-class rooms."

Scooter and the pups entered and pulled up short. "Wow! This is more than a room."

Robert placed the suitcases on webbed stands and headed out. "Call us if there's anything you need, sir."

Scooter tipped him. "Thank you, Robert. Everything looks perfect."

The instant the door clicked shut, Gabby bounded in two strides up on the king-sized bed. *This bed makes yours look like one of the squished sofa cushions, Scoot.*

"Get off that bed! Didn't you see those two doggie beds over beside the sofa?"

Gabby hopped down onto the light blue carpet. *I saw them, Scooter. Is that where we sleep?*

Scooter pointed at the dog beds. "Yes. And even though this hotel allows pets, that doesn't mean we will mess it up."

Gabby mumbled as she walked over and sniffed the large, red plaid round bed. *Dogs don't sleep in this thing, Scoot.*

"Why do you say that?"

Because it doesn't smell like a dog.

Scooter chuckled. "In case you haven't noticed, this is a fancy hotel. I'm sure the dog beds are professionally cleaned after each guest leaves. If they weren't, you could get fleas."

I don't ever want fleas again, Scooter.

Me, either.

"I'm sure you don't." Scooter walked into the navy blue and white tiled bathroom. "This walk-in shower is big enough for four people." He noticed the gold-plated fixtures on the huge tub and sink twinkling from the overhead lights. "It's so beautiful, I hate to touch anything, but I need a hot shower and then to crawl into fresh clothes for our studio visit," he mumbled, returning to the main suite.

Flash was curled up in the doggie bed, licking his front paw. "Is it comfortable, Flash?"

Yep. It's real soft.

I've got an idea, Scoot-toot.

Scooter kicked off his Top-Siders and began unbuttoning his shirt. "Let's hear it."

Well, you have a bigger soft bed than you need, and I hate to see it go to waste. So, how about you put our doggie beds on the foot of your bed? See, that way, we won't mess it up with our fur.

Scooter flipped his shirt onto the bed in question. "I'll think about that while I take a hot shower." He chuckled. "Girl, does your conniving ever stop?"

Gabby looked into his eyes and cocked her head. *Don't forget who's responsible for getting us here.*

Scooter headed for the bathroom. "I knew you'd remind me."

Twenty minutes later, Scooter emerged from the steam-filled bathroom wearing a fluffy, blue robe with the hotel's logo embroidered on the pocket. He found his furry friends sound asleep in their plaid beds. The precious scene brought a smile to his face as he recalled their lonely, difficult situations before they came into his life. Truthfully, all of them had benefitted with a better life after finding one another.

As quietly as possible, Scooter selected his clothes from the suitcase, deciding to go casual and comfortable to meet the Disney people. He climbed into a pair of khaki slacks, stepped barefooted into his Top-siders, and pulled on a white polo shirt. When he returned from the bathroom after combing his blonde mop and brushing his teeth, he checked his watch, glad Captain Blow reminded him to reset it to West Coast time. "I've got a little over an hour to relax," he whispered, stretching out on the super-soft bed, propped on the fluffiest pillows he had ever parked his head on. "Nice. Real nice," he whispered as his eyes closed.

A loud, high-pitched yip snatched Scooter from a relaxing slumber. He leaned over to see Gabby beside the bed. "What?" No sooner than he had spoken, the chirp of the phone had him scrambling for the receiver on the nightstand.

It's been ringing, sleepyhead.

"Hello?" Scooter said, blinking blurry eyes while listening and nodding. "Okay, that's fine. We'll be down in five minutes. Thank you." He put the receiver in the cradle and sat up.

Who was it?

Scooter hustled to the bathroom, side-stepping a drowsy Flash. "The clerk called to let me know our limo would be here in five minutes. I'll be out in a minute." He closed the door.

Scoot moves faster after waking up than I do.

Gabby yipped once. *He had to go to math class, buddy.*

Flash yipped. **Oh. Well, so do I, Gabby.**

Me, too. Scooter will find us a place.

Scooter came out smiling and holding a blue package. "Okay, I'm wide awake and ready to go."

What's in the package, Scoot?

Scooter flipped the light, plastic-wrapped package up in the air and caught it. He deepened his voice like a TV announcer as he read from the package, "Number One friend of your puppy. The new and improved Wee-Wee Pads are perfect for training your pups in the house or when the weather is bad."

Gabby cocked her head and gave him 'the look'. *You are toying with me again, Scoot.*

Unable to contain his laughter, Scooter shook his head. "No joke," he said between sniggers as he opened the package and removed a light blue rectangle with padding on one side. "See, I'll spread this on the bathroom floor, and then – "

Don't bother! I am not going to squat over that thing and do my business, either number. I can hold it until we get outside. She shook her head and looked at Flash. *How about you?*

I can wait.

After carefully folding the sheet of plastic and padding, Scooter returned to the bathroom. When he came out, he was holding four plastic bowls with the Purina checkerboard logo on each. "I found these in the closet. I'll fill two with water for you in case you want a drink before we go downstairs." Another burst of laughter exploded. "I'll bet you guys are real thirsty."

Not me.

I'm not, either.

Scooter's side ached from laughing as he bent over and placed the bowls on the floor. "Okay, let's go see the Disney studio and meet the folks. Now, remember, no talking or acting up. We need to make a good impression and behave like we know what we're doing."

CHAPTER 12

The early afternoon California sun delivered perfect warmth for a November day. The cheerful driver opened the door and Scooter and his companions slipped into the rear seat of the limo. "I hope you all had a chance to relax a bit before your big afternoon."

"We did. And our room is awesome, too," replied Scooter.

"Good. Our ride to the studio will be about five minutes," the driver said, gently closing the big door.

Scooter took a deep breath and released a nervous sigh. "Okay, pooches, we're going to meet several people this afternoon. Just be your normal, nice selves, and you'll be a hit. And hold back – "

Gabby's words cut him off. *We know, Scoot. No yakking. But I'll tell you this, pal...you better find us a place to hold math class, and not on a silly Wee-Wee Pad. You catch my drift?*

"I'm sure we can find a place, Gabby. You won't be the first animals to visit the studio," said Scooter, giving her a wink.

I wonder if they make those pads for humans.

Before Scooter answered, the limo driver made a left turn and slowly pulled into the huge entrance to Disney Studios. They stopped at the guard shack while the driver signed in. The guard said he would call Ms. Robbins to let her know they were on the way. With a friendly wave from the guard, the limo moved forward. Scooter looked at Gabby and Flash, wondering what thoughts were zipping around in their heads. "Well, the beach bums are now inside the famous Disney studio. You ready?"

Too late to turn back now, Scoot.

This is neat.

The driver lowered the tinted divider. "We're going to drive around back where the offices for directors and producers are located. Ms. Jan Robbins will be waiting for us. She will notify me when the meeting is finished, and I'll be back to pick you up and carry you wherever you're to go. Enjoy your visit."

"Thank you, sir."

Several minutes and turns later, they pulled into a large parking lot in front of a three-story tan building with double glass doors. An attractive, short-haired blonde stood beneath the blue awning, waving. The driver tapped the horn once. "Good afternoon, Ms. Robbins. I have a special delivery for you." Scooter quickly leashed the pooches and slipped out as butterflies filled his stomach.

"Welcome to Disney studios, Mr. Bissell. I hope your trip was pleasurable and uneventful." Jan shook his hand, and, before he spoke, immediately focused her attention on Gabby and Flash. "Well, aren't you two the cutest pups in California?" She petted both of them, and they gobbled up the attention.

Scooter released a tense sigh. "Everything has gone finer than frog's hair. You all are certainly accommodating and professional, Ms. Robbins."

She stood. "Please, call me Jan. One thing you'll find is that Disney settles for nothing less than perfection for their movies, employees, and patrons. I'll admit, it's a job, but it doesn't feel like one. Anyway, this afternoon, we'll do a walk-around orientation of our various studios and related facilities. If you have any questions, feel free to ask."

"Good. Maybe seeing a little bit about how the movie business works will calm my nerves. Oh, and call me Scooter."

"Scooter it is," she replied with a wink.

Jan looked at their driver. "Thank you, Lewis. I'll call you when we're finished. Tonight at seven o'clock, we'll have dinner at Olive's Bistro for Scooter."

Lewis nodded. "I'll await your call, Ms. Robbins." He waved to them and slipped into the long, shiny limo and pulled away.

Scooter asked, "Are the little ones allowed to go on the tour with us, Jan?"

She smiled and reached for Gabby's leash. "You bet, if you don't mind. We're pet friendly, especially when it comes to dealing with a potential star."

"No, not at all. I'm sure they'll enjoy seeing new places like this. Right, Gabby, Flash?"

Both yipped and swished their tails.

"I see they're not only darling, but very intelligent."

Scooter chuckled. "Oh, yeah. Sometimes too smart. I do have one question. Is there a place for them to TCB? If you've got a bag, I'll pick it up."

Gabby yipped. Scooter was unsure whether she was upset because he mentioned their 'business' to a stranger or because she really needed to go.

Jan replied, "Yes, indeed. We have a grassy, secluded area beside the building." She returned Gabby's leash to him. "I'll go get a couple of bags." She turned and entered the building.

Yes, we have to go, Scoot, but did you have to make a big announcement?

"How else was I to find out? And don't worry, she's not going to watch. Remember about holding your tongue around people. Okay?"

They both yipped as Jan hustled up to them. "Here, Scooter. Just walk to your left and then take a right. You'll see a large oak in the middle of a small yard with a couple of cement benches. Anywhere around there is fine. Also, there's a trash can there. While you do that, I need to get some brochures from my office. I'll meet you back here in a few minutes."

"Thank you, Jan." Scooter led them across the pavement and into the private area. After five quiet minutes, they moseyed up to him. *Okay, Scoot...I'm ready to check out this fancy place. Oh, we'll be very hungry when we're finished, and I heard the nice lady mention dinner. Do you think Flash and I are invited?*

Scooter walked over, bagged their deposits, and dropped them into the plastic can with a picture of Mickey Mouse printed on the side. "I doubt it. But the restaurant is in our hotel, so I can bring you some of my dinner after you've eaten your Puppy Chow."

We don't have any dog food, Scoot.

Nodding, Scooter replied, "Yes, we do. In the bathroom closet where they keep your Wee-Wee Pads. There's a list of dog foods they stock for doggie guests. And Puppy Chow is top on the list. I'll get some from the nice man in the lobby."

Hey, Scoot. There's another picture of the mouse. You weren't kidding about Disney and his mouse.

This mouse looks friendly. There was a real big mouse with yellow teeth that lived near the trash cans at Miss Celie's diner. He came out at night. I was scared of him.

"That was probably a rat, Flash. Disney's cartoon animals are all nice, and act like humans."

Good.

When the trio came around the building, Jan was waiting. She handed Scooter several folded brochures, along with a laminated card with 'VIP' in the center and bordered with Disney cartoon characters. "Clip this on your shirt, Scooter. Since this tour is only for our special guests, it makes the security guards' jobs easier."

After Scooter gave her Gabby's leash, he clipped on the badge. "Okay, Jan, we're ready."

They strolled along the spotless walkway behind the production buildings. Scooter was impressed with the overall layout, manicured grass and flowerbeds along the way. Recalling what he had heard earlier from Lt. Wilson, there were an abundant number of squirrels. They leaped across the grass and scooted around in the branches of huge oaks, barking and squeaking. Gabby moseyed down the path, her head swiveling from side to side, taking in as many sights as possible. Little Flash pranced on stubby legs, his snoot held high, no doubt catching whiffs of the furry creatures.

Being the perfect guide, Jan pointed out cinderblock buildings and fancy Quonset huts, explaining what went on behind closed doors – editing, animation, and sound studios. Scooter realized from only this small peek at a renowned movie production company that a ton of specialized work went on behind the movies and shows millions of people enjoyed. Swamped with awe and questions, he again remembered the sole reason they were in California – Disney wanted to make a movie about his Gabby. That thought alone had the potential to cross his eyes and short out his brain waves. "Jan, this is some place. It's mind-boggling to realize that so many professionals work together to create your movies the world loves so much."

Jan giggled. "After working here five years, I'm still learning new things. The developments in technology change daily. Disney takes pride in being on the cutting edge."

What happened next played out in slow motion. Scooter watched the lead squirrel race down the trunk of an oak with another squirrel inches behind. As they neared the green grass, both leaped into the air and hit the ground, only fifteen feet in front of them. Flash also closely observed the antics. In a split second, he decided to join in the chase – before Scooter had a chance to react and tighten his grip on the nylon leash. The little stubby-legged pup broke free in hot pursuit of the fast-moving furry animals. "Flash, no! Come back here!"

The red loop on the leash never touched the ground behind Flash as he quickly gained on the squirrels. His deep howls filled the quiet area. The furry-tails' only safety was another large tree, twenty yards ahead. Jan moaned, "Oh, my." Gabby released several high-pitched yips. Scooter broke into a hopeless sprint and yelled another order for Flash to stop. Suddenly, a red golf cart emerged between two huts onto the walkway, quickly swerving, barely missing the frenzied squirrels and Flash. "What the…" screamed the driver when he righted the cart and passed Scooter.

Doors on the buildings and huts flew open, followed by shocked staff with wide-open eyes and mouths. Scooter ran past them panting, "I'll get him." When the squirrels determined they were close enough to the tree, they leaped several feet into the air, latched onto the rough bark, and quickly clawed their way to the top. At the tree, Flash pulled up short. His front paws hit the trunk, and he stood howling up at his prey. Scooter neared the tree and put on the brakes. His Top-siders lost their grip on the green grass, and he landed on his butt. He slid up and latched onto the leash. "Easy, Flash. They're gone, buddy." He pulled the panting beagle to him and held him close. *Almost got 'em, Scoot.*

When Jan and Gabby approached, Scooter was standing and brushing grass from his pants as balls of sweat rolled down his face. "Well, it appears Flash likes squirrels," Scooter said between gasps.

Gabby eased up beside Flash and nudged him, but thankfully remained silent. Jan giggled. "I must admit, Scooter, when I first saw the short-legged beagle, I wondered how he got his name." She reached down and stroked Flash. "But now I know. You are one fast pup."

Scooter swiped his forehead with a handkerchief and sighed. "I'm sorry for the commotion, Jan. I hope we don't get you in trouble."

"Not at all, Scooter. This was child's play compared to what happened last year."

"Really?"

"A well-known raptor trainer brought his hawk outside a studio for fresh air. You know, they're trained to sit on the handler's arm. Well, one of our resident squirrels was entertaining himself by jumping from tree to tree. Evidently the hawk couldn't take that type of taunting, and into the air he went. I heard the time it took for him to get airborne, dive, and capture the squirrel took only several seconds." She shook her head. "Poor squirrel."

"Oh, what a shame." Scooter knelt beside Flash. "Little buddy, these squirrels live here. They're not really wild. I know it's hard for you to hold back your natural tendencies, but remember we're the visitors. Understand?"

Flash looked up at Scooter with a sorrowful expression and yipped once, and then bowed his head.

Jan quickly placed her hand over her mouth to stifle a giggle. Between her fingers, she said, "You sure have smart puppies, Scooter."

Scooter smiled and nodded. "Yes, they're a handful. I promise we'll behave if you're still willing to show us around."

"You bet! See, I was serious when I said working here was a blast." She turned back toward the buildings. "We sort of zipped past one of our sound studios you should see. This large building is where individual stages are constructed to re-create the interiors of rooms or offices used to shoot scenes during a movie."

Scooter gripped Flash's leash a bit tighter as they walked back to the area of trees and squirrels. "That's cool. Disney will really need to use their creativity when they build my cottage interior."

"Why? I think any cottage on the beach would be awesome."

"Well, let's say that mine falls in the category of drab."

Gabby yipped twice.

They approached a huge cinderblock building with a bright red '4' painted on the door. Jan lightly knocked twice. Within seconds, a uniformed man opened the door and smiled. "Howdy, Miss Jan." He looked at Scooter and the pooches. "I knew you all would be back after the chase." He extended his hand to Scooter. They shook.

"Filming today, Larry?" Jan asked.

"Yep, a heartwarming Christmas special. It's about a family finally getting back in their house after a hurricane. From the snippets I've seen, it's pretty interesting. You all come in." He stepped aside and held the door.

Scooter leaned close to Jan and whispered, "Do we have to be perfectly quiet?" He nodded his head toward the dogs.

"Not perfectly. They frown on anything loud, though." She glanced at the pups.

Scooter knelt between his companions. "They're making a movie inside. We have to be very, very quiet. No barks or yips. Okay?" Their silence was a satisfactory 'yes'.

One of the sets was a living room decorated for Christmas, complete with tree and gifts. The actors appeared as normal as any family, opening presents and talking and laughing. Several large cameras, each one mounted on a rolling platform, strategically placed and manned by a man wearing a headset, captured the images from different angles. Four booms hung from aluminum rafters above the set, holding fur-covered microphones and recording the audio. Bright lights were also positioned in certain positions around the stage, as were large squares of a reflective material. After a particular scene was completed, an unseen voice would yell, 'Cut!' The make-up people would appear and make small changes, and the actors would relax as the director approached and quietly discussed something with them. After a few minutes, they returned back 'in character' and either repeated the scene or performed another one. Scooter listened and watched every movement in wide-eyed amazement. *I wonder how Gabby would handle the precise structure of doing everything the director demanded. We'll see.*

Several scenes and twenty minutes later, Jan whispered, "Ready to visit the editing hut?"

Scooter nodded and gently tugged Flash's leash. "Let's go, buddy."

Gabby and Jan led them to the exit. Jan thanked Larry, as did Scooter, and they stepped out into California sunshine. While they walked, Jan explained, "We have several sound studios on premises engaged in different projects. Our outdoor scenes are filmed at other locations we either rent or own, depending on what is required. In other words, for beach scenes we get permits allowing us to fence off an area on the coastline. If we need mountain or desert areas, those are also at our disposal. Tomorrow while we meet with the contract lawyer and screenwriters, our qualified animal handlers and trainers will take Gabby and the three other dogs being considered for the part to the coast for an initial viewing of their abilities to obey with different commands."

Gabby yipped. Jan giggled.

"Oh, I see. Everything seems to be on track. You've mentioned several things that haven't even crossed my mind."

"Once a project is approved, Disney assigns their people to it, and the wheels are in motion. If you approve the contract, and the main dog is selected, along with a qualified fill-in, the actors we've chosen and contracted with are notified. Then, the director brings everyone together and lays out the schedule. I know everything sounds like a tangled ball of twine to a layperson, but Disney has been at this for generations. They have every area of production down to perfection."

Scooter knew Gabby and Flash were hearing a lot more information than the bit of drivel he had spouted, as if he knew, to them. No doubt, tonight after dinner, Gabby would be overflowing with questions. He hoped to have a few answers, knowing tomorrow she would be whisked away with strange dogs and people, on a strange coast, and asked to follow specific directions. "You mean actors have already been selected?"

"Yep. And you will be surprised to know who has agreed to play you, Scooter." Jan let out the perfect 'wolf whistle'.

Gabby and Flash yipped twice.

This nugget of information caught Scooter by surprise. The actors had never entered his thoughts, certainly not an actor playing him. But, in reality, if the movie is about Gabby, then a 'Scooter' would play a major role. *A fake Scooter and his companion.* "Who's playing me, Jan? And what's with the whistle?" His curiosity was piqued.

Jan nudged him and laughed. "That info will be revealed tonight at dinner by the director. As you know, well-known, popular actors normally make successful movies."

Scooter looked into her captivating hazel eyes and unleashed his best smile. "How about a hint? Maybe a movie this person starred in?"

Jan looked at her watch and giggled. "In three hours, you'll have more than a hint."

They spent fifteen minutes in the spacious, high-tech editing hut. Scooter's eyes zipped from station to station and screen to screen as the professionals added, deleted, and highlighted film frames. Strangely, the old song 'Freeze Frame' by the J. Geils Band came to mind. "I assume the director oversees and approves the movie after edits?"

"You bet. In fact, his staff also adds 'fresh eyes' to post-edits." She ran fingers through her blonde hair. "Since you're a published author, I'm sure you're very familiar with edits."

"You all haven't left out anything, have you?"

Jan smiled. "We try not to. However, in your case, we didn't have to dig. See, your screenwriters are friends of ours, and they told us about your upcoming novel. Disney has filmed a couple of their submissions, and they proved to be top-sellers. You are very fortunate to have them working with you."

They paused at the door of an amazingly large, four-story brick building. "Oh, that's right. Well, I had nothing to do with getting the Sizemores to write the screenplay. They're very good friends of my publisher, Jason Goldberg. To be honest, Jan, everything from the acceptance of my novel to the making of this movie has happened so fast, it feels like a dream. I expect to wake up anytime." He chuckled and wiggled his fingers in front of his eyes.

"When does your book hit the market?"

"Jason expects to have me on one of many signing tours in two weeks, beginning in West Virginia where the novel is set. It appears my schedule will surpass my definition of 'busy', and all while this movie will be underway."

Jan giggled as she knocked on the steel door with 'Costumes' in gold letters above a brass 8. In a matter of seconds, an older lady with wire-rimmed glasses and grey hair in a tight bun opened the door. "Good afternoon, Jan. I've been expecting you and your guests. It's not often I'm visited by two cuddly puppies." She shook Scooter and Jan's hands, then knelt down and hugged Gabby and Flash. "You two are the most adorable sweethearts I've ever seen. Welcome to my house of clothes and wigs." She stood and held the door open for them.

"Thank you, Stacy," said Jan. "We're running a little behind, so I'll quickly show them around the various departments. We wouldn't dare be late for Scooter's introduction dinner this evening."

Stacy nodded. "By all means, Jan. You know your way around. If you need anything, just holler. I'll be in the inventory office."

For nearly forty-five minutes, they looked at costumes covering, in Scooter's mind, clothes and fashions from the time humans stopped wearing fig leaves. "I'll bet moths would love to get in here." He would never admit it, but fashion was not high on his priority list. However, Jan was well-versed and helpful when explaining the major changes to fashion and how they came about. Scooter did enjoy the period from the Roaring Twenties up through the Fifties.

"Scooter, this place is not only treated weekly for moths and silverfish, but other pest preventions are used, like ultra-violet lights and sticky traps. And we have our own first-class dry cleaning facility on the premises."

"I'm no longer surprised at anything, Jan. It shows what a sheltered life I've led."

Jan glanced at her watch. "There's one more section I want you to see before we head back." She increased her gait and headed down another aisle. "I'm sure this collection is right up your alley."

After two more turns and a flight of stairs down to the second floor, Jan stopped and waved her arm like a host on a game show. "Welcome to the Ocean Wear Collection."

Scooter stepped through the entry, and, upon seeing the numerous racks of beachwear and swimsuits, felt his eyes cross. "Wow! These clothes date back to the 18th century. Will you look at these threads? And they go all the way up to the stuff I wear." He sighed. "I could have a blast wearing some of these older duds on the beach. It's so retro."

Jan giggled. "I knew this assortment would get your attention. Neat, huh?"

"Better than neat." Scooter reached over and scratched Gabby's ear. "You think I'd look good wearing this while surfing?" He held up a man's one-piece, yellow and black striped bathing suit. Gabby and Flash both yipped.

"It's almost like they understand you, Scooter," said Jan. "Maybe it's my imagination."

Scooter chuckled. "Let's just say we bonded really fast. Right, pooches?"

Again, showing off for Jan, they yipped, twice this time.

"Well, it's time we leave the museum of threads and get you back to the hotel. I'm sure you are starving. Tonight will be very enjoyable. We do a lot of business with Olive's Bistro, and we reserved a meeting room in the restaurant. That means Gabby and Flash have the honor of attending." She leaned over, not seeing Scooter's jaw drop. "Will you like that, pups?"

Gabby cheered with two high-pitched and one deep yip. Flash followed with a low howl. Scooter shook his head, realizing they were showing off, but he wondered if Flash's quiet howl was due to his worry about being scolded for his 'break-away' stunt. "Okay, Miss Jan said it's time to go. You need to rest because you're going to the fancy restaurant tonight."

When they reached the office building, Jan excused herself to go inside and call Lewis to come pick up Scooter. No sooner than the door closed, Goofy and Pluto appeared from behind the building and slowly approached. Scooter beamed. "Look who came to see you!"

Gabby backed up, emitting a low growl. Flash froze. Goofy eased up, and in his silly voice said, "Hi, Gabby and Flash. I'm Goofy." He released his trademark laugh. "I've never been to Virginia Beach. Can I come visit you one day?" Then Goofy did a little dance and pointed to Pluto.

That's a good name for you, Goofy.

"Hey, my name's Pluto, and I'm a doggie like you. Nice to meet you both. Can you dance like us?" Pluto proceeded to dance like his big buddy. "Come on, join us."

Flash looked up wide-eyed at Scooter. ***They're real big dogs, Scooter.***

"They're very famous dogs, too."

Goofy stopped dancing and bent down. "Gabby, I heard we're making a movie about you. That's cool." He put his paw on Pluto. "My buddy and I have been in a whole lot of movies, well, cartoons, but it's sort of the same thing."

Scooter, are they for real? She looked at Flash. *Do they smell like dogs?*

No.

Jan walked out of the door, laughing. "Well, my two big puppies came to see my little friends. Hey, Goofy and Pluto."

The big dogs hopped over and hugged Jan. "Jan, you're still as cute as you were yesterday." Pluto laid his head on her shoulder. "You got any treats for us?"

"As a matter of fact, I do." She pulled two Snickers candy bars from her pocket and handed one to each famous, furry dog. "Okay, see you later. We've got to get ready for tonight's dinner to welcome Flash and Gabby. Thanks for stopping by."

Pluto and Goofy waved and trotted back behind the building. Scooter hollered, "Nice meeting you!"

Jan knelt beside Scooter's pups. "Wow! Our two famous doggies came over just to meet you. That's neat. Maybe Scooter will show you some of their cartoons on Saturday morning." She winked at Scooter.

"Surprises never cease around here, Jan."

"Remember, Disney is all about making dreams come true."

Scooter nodded. "And they do a fantastic job, too. I'm glad you'll be at the dinner tonight. You've been so helpful today, I'm sure we'll need you to hang with us tonight."

"I wouldn't miss it."

Both pups yipped.

"You're a hit with my furry friends, too."

"Yeah, we bonded. I guess it's because they know I love puppies." Jan giggled. "I'll let you in on a little secret, if you promise to keep it."

"I promise."

Jan stood on her tip-toes and whispered into his ear. "I have a sweet little doggie named Gabby, too."

Leaning back, Scooter looked at her. "Well, I'll be doggoned. No wonder you reached for Gabby's leash."

Jan nodded. "But I also love little Flash."

Lewis appeared, bringing the long limo to a stop. "Howdy, friends."

Jan waved. "We had a productive afternoon, Lewis. You need to get Scooter back to the hotel so he and his furry companions can rest up for a big night."

"Will do, Miss Jan."

Scooter leaned over. "I'd like to give the pooches an opportunity to TCB before we go. I don't think we'll need the bag."

"Certainly. I'll wait here."

Scooter led them around the corner and into the secluded area. "Better take care of business now, unless you want to experiment with the Wee-Wee Pads." He laughed.

Gabby paused in mid-stride and eyed him. *I don't see how you can cut jokes and laugh when we're so over our heads we can't see daylight.*

"Sure beats crying, girl. Remember what I told you? Whatever we do will be fine as long as we stick together. Now, go do your business. I want to take a shower and relax before tonight's shindig." Gabby shook her head and trotted away.

Flash finished and eased up beside Scooter, looking at him with puppy-dog eyes. *I'm sorry about running after the squirrels, Scooter. I don't know what got into me. I won't do it again.*

Scooter got down on his knee and hugged the trembling beagle. "I understand, pal. No one got hurt, and nothing was broken. You really are super fast."

Thanks, Scoot. I am having fun. But there were humans inside the dogs, not real dogs.

"Yes, they were. Disney has humans play all of their famous characters. Kind of cool though."

Gabby trotted up. *Let's get out of here, Scoot. I'm starving and sleepy.*

The trio climbed into the limo, waved good-bye to their new friend, Jan, and Lewis drove them out of Disney Studios and back to the hotel. Tonight, more new people would gather to dine and meet Scooter and his trusty partners. Scooter whispered, "Life's good."

CHAPTER 13

While the exhausted canines devoured their Puppy Chow, compliments of the hotel, Scooter hopped into the steam-filled shower and exhaled deeply to relieve his tension. "If today is a red letter day, what will be tomorrow's color?" Thinking ahead to the introduction dinner set to kick off in an hour, Scooter bowed his head beneath the hot, pulsing water and let it roll over his body, contemplating the professionals he would meet and the information they would convey. Each one would surely be sharing his respective goals and requirements. Even though Scooter desired to spend more time in the muscle-relaxing water, it was time to get the show on the road.

Scooter sliced the day's stubble from his face, brushed his teeth, and combed his shaggy mop. With a monogrammed towel wrapped around his waist, he entered the main suite and found both pups stretched out in their beds, dead to the world. "God love 'em," he whispered, opening his suitcase. He selected a light blue dress shirt, navy slacks, and Bass Weejuns. As he slipped his bare feet into the comfortable loafers, he sat on the bed, staring at the face in the mirror. "Gabby was right, we're in over our heads, and we've not even officially started." After practicing a couple of smiles, hoping to loosen up his facial muscles, thoughts of Darla Kay squeezed into his cluttered mind. "I'd better call her."

East Coast time would make it nine p.m., so Scooter quickly dialed 'O', and punched in his credit card number, then her home number. He waited patiently until her cheerful voice replaced the dull tone. "Hello."

"Hey, girl! What's happening at the beach?"

"Scooter! All's fine here...how is California?"

Over the next fifteen minutes, Scooter shared the day's experiences from boarding the Disney jet to the present. Darla Kay's replies showed she shared his excitement. Scooter felt better after telling her how this project was larger than he had ever imagined. "Making movies appears to be very technical and in-depth, and I've only seen a smidgeon so far."

"You will do fine, Scooter. And don't be surprised how Gabby performs tomorrow. She's one tough competitor."

"I don't disagree with that."

Darla Kay asked, "Since Gabby didn't care for flying, could she handle the trips back and forth?"

The cold, steel fist tightened its grasp on his stomach. So far, that question, and the possible answer, had remained tucked beneath the surface. "We'll see, Darla Kay." Knowing it would most likely help him to voice his concerns about leaving Gabby behind, he almost replied, 'Gabby told me she would rather stay than fly.' Thankfully, he stifled the words instead of shooting them across the country. "Everything hinges on whether she's selected for the part. The director's assistant said there will be three other dogs in the tryouts. And I guarantee they have previous movie experience. So, time will tell."

"You're right. Like the song says, 'don't worry...be happy'. So, are you looking forward to tonight's dinner?"

Scooter chuckled. "Is 'I'm starving' a sufficient answer?"

Darla Kay giggled. "You know what I mean, Scooter. This is your opportunity to meet talented movie people who work with a renowned company. That has to be exciting."

"I guess so, but it doesn't compare with grilling steaks on the deck and watching glassy waves roll onto the beach with you. Anyway, before I go, here's a little nugget of casting info. Jan, the very nice and helpful assistant to the director, told me the actor they've booked to play my part is some real famous guy." Scooter's best smile appeared on the face in the mirror.

"Oh, my! Who is it?"

"Jan said I'll have to wait until tonight, because Mr. Whoever is attending the dinner."

"Oh, Scooter, now that's thrilling! Hey, I can think of several handsome actors who could portray you. Please call me when you find out...please?"

Scooter chuckled. "Aw, it'll be late your time, and I wouldn't want to wake you. I'll surprise you tomorrow, between meetings. Anyway, I've got to go brush the pups and make them look spiffy for the guests."

"Okay. Give them a hug from me. And Scooter, thank you for calling. Have a great time tonight. I'll be waiting for your call tomorrow."

"Good night, Darla Kay. I'll call you when we get a break." He placed the receiver in the cradle as Flash eased up beside his leg. "Did you have a good nap?"

Flash pawed his muzzle. *Yes.*

"I hope my talking to Miss Darla Kay didn't wake you."

No. Gabby yipping in her sleep did. Scooter, I'm nervous about tonight.

Scooter picked up the little beagle and set him on the bed. While he stroked the floppy ears, Scooter said, "So am I, Flash. And so is Gabby. But we have to meet the people who will be making the movie." Scooter stepped over to his suitcase and pulled out the dog brush. He gently brushed Flash. "Just stay with me and expect lots of people to pet and make over you. And I'll slip you and Gabby small pieces of my food, too. Don't worry, we'll have fun."

When do we go back home?

"Sunday afternoon. That's the day after tomorrow. Why? Are you homesick?"

I miss the beach and our cottage.

Scooter took a deep breath. "You really like living with us, don't you?"

Flash nudged Scooter's leg. **You and Gabby are nice to me. I love you both.**

Scooter finished the brushing. "And we love you, too." He noticed movement across the large room. Gabby was up, performing her full body stretch. Her back arched in an inverted 'U'. "Speaking of Gabby, she's awake." Flash turned toward her, his tail wagging.

Gabby completed her wake-up ritual and moseyed over. "Are you rested up for tonight, girl?"

She held up a front paw and yawned. *I'd rather be having grilled steaks on our deck, Scoot.* Her statement was followed by a yip.

Scooter laughed and rubbed her black head. "You were eavesdropping while I talked to Darla Kay."

I thought she was asleep.

"She's sneaky, Flash."

No, I wasn't listening. I was dreaming about steaks. Did you really call Darla Kay? She hopped up on the bed beside Scooter and looked into his eyes.

Scooter began brushing her. "I know your tactics. You always keep an eye or an ear on me and Darla Kay."

Gabby lifted her head so Scooter could brush under her neck. *Let's change the subject. Tell me what's going to happen tonight. I've been to a restaurant before. Remember?*

Scooter nodded. "Yes, I remember. And I want you to behave as nicely as you did in New York. And, I want you to stick with Flash since this is his first time. Will you do that?"

Gabby rolled over and lifted her paws in the air. *Do my belly, Scoot, it itches. I think the doggie bed has fleas.*

Scooter performed her request. "There are no fleas in the bed. But if you two are nice and gentle tonight, and don't talk, I'll put your beds on the foot of mine. How's that?"

Now you're talking, Scoot-toot.

Will you put my bed in the chair?

Scooter glanced at his watch and stood. "I will, Flash. Now let's get ready. We've got fifteen minutes."

Both pooches leaped from the bed and hit their water bowls. Scooter checked himself out in the mirror. "Since I haven't found a place outside for you to do your math, it looks like it's Wee-Wee Pad time. Who wants to go first?" He covered his mouth to prevent Gabby from seeing his smile.

Gabby's head jerked up from her bowl. *Forget the pads, Scoot. Either find a place outside or let me stand in the shower.* Flash looked up and stared at her. *You can go in there, too, Flash. Scooter can run water on the wall and wash it away. Right, Scoot?*

Scooter leaned over, hands on his knees. "You are not going to wee-wee in the shower. If the pads are not an option, let's leave now, and I'll ask the clerk if there's a place around back."

It would be a lot easier.

After leashing his cute canines, Scooter followed them into the hallway. "The talking stops now, and your best behavior begins. Got it?"

Both yipped. "Good." Scooter took a deep breath as they started down the stairs.

The clerk grinned when Scooter asked the important question. "Yes, sir. Go out the front door and turn left. When you get around back, you'll see the sign in the middle of a small grassy area. This area is strictly for our pet guests. If you need a plastic bag, there's some in a box beside the sign, along with a covered trash can for your convenience."

Scooter thanked him. "Come along, Gabby and Flash. I'm sure Flash's nose will lead us right to it." Gabby yipped and wagged her tail. Flash remained silent, focusing on his sniffing task.

CHAPTER 14

On this warm Friday evening, diners flowed into the lobby of the Coast Anabelle Hotel, heading for Olive's Bistro. Many were finely dressed, in Scooter's opinion, while others wore something one notch up from casual. No matter their dress, all of them cooed over Gabby and Flash as they entered. Scooter nodded, preparing for the 'meet and greet' evening. He pulled up to the desk and asked where their meeting room was. The friendly clerk pointed toward the hallway on the other side of the main restaurant. "Take the first door on your right. Enjoy your dinner." Scooter thanked him and led the pooches along the wall of the main restaurant and into the hall. "Okay, time to put on a happy face," he whispered to them as they approached the door.

Scooter drew in a lung full of air and raked trembling fingers through his hair. When he pulled the heavy door open, two sounds greeted him. The first, a pleasant sound of a jazz trio. The second, the voices of twenty to thirty people talking and laughing in small groups. Thankfully, his eyes found and met Jan's. Tonight, she wore an attractive low-cut, light blue dress above the knees, and navy high heels. Her blonde hair was perfectly styled and framed her smiling face. With a quick wave, she headed toward him. "Okay, here comes Miss Jan. Be nice."

Jan gently shook his hand. "Nice to see you again, Scooter. I hope you are ready for an exciting evening." She reached down and greeted each pooch.

Scooter took another deep breath. "You look very nice, Jan. I'm glad you were keeping your eyes open for us. At least we know one person here tonight."

"Well, thank you. I prefer casual, but this dinner is special. My pleasurable duty for the evening is to introduce you to everyone. In other words, the pooches and I will be your sidekicks."

Scooter chuckled as he spotted the screenwriters, Paul and Ruthie, moving around the white linen-covered tables set with crystal, china, and silverware. "I wouldn't have it any other way, Jan." He handed Gabby's leash to Jan. "Here come the Sizemores. Have you met them?"

"I sure have. Nice people," Jan replied, turning toward them and waving.

When Scooter had first met the Sizemores, he guessed them to be in their early-forties. Paul was short and stocky with thinning black hair and a moustache. His wife appeared to be a couple of inches taller, but her bountiful auburn hair may have created an optical illusion. Her deep blue eyes, small nose, and full lips accented her cute face. They made the perfect-looking couple.

Paul stepped up, holding a flute of bubbling champagne in his left hand and extending his right. "Scooter, it's so nice to see you again. Big evening, buddy."

"That's what I'm told, Paul. I do want to thank you and Ruthie for your time and creativity to write the screenplay. I've not read it yet, but Disney must have liked it written out."

Ruthie stood after greeting Gabby and Flash and gave Scooter a light hug. "You're looking well, Scooter. Are you as nervous as we are?"

Scooter chuckled. "So nervous is normal? Good, count me in. I will say, my new friend, Jan, has made today as smooth as possible for us. I hear you have met."

"I'm glad you could attend tonight, since you've been busy editing the script. However, as you are aware, working with Disney is not really work, right?" She winked at Scooter.

Ruthie replied, "Very true, Jan. As you know, we're going to sit down with Scooter tomorrow and expand the ending. That should be no trouble, now that we've seen the new addition." She nodded down toward little Flash. "He will be perfect."

Scooter heard those words, and they immediately circled around inside his already full head. *Are they thinking of adding Flash?* In an effort to remain calm, he said, "A new ending?"

Paul nodded. "It's not a big deal, Scooter. The producer and director want the main thread in the movie to subliminally suggest that people adopt unwanted pets. We feel since you and Gabby found and took in Flash when he was a stray, that would be the perfect ending. Don't worry. Tomorrow, we'll get the story of how you found him, and all of his traits, and the ending will show several scenes of you three at the beach."

"Okay. That sounds good," replied Scooter. His mouth was as dry as sand. He looked at Jan. "Would you point me toward the bar? I'm a mite thirsty."

Jan replied, "Tell me what you want, Scooter. I'll get it while you're talking."

"I appreciate that, dear. I'll take a club soda with ice and an olive. Thank you." Jan handed Gabby's leash to Ruthie.

Paul nudged Scooter. "Here comes another one of Disney's talented assets."

Scooter turned to see a middle-aged lady working her way through the maze of tables. She wore a bright flowered blouse and tan slacks. Her hair was light brown with sprays of gray. "Who is she?"

"Only the best animal handler they have. She'll be tending to Gabby tomorrow, and if she's selected for the movie, Vennie will stick to her like fly paper."

"Good evening, Paul, Ruthie," said Vennie, shaking their hands. "How are my two rescue pooches, Ruthie?"

"They're just fine, Ven. You haven't been over to see them in a while. I can tell they miss you."

Vennie nodded. "I know. I've been busy working with two wild and crazy spider monkeys for a children's special due out this summer." She turned toward Scooter and smiled. "And you must be Mr. Bissell." She extended her band-aid speckled hand and noticed Scooter's eyes checking it out. "Those monkeys are spastic little rascals, but I love them. It's a pleasure to meet you."

Scooter chuckled. "The same here, Vennie." He nodded toward Paul. "You come with high credentials. Oh, and please call me Scooter. And I can guarantee Gabby won't challenge you as much as the monkeys." He looked down at the quiet pooches. "The black one is Gabby. The beagle is the newest member of the family. Meet Flash."

Vennie knelt and pulled both pups close, giving them a hug. "It's my pleasure to meet you both. I look forward to spending time and working with the two of you." Gabby's tail flipped from side to side. Flash nuzzled her hand, smelling the antiseptic and monkey scent.

Jan approached and handed Scooter a glass of club soda with two olives. "Thank you." He took two long sips. "Oh, that hits the spot."

Vennie and Jan shook hands. "I knew you wouldn't miss tonight, Vennie."

"Never miss the opportunity to meet new pups," replied Vennie. "So, Scooter, are you excited about having a movie made about your Gabby?"

"Vennie, if I was any more excited, I'd explode. However, right now, nervous is overshadowing excitement." He swiped beads of sweat from his forehead. "Everything is so new and way over my head."

Vennie laughed. "Relax. Have no fear, because you're in good hands with Disney." She stood and looked toward the entrance. "Here comes the main man."

Scooter turned to see a tall, thin man in a navy suit, white shirt, and red tie. His tan face displayed a pleasant, but confident look. Ruthie said, "Wayne 'Gets It Done' Zurl will be directing this project, Scooter. A more qualified man you will not find."

Scooter smiled at Ruthie. "I'll admit my nerves are beginning to relax as my discombobulated questions are answered by real-life, highly qualified people. So far it sounds like we have the A-Team."

"I'm sorry the producer, Thomas Winton, won't make it tonight. He's in LA for a seminar. He and Wayne work on many projects together and are usually found on the same page, so no worries on our part," said Paul.

When Wayne Zurl finally was free from a group of guests, he strolled up and extended his hand to Scooter. "It's a pleasure to meet you, Mr. Bissell. Wayne Zurl, at your service." Scooter noticed the firm, confident grip; he liked that in a man's shake.

"My pleasure, Wayne. You also come with high ratings. And I'm way too young to be a Mister. I'm just plain old Scooter." He pointed to his furry companions. "The black one is Gabby. And Flash is our newest."

Zurl quickly dropped to his knee to greet both dogs. "Scooter it is." There was no doubt Wayne liked dogs as much as the others. The fact they all were canine lovers convinced Scooter this movie would be all right. If he had to leave Gabby here for the shoots, she would be in good hands.

When Wayne finished his warm introduction to both pups, he stood. "It's nice to see all of you here tonight," he said to the others. "I knew everyone would make Scooter and his friends feel welcome." He paused and looked around the room, appearing to be in search of someone. He leaned toward Jan. "Any sign of Kevin?"

"No, sir. But his secretary called me before I left the office and confirmed he would be attending."

Zurl nodded and scratched his balding head. "And Meg is still out of country, right?"

Jan replied, "Yes. She's due back in three days and will be ready."

Scooter listened closely when the two names were mentioned, his mind running through famous actors by first name. Maybe if his head were clearer, putting last names with the first ones would be simpler. However, now was not the time to test his movie trivia skills, so he decided to jump in and ask. "I'm assuming these are the two main characters, right?"

Zurl chuckled and looked at Gabby. "Close, Scooter. A black lab, whichever one is selected, will be the main character. But yes, Meg Ryan will play Darla Kay, the teacher in charge of the special children. Oh, and by the way, we have selected six very talented child actors for those parts. They are delightful to work with, and we've used them before in movies and TV shows."

Scooter dropped the silly grin and leaned forward, expecting to hear more about this Kevin who would play him. *Might as well ask.* "And Kevin plays me?"

The others chuckled, and Ruthie whistled, just as Jan had done earlier. Zurl laughed. "Well, since he'll be here in a while, I'll let Ruthie tell you." He smiled at Ruthie. "Ruthie?"

Ruthie grinned from ear to ear and looked at Vennie and Jan. "Drum roll, please." The two ladies quickly responded with a low buzzing. "Scooter, you will be played by Mr. Kevin Costner." She fanned her face with both hands. "What a hunk!" The girls whistled in agreement.

Scooter's legs turned to noodles. Just hearing Meg Ryan would be Darla Kay caused his heart to beat out of rhythm. He couldn't wait to tell her. Now, Kevin Costner would be him. His eyes blurred as he looked around the group, struggling for a reply. The goofy grin reappeared.

The entire group laughed. Zurl gave him a pat on the back. "You look a might surprised, Scooter. Wish I'd have gotten that look on film. It would become one of my teaching tools."

"Wow! You folks are serious about producing a first-class movie about my Gabby."

Jan said, "I told you."

A young man stepped up beside Wayne and whispered something to him. Wayne nodded. "Thank you, Rick. I'll go meet him."

"If you'll excuse me, I'll be back in five."

Wayne headed for the door as Scooter drained his club soda. "Good drink." Jan slipped up and took Scooter's glass. "Time for a refill." She hurried off toward the bar.

Vennie said, "Would you mind if I escorted Gabby and Flash around to meet the others before we eat?"

Without hesitation, Scooter handed her both leashes. "They love people, Vennie." He bent over and whispered to them, "You all be polite and do what Vennie says. Okay?" Both yipped. "Good."

As they departed, Jan stepped up and handed Scooter another refreshing drink. "Thanks, Jan. Am I embarrassing myself too much?"

The short blonde giggled. "You're doing fine. I was impressed how calm you remained when you heard Meg's name." The others laughed. "I was expecting a real wolf whistle."

Scooter sipped the cold drink. "I'm in a mild form of shock. But I'm positive Darla Kay will go ballistic when I tell her who's playing us. And she's a huge Kevin Costner fan."

Ruthie said, "Show me a woman who isn't."

"I'm surprised Kevin has time to do a movie about a dog." Scooter fished out an olive with the little red swirl stick.

Paul replied, "You're lucky, Scooter. Kevin just finished 'Wyatt Earp', and when he read our script, he said this was the perfect movie to play himself and work with a dog. Not to mention, he loves the beach and surfing."

Scooter shook his head. "Please ignore this stunned look plastered on my face. It could very well become permanent if I don't wake up soon."

"You'll wake up tomorrow, Scooter. We'll be in meetings for most of the day, dealing with the script, shooting schedule, and the contract. When we're finished, we will go down to the coast and see how the auditions are coming along," said Ruthie. "I recommend you get a good night's rest."

Before Scooter responded, a commotion behind them grabbed everyone's attention. Scooter turned, seeing several people walking along and talking to Zurl and Costner. "Yeah, I'm dreaming," Scooter whispered. "Pinch me, Jan."

Ruthie and Jan released sighs that sounded more like drawn-out swoons.

Paul chuckled. "Women. Come on, girls. Kevin's a normal man."

Ruthie gave him 'the look'. "Oh, he's a man, Paul, but way above normal. Right, Jan?"

Jan quickly nodded, keeping her eyes on the blond, boyish-looking man in faded jeans, a white dress shirt with the sleeves rolled up to his elbows, and brown cowboy boots. "Very right, Ruthie."

When others in the meeting room saw Costner's entrance, the buzz quieted briefly, then continued. Scooter hoped he wouldn't say anything silly enough to cause Costner to back out of the movie. *Even a fool is not known if he keeps his mouth shut.*

As Zurl approached with Costner close in tow, Scooter relaxed when he saw the familiar grin and twinkling blue eyes on the actor's tan face. He also picked up on the fact they were both six foot tall and had the same body type and shaggy hair. *Disney doesn't miss a trick.*

Zurl looked closely at both men. "Kevin, I know you've read the publisher's bio on Scooter, as he prefers to be called. Now you may observe for yourself." Zurl chuckled. "Scooter, meet the 'on screen' Scooter." The two Scooters shook hands. Scooter noticed Costner also had a firm grip. *Good.*

"Nice to meet you, Scooter," said Costner in his typical laid-back fashion. "From what I gleaned from the script, my goal is to play a beach bum who writes novels, loves to surf, grills burgers, and has a tender heart for special needs children." He chuckled. "And, most of all, he loves pets nobody else wants. Am I close?"

Costner's perfect description of Scooter's lifestyle stunned him. It was amazing that it came from a famous actor who received the information only from others' observations. "So far, you're riding the wave perfectly, Kevin."

Kevin slapped him on the back. "I jumped on this movie for several reasons, Scooter. After finishing *'Wyatt Earp'*, I need to get back to reality and a project that will touch peoples' hearts in a warm, feel-good way. I'm honored Tom Winton asked me. I respect Tom as a producer, and my talented friend Wayne. I'm open to learning anything else about you that will help me portray you as accurately as possible."

"Okay, but there's not much to me, Kevin. I'd say you have me nailed down pretty well already."

Wayne held up his hand. "We can continue this conversation over our gourmet meal. I'm sure everyone is hungry. Later, they want to hear a word from Kevin, after he meets the pups."

Kevin smiled broadly. "I'm glad to hear that, Wayne. I'll meet them tonight and spend part of tomorrow on the coast during the canine auditions. And, yes, I'm starving."

CHAPTER 15

The trio from Virginia Beach housed in Room 213 of the Coast Annabelle Hotel crashed like string-less puppets after the evening's introduction dinner. After a few compliments from Gabby and Flash about the delicious filet mignon, Scooter congratulated them for being so well-behaved and friendly to everyone. They completed their short conversation to hit the sack quickly. Scooter had placed Gabby's doggie bed on the foot of his and Flash's in the fancy wingback chair, then watched them perform their routine spins and drop. "Sleep tight tonight. We've got a busy day tomorrow."

"Five-thirty." Scooter stirred and looked blurry-eyed at the digital clock on the nightstand. "I feel like I just crawled into this comfortable bed." He put his hands behind his head, closed his tired eyes, and allowed his jumbled thoughts to run freely, hoping they would find a logical order.

Today would take them a step further into an uncharted future. The idea that Gabby, if selected for the movie, would remain in Burbank in lieu of flying several times from coast to coast weighed heavy on Scooter's mind. After meeting most of the main people involved in the making of the movie, he was assured she would be cared for. Ruthie and Paul had already mentioned Gabby was welcome to stay with them and their two rescue dogs. Also, the renowned animal handler, Vennie Ramos, offered to have Gabby stay with her on her five-acre farm. Almost pleading, Vennie's reasoning made good sense, since she would be on the set anytime Gabby was in a shoot. Her reputation for the care and training of all types of animals and birds was comforting, and Scooter knew Gabby would enjoy seeing a wide array of creatures…as long as she remained number one.

Not knowing for sure what his book signing schedule would be, or exactly where it might take him, Scooter was sure he would find a way for him to come visit. And if there happened to be a couple or three-week break in filming, he might persuade Gabby to make a flight. Enticing her with a return for a quick visit to her home beach might do the trick.

His thoughts switched over to today's scheduled meetings with the Disney lawyer and the contract and giving information to Paul and Ruthie for a new ending. Scooter shut down his mind, deciding to trust his ability to handle those. Those details did not even compare to being separated from Gabby for any length of time. He crawled out of bed, deciding on a hot wake-up shower.

The soothing water instantly recharged his battery and cleared the cobwebs from his head. As he towel-dried his hair, a terrific idea formed. Since the meetings and Gabby's auditions were set to begin at nine o'clock, they had three hours to kill. "I'll reward them with a morning beach walk on a new coast. It will allow me to see where my black lab will be performing for the movie professionals. And, Gabby will get a preview of the California beach, too. Man, I feel like a parent wanting to go to school with their child on the first day." He slipped into his knock-around clothes.

As he opened the bathroom door, he heard Gabby and Flash talking. He paused to listen.

The lady who was scratched up by the monkeys was real nice to us. She works with the movie people and animals. I think her name was Vennie.

I liked her, too. But I don't think I've ever seen a monkey. Have you?

No. They don't live at our beach. Hey, I noticed Scooter was nervous at first, but then he relaxed. I'm glad he didn't tell any jokes. Gabby yipped.

The steak was good. It was better than he cooks at home.

Scooter stifled a laugh and continued his eavesdropping.

I like the lady they call Jan. She's friendly and giggles a lot.

And she didn't get mad at me for chasing the squirrels. She gave me a piece of steak under the table. Did you get one from her?

Yep. Oh, did you think the man who is going to play Scooter looked like him?

A little bit. Why won't they let Scooter in the movie?

Because he's not an actor, Flash. They only use real actors.

You're not a real actor.

It's different for dogs. See, that's why they have Vennie. She tells me what to do, and I do it. That's simple. Scoot would want to do everything his way. You know how he is.

Scooter got his hand over his mouth in time to silence the chuckle.

But isn't that what the movie is about? You and Scooter?

Yes. It's a movie about Scooter adopting me and all of the cool things I did.

Then Scooter should be himself just like he is at home. Maybe I don't understand.

You'll learn. Maybe one day they'll do a movie about you.

I don't want to be in a movie, Gabby. I'm happy to take life easy.

Scooter decided he had heard enough. It was time to come out and surprise them with the beach walk. When he stepped from the bathroom, the light of a new day spilled through the window. The two pups were stretched out on the carpet at the foot of the bed. "Good morning!" Scooter announced as he trotted over and rubbed their heads. "You two are looking perky."

Easy, Scoot. We just woke up. What's with all this excitement?

Hey, Scooter.

"Hello, Flash. It looks like Miss Maybe A Movie Star is a tad grumpy."

I'm not grumpy, and I'm not a movie star.

Scooter dug his flip-flops from the suitcase. "You might be. Today's the big day for tryouts."

Whatever.

Scooter clapped his hands, causing Gabby to jerk her head up from her paws. "Since you both were such nice pups last night, I am rewarding you with an early morning trip to the beach. We'll take a walk beside the ocean, and when we come back, I'll have breakfast delivered to our room. You ready?"

We're getting on the plane and going home?

No, Flash. There's a beach not far from here, right, Scoot?

"Yepper. I'll call the clerk and have him get us a cab. We'll be on the Santa Monica coastline in thirty minutes. And Gabby, that's where they hold part of the auditions today. So you'll get a peek at it before you have to do your thing." Scooter walked over to the phone and hit '9'. When the clerk answered, Scooter requested the cab. "Okay, that's fine. We'll be downstairs in a few minutes. Thank you."

"Let's head down. By the time you take care of business, the cab will be here." He clapped his hands again. "This will be neat. I've never seen the Pacific Ocean up close."

Scoot, go easy on the clapping. I'm still half asleep.

Thirty minutes later, the bright yellow taxi delivered Scooter and the pooches to the end of Colorado Avenue and the famous Santa Monica Pier. "Okay, friends," said the driver. "Looks like we've got another beautiful day. If you like, I'll come pick you up whenever you say."

Scooter let the eager doggies out, holding firmly onto the leashes, knowing how much they wanted to run and play. He paid and tipped the friendly driver. "That would be perfect. How about forty-five minutes?"

"Thank you, kind sir," the driver said after seeing the tip. "Count on it. I'll see you at exactly seven-thirty. Enjoy yourselves." He tooted the horn as he pulled away.

Scooter walked toward the ocean for a wide-open view of the Pacific. White crests foamed from the blue swells in perfect rhythm and rolled onto the sandy beach. He filled his lungs with salty air. "Well, what do you think of this beach? There are more people here than at ours."

That pier is a lot bigger than ours. In fact, it looks bigger than Sandbridge.

Scooter eyed the famous pier. "You are right. This pier is over eighty years old. It has a carousel, aquarium, shops, pub, and restaurants."

Wow! Our pier is only for fishing.

"Right you are, Flash. The fishing part is way down on the end. Come on, let's walk down on the beach and get our feet sandy and wet. It'll be like home."

They maneuvered their way onto the beach and Scooter kicked off his flip-flops. "Man, I love the feeling of sand under my feet." He raked his bare feet back and forth like a chicken scratching dirt in search of corn.

Gabby looked at Scooter and then over at Flash. *Sometimes I worry about him, Flash. Give him a minute, and maybe he'll remember to unleash us. We won't run away.*

I want to get my paws wet, Gabby.

Scooter completed his silly act, mainly done to get Gabby back into her normal mood. "Hey, let me take the leash off, and you can run on the beach. Go get 'em, Pacific pooches!" He chuckled and unhooked the leashes.

As Gabby sprinted across the sand, Scooter heard her say, *Flash, he's always playing Mr. Funny.*

Scooter watched closely as they neared the water line. He knew, compared to Sandbridge, the water here would be much colder and he wanted to see their reactions when they splashed into the shorebreak. He didn't have to wait long. Gabby reached the white water first. She yipped, leaped into the air, and landed, belly-deep. Instantly, she released two high-pitched yips and one long howl as she turned and sprinted up on dry land.

Flash met her as she raced back up, thinking she was only running, having no idea what was in store. He bounded into the water, and his short legs put the water completely over his back. Flash didn't yip or howl…he barked several times and backed out as fast as possible. Then he turned and stumbled onto the warm sand.

Scooter sat down and laughed until his sides ached. "Yes, we love the Pacific Ocean!"

Both pups completed full body shakes and walked up to Scooter. "Come on in, the water's fine." His laughter continued.

If those movie people think I am going to swim in their icy water, they've got another think coming. I have better things to do than freeze my feet and ears off. No way, Scoot.

She's right. It's really cold. I'm glad our beach has different water.

"Since I've never been in this water, maybe I should give it a try. You think?"

Gabby and Flash yipped in sync.

Oh, yeah, Scoot. But it's probably warm to a tough surfer like yourself. Gabby looked at Flash and nodded.

Just get your feet wet, Scoot-toot.

All in the hope of giving his furry friends a fond memory, he had withheld one other nugget. When he had stepped from the steamy shower earlier, the idea hit him. He had chuckled the entire time he was putting on his bathing suit and extra T-shirt, and then slipped into his baggy khakis and Dewey Weber T-shirt. Now, he was about to make a fool out of himself for their enjoyment. *I'm crazy.*

"Okay. If you all were brave enough to go in, I will, too." In slow motion, he peeled off one T-shirt and dropped it onto the sun-kissed sand. Then he unbuckled his belt and dropped his pants, leaving him standing in a pair of flowered surf baggies and a ragged Raven T-shirt. "I'm ready!" He clapped his hands, refusing to think about the cold water.

I dare you, Scoot!

Don't do it. It's really cold.

"Gabby said I was a tough surfer, so it won't be cold to me. See ya!" He reached down, rubbed their heads and noted their wide-open eyes of surprise, then sprinted to the ocean. When his feet hit the white water, needles of ice shot up his legs. He continued forward, spreading the frozen chills to his knees, waist, and chest. Then he inhaled a huge breath of air and dove into the swell. The icy shock almost stole the air from his lungs as he surfaced. He stood in neck-deep water and forced a broad smile onto his frozen lips, waving to his spellbound pups. "Come on in…the water's fine!" Then his teeth began to chatter. He moved toward the shallows, quickly rubbing his numb arms. What he saw next totally blew his mind. Gabby ran toward him at full pace. She leaped the shorebreak, hit the water, and paddled for all she was worth. He felt his throat tighten as hot tears filled his eyes. *She's practicing for the audition. That's some pooch.* "Come on, girl!"

They met in waist-deep water, and Scooter pulled her tight against his chest. "Why did you come out with me in this freezing water, Baboo?"

I'm not letting any strange dogs show me up. Remember when I saved little Kay? You told me I was a tough pup. Now we're both tough, Scoot-toot.

Scooter hugged her and swallowed the growing lump in his throat. "Yeah, Gabby, we're both tough."

Flash was waiting for them when they walked onto the damp sand. ***Wow! You both surprised me.***

Scooter backed up while Gabby shook. *I'm hungry.*

"We all are." He looked at his watch. "Let's go up and let me step into the restroom and get some dry clothes on. The cab will be here in a few minutes." He got down on one knee and pulled both of them close. "I'm proud to go anywhere with you two."

CHAPTER 16

The timing proved to be perfect. After a thawing-out shower, Scooter finished dressing as a double-knock sounded on the door. "Our breakfast has arrived," he said to the laid-back canines. He opened the door to a young man dressed in a white coat and dark slacks. "Come in," Scooter said, stepping back. Gabby and Flash watched in amazement as the cart, draped with a linen sheet, was rolled in. With precision, the man whipped the linen from the plates. "Enjoy your breakfast, sir. When you're finished, just put the cart in the hallway." Scooter tipped the friendly fellow and replied, "Thank you. I'm sure we will clean our plates."

Now, Scooter, I've got a great idea.

As Scooter put a cup of Puppy Chow into their bowls, he grinned, knowing Gabby's statement would include food and eating. "I dare to ask, but what?"

Maybe once a week, Flash and I could tell you what we want for breakfast. You would go into the kitchen, fix it, and then deliver it to the bedroom. Wha'cha think, Scoot-toot?

Flash looked at Gabby as if the cold water had affected her brain.

Scooter chuckled and began to break strips of bacon into little pieces and sprinkle them on the dog food. "There may come a time when I'll do that. I promise you, Gabby, it will be a special occasion. Now, eat up. We've got one busy day ahead of us." He placed the bowls on a towel on the carpet.

Oh, that smell so good. Flash, if you don't want all of your bacon, I'll take it.

I'm hungry.

Pig.

Scooter pointed at her. "Gabby! That's not how we talk to each other. Now apologize, young lady."

I'm sorry, Flash. You're not a pig.

Flash's tail swished from side to side. ***I know you didn't mean it. But I'll share with you if I can't finish.***

Scooter nodded his approval to Flash. After adding a pinch of salt and pepper, he sipped from a large glass of tomato juice and glanced at the clock on the nightstand. "I have time to call Darla Kay and tell her who's playing me and her. She'll go ballistic." He punched in the necessary numbers and nibbled on a piece of cheese toast while listening to the dull ring. After seven or eight, the recorder answered with Darla Kay's sweet voice asking the caller to leave a message. *Since it's Saturday, she's probably out somewhere.* After the beep, he gave her a cheerful greeting and explained a bit about their agenda for the busy day. With a smile on his face said, "I heard last night who will be playing us. Since the Disney folks seem to know everybody in the biz personally, they only used first names. You probably know who they're talking about, but I didn't ask, preferring they not know I'm a beach bumpkin. Anyway, some dude named Kevin is playing me. I met him, and he's cool. He just finished filming some cowboy movie. And a young woman named Meg will play you. So that's the scoop from Burbank, dear. I'll be home Sunday afternoon. If you have no plans, let's do a cookout at the beach. I'll call when I get home. Have a super day."

Gabby had devoured her breakfast and was sitting two feet from Flash, staring, while a string of drool dangled from her mouth. Flash, lost in his own world, ate at the normal slow pace. Scooter smiled and picked up another piece of toast and mentally checked off his upcoming tasks. Then Gabby's audition slipped into his thoughts, pushing his menial tasks to the back burner. From the remarks she made on the beach, she let him know the audition would receive her all-out best. And, if selected, that would be great, but then the decision to stay or do the flying thing must be made. *Well, at least she will be in good hands, and no matter her decision, Flash and I also have an agenda. What will be...will be.*

With breakfast behind them, Scooter put the cart in the hallway. "It's time to go downstairs. The limo will be here in ten minutes. You can TCB, and then it's off to the studio. Who's excited?"

I am, Scooter. This is fun.

Gabby stretched and yawned. *I'm ready, now that my tummy is full. Thanks for taking us to their beach. I feel better now that I've seen it and been in the water.*

"Good, I'm glad. Now, Gabby, you have no need to be nervous. See, you've got an edge on the other dogs."

How? They live around here and have probably been in movies.

Scooter looked in the mirror and raked his fingers through his still damp hair. "You will understand exactly what the director is asking to be done. The others will rely on hand signals from Vennie. You'll be able to perform with precision, and, knowing you, I can see you adding a creative touch."

Oh. I see, Scoot. I will do my best because I don't believe in quitting or giving up.

"That's my girl. Now, let's go do this thing. Remember, we're all in this together."

Lewis pulled the limo up to Jan's office building. "Have a productive day, sir. I'll be in touch with Miss Jan when it's time to pick you up." Lewis held the door open for them to slide out.

"Thank you, Lewis." Scooter handed him a tip. "We've got a busy one."

As Lewis pulled away, Jan emerged from inside with a smile larger than a Sandbridge sunrise. "Good morning!" She leaned down and greeted Gabby and Flash. "Gabby, I'm pulling for you today. Vennie will be here shortly to take you to the sound studio for the first part of the audition. Then you will be taken to the beach to see how you do around the water. Just be yourself, and you will be a hit." Jan looked up and winked at Scooter. "Relax, Scooter. You look like a parent waiting for his child to step onto the stage for a school play." She giggled and gave him a gentle pat on the arm.

"A perfect description as to how I feel, Jan."

Jan pointed. "Here's our talented animal trainer now." She waved to Vennie as she pulled up in a new Ford pickup with several large cages in the back.

"We've got a beautiful day for auditions," Vennie chirped, climbing from the truck. "Good morning to all." She knelt and greeted the pups. "You all look ready to grab this day by the tail and enjoy it."

Scooter smiled. "If Gabby gives you any grief, just give her 'the look'. I'm only teasing. She's a good pooch, and I believe she's ready."

"No worries, Scooter." She looked at her Mickey Mouse watch. "Hate to do it, but we've got to run. Wayne's meeting us in five minutes at the studio. It's set up to look like a real living room and kitchen."

Gabby yipped. "I'm sure you heard 'kitchen'. Now you go with Vennie and do your best. I think we'll be over to see you at the beach this afternoon." Scooter hugged her close and whispered, "Knock 'em dead."

Flash released two yips. Gabby nudged him.

Vennie opened the passenger door. "C'mon, Gabby. You can ride up front with me." Gabby leaped into the cab. As they drove off, Scooter felt a twinge of sadness and pride. Flash moved up against his leg, tail wagging.

Jan said, "Okay, let's go inside and begin. Paul and Ruthie will be here shortly." She led the way through the glass doors. "Welcome to my world."

The morning slipped into afternoon quicker than a bluefish through a school of baitfish. Scooter detailed for Paul and Ruthie how he found little Flash abandoned in the woods on the Eastern Shore. When he described the pup's physical condition, Ruthie and Jan's faces filled with compassion. They both looked at the now-healthy beagle sleeping soundly on a white towel on the carpet. "He's come a long way, Scooter," said Ruthie. "It breaks my heart to think about all of the unwanted and mistreated dogs and cats thrown out like trash. And with our two rescue dogs, Paul and I realized how much they appreciate having someone care for them. But the truth is, they also add to our lives."

Jan nodded. "So true."

Scooter shared how quickly Flash bonded with Gabby and accepted that he now had a home and was loved. When he told about Flash and the special needs children, he felt his emotions bubbling up, but he kept them at bay. However, Jan and Ruthie's eyes became moist. Then their eyes grew wide with astonishment upon hearing about Flash finding Darla Kay's bracelet.

Paul stayed busy taking notes. When Scooter paused, Paul said, "It sounds to me like this information provides the ending Wayne wanted. It shows the rewards of adoption, for the person and the animal."

Scooter sipped his Coke to hide his grin. If only he could tell them about his pups' unique ability to speak. *Talk about a fantastic movie.*

Jan glanced at the large Mickey Mouse clock on the wall. "Well, it's almost one o'clock. Let's walk over to the cafeteria and grab some lunch. The attorney meets with us at two-thirty to go over the contract." She closed the leather folder in front of her and stood. "Are you two going to the auditions after lunch?"

Paul nodded. "Wouldn't miss them. Then we'll head home and work on the ending so Scooter can read over it tonight. We'll see them before they fly out tomorrow afternoon. Does that sound good to you, Scooter?"

"Finer than frog's hair, buddy. I'm enjoying riding this wonderful wave."

On their way across the lot to the cafeteria, Jan explained how delicious the food was. "From the visitors' reviews, it's one of the favorite places to visit while touring the studios."

Paul and Ruthie agreed. "For a cafeteria, it's four stars, Scooter," said Paul.

Scooter pushed his chair back from their outdoor table and swiped his mouth with the linen napkin covered in Disney cartoon characters. "You weren't joking. That's the best cheeseburger I've ever had. My famous beach burgers don't compare." He handed Flash a French fry. "We'll have to keep this a secret from Gabby, little buddy." Flash yipped.

Paul laughed. "I think he understands you, Scooter."

Ruthie smiled. "They have more sense than people give them credit for, right, Scooter?"

The butterflies found room to flap their wings in his taut stomach. "You're right, Ruthie." In hopes to nip the discussion about intelligent animals communicating with their human companions, he said, "I wonder how Gabby's doing?"

"Well, they've probably had a snack for lunch and are getting ready to head to the pier for the afternoon. It's a beautiful day to spend on the coast," replied Jan, standing. "And we will be spending the next couple of hours reading a contract." She shook hands with Paul and Ruthie. "So you go and enjoy the afternoon. Tell everyone we'll be there as soon as possible."

"Somebody should enjoy the beach today besides the pups," said Ruthie. "We'll probably be home writing the ending by the time you get there. See you in the morning, friends."

Jan and Scooter waved as the couple drove away from the office building. "Scooter, you'll like our lawyer. He's laid back and explains everything in layman's terms. Feel free to ask him any questions you have. In my opinion, there is no stupid question when it comes to legal jargon." Jan giggled and held the door open for him.

"After that delicious lunch, laid back sounds good to me," Scooter replied.

Jan looked through the large window of the conference room and spotted Blaine Lucas sitting at the table, scanning pages of the contract. "He's always on time, and he's a master with numbers, Scooter." She opened the door and said to Blaine, "Good afternoon." They shook hands. "This is Scooter."

"Nice to meet you, Scooter. That's a cool name." He gave Scooter a firm handshake. "I'll do my best to make this as painless as possible."

"Jan said you can explain difficult legal lingo to dummies. When it comes to that stuff, I qualify. Nice to meet you."

Jan giggled. "I didn't use the word dummy, Blaine. You'll quickly learn Scooter's as laid back as you are. Shall we get down to business? The sooner we're finished here, the sooner we can hit the beach."

"Sounds good to me." Blaine slid a stack of pages toward them. "I've drawn up two different contracts." He looked at Scooter over rimless, tinted glasses. "One is between Dooley Bissell, your real name, for legal reasons." He smiled. "And Disney." Setting that stack aside, he picked up the other. "And the second contract will be valid, if you accept the terms, and if Gabby is selected for the movie. Of course, you are what we call her guardian. You'll see a considerable increase in monies and royalties compared to the first contract. Why don't you and Jan take as much time as you need and read over both of them and jot down any questions? I'll be back in fifteen or twenty minutes. I need to make a couple of phone calls to headquarters."

"Thank you, Blaine," said Jan. "Feel free to use my office."

In silence they read over the contracts. Scooter thought his eyes would pop from their sockets when he counted the zeros in the first contract, just for the use of his story. *Good-googly-moogly. We're talking several million without Gabby starring, and I haven't even seen the royalty percentage.* He slowly set the contract down, took a deep breath, and grabbed the second one. His heart rumbled like a roll on a snare drum upon seeing the difference in the amount of the payment in the first one compared to what it would be if Gabby was featured. Sweat bubbled on his forehead. *Wow! They must think the movie will be a super hit.* His hands began to tremble and his breathing quickened. He blinked his eyes several times to erase the blur, then he scanned the page until he found the section on royalties. *Holy moley! That's a generous percentage. Works for me.* He placed the contract down and stood. "I need to walk around a minute, Jan." She remained silent. Scooter eased up to the window, gazing down three stories and taking in the massive grounds. Struggling to level out his breathing, a smile creased his face. *We can do a lot of good with that amount of money. That's what Gabby and I had pledged to do, help others whenever we could.* He closed his eyes to the world of Disney before him. *Gabby, even if you aren't selected, we can still do a lot.* Scooter slowly shook his head, moved back to the table, and sat.

Jan put her copy down and stood. "Would you like something to drink, Scooter?"

Nodding, he looked up into her eyes. "Thank you. A glass of water would do wonders."

"I thought so. I'll be right back." She hustled from the room.

Scooter lowered his head to his hands and released a long sigh. His thoughts swiftly moved to the Santa Monica coastline and Gabby. Silently, he wished her luck. He slipped from the padded chair and knelt beside the sleeping Flash. He put his still trembling hand on the soft fur.

"Here's your water, Scooter." Jan handed it to him and raised her glass. "Cheers!"

"Cheers! Thank you, Jan. You've been a great help. We really appreciate all you've done."

"Aw, you're welcome. It's been my pleasure. I told you this was a fun job."

They returned to their seats at the shiny mahogany table. "Jan, I'm far from a legal scholar, but I know Disney is a trustworthy company and renowned institution, so I doubt there's any fine print to Disney's advantage contained in either contract. In other words, from what I read, everything looks fine to me. I respect your opinion. What do you think?"

Jan sipped her water and set down the glass. "In my five years with Disney, I've never heard a word about sleazy business practices, either within the walls or from the vast amount of people they serve and work with. However, as my mother used to say, my mouth is not a prayer book. Anyway, if I were in your shoes, I would trust Disney." She looked at him seriously. "But, Scooter, it's your decision."

Scooter drained his water. "My life has changed so dramatically since Gabby came into it, I couldn't begin to tell you. And nothing we've been involved in has been sour." He nodded down to the sleeping Flash. "As soon as we found this little fellow, it was her idea..." Scooter caught himself. "I could tell, you know how dogs and cats are around a newcomer? Well, Gabby and Flash instantly hit it off. So I figured he would be a welcomed addition. And we made the right decision. Now this major change is because of Gabby, since it was her brave actions that put me and my novel in front of a big-time publisher. Knowing how well things have worked out whenever Gabby's been involved, I believe accepting the contracts would be in our best interest." Scooter pawed sweat from his brow. "Whew! Did you understand any of my babbling?"

"Yes, Scooter. And I agree with everything you said. Congratulations!" She leaned over and hugged him. "I'll go see if Blaine is ready, then call Lewis to come pick us up. Do you have any questions for Blaine?"

Scooter shook his head. "Not really. At least nothing that would prevent me from signing. And, honestly, I'm getting itchy to hit the coast and see my other special pooch in action."

CHAPTER 17

Scooter expected more people on the coast than earlier that morning, but nothing like the parade of colors, bathing suits of all styles, and an eclectic selection of humans dotting the beach and boardwalk. Hair-dos ranged from 'bed-head' hair to styled, heavily sprayed and wildly-colored-hair, and everything else in-between. He, Flash, and Jan slipped from the limo. Jan asked Lewis to come pick them up in two hours. "They should be finished with auditions by five, Lewis." Scooter slipped him a ten spot.

Lewis smiled. "It's a real pleasure serving you, Scooter. I'm rooting for Gabby."

Scooter replied, "I'll tell her, friend." As Lewis pulled away, Scooter stood tall in the hope of spotting the dogs and Wayne and Vennie. "I don't see them, Jan."

"Disney gets a use permit to cordon off a section of beach. It's just down a ways to our right. Come on, follow me."

Scooter's nerves tightened. As they maneuvered through the crowd, he paused and removed his Top-siders, instantly savoring the warm sand beneath his feet. His thoughts came to rest on Gabby down here in the midst of strangers and doing her best to follow Wayne's directions. *She's one brave, determined doggie.* He glanced down at his little beagle plodding through the sand. Flash's tri-colored tail was straight up, as was his muzzle with its black nose twitching. "Are you excited, Flash?"

The beagle's response, a high-pitched yip.

Jan turned and looked at Scooter with questioning eyes. Nodding her head slowly, she said, "It sure sounds like he understands you."

"Maybe, but I think it's more about hearing his name." Scooter was satisfied with his reply.

They finally breached the largest group of people, opening up the view of the Pacific Ocean. Waist-high, choppy waves rolled onto the shore. Several surfers in black wetsuits straddled their boards, waiting for one wave with a bit of form. The sight told Scooter two things: the water was cold and rough. *How are the dogs supposed to swim in that stuff?*

"There they are, Scooter," announced Jan, pointing. She increased her pace. "I'm so excited, and I know you are, too."

Scooter sped up, as did Flash. "The word excitement doesn't fully define what I'm feeling now." He chuckled. "But it's an important ingredient."

Yellow plastic fencing with the Disney logo stenciled every three feet cordoned off a large area. It was filled with a few chairs, umbrellas, blankets, and three dogs that could be Gabby's identical twins. "Wow!"

Jan giggled. "I see Gabby. Do you?"

"Ha! Which one?"

She nudged Scooter. "See the tall girl with short blonde hair and big sunglasses?"

"Yeah."

"That's Vennie's assistant, Bobbi Frazer. She's also a talented animal trainer, but her specialty is dogs and cats. Look, she's saying something to Gabby."

"Oh, I see her. I hope Gabby's paying attention."

Flash yipped and pulled forward toward his canine companion.

When they stopped at the fence, Jan led them past several onlookers and over behind Bobbi and Gabby. She tugged on Scooter's shirt sleeve and whispered, "Don't say anything to Gabby. We don't want to break her concentration."

Scooter nodded and knelt beside Flash. "Let's be quiet." When he stood, Jan's eyes were focused on him, a smile tightening her full lips. He shot her a wink and looked back to Gabby.

Wayne wore a pair of navy shorts and white polo shirt with the head of Mickey Mouse embroidered on the pocket. He held a clipboard in one hand and fingered his thinning dark hair with the other. His focus was on a pure black lab sprinting between five plastic orange barrels spaced between him and Vennie. Behind Vennie sat two more black labs, tongues hanging and ears perked.

Bobbie stood, gave Gabby a pat on the head, and led her to the first barrel as the other lab completed the mini-obstacle course. Scooter held his breath. *Come on, Gabby...pretend there's a big burger waiting at the finish line.*

"It looks like they're about halfway through these auditions," Jan whispered.

"And they're dry, which means they haven't hit the waves yet."

Vennie held up her hand and looked at Wayne. When he nodded, she dropped her hand. Gabby reared up on hind legs, paused, and took off in a flash. She came upon the first barrel and never slowed as she leaned in toward the barrel and shot between it and the next one, increasing her speed. Sand flew up in her wake. She lowered her head, made the next cut between the barrels, never touching them, then lowered her rear end and shifted gears. Upon rounding the final barrel, she pulled up so fast, a flurry of sand sprinkled Vennie. Gabby's tail whipped from side to side, and she yipped once. Vennie hugged her. "Good girl, Gabby. Well done," she said enthusiastically, fishing a treat from her pocket and handing it to the panting pup.

Chills covered Scooter's arms, and his eyes blurred. He drew Flash close. "She ran fast, buddy." Flash leaned his head against Scooter's thigh.

Zurl moved over beside Bobbie and said something while pointing to a black and white blanket. Bobbie nodded to Vennie. "Wayne wants them to trot over, step onto the blanket, and lay down."

Vennie knelt beside one of the other labs. Scooter wondered if she was explaining to them what to do, or just encouraging them to follow her hand signals. She spoke to each dog, then walked the thirty feet and stopped behind the blanket. All of the dogs sat obediently on their haunches, ears upright, watching Vennie.

Gabby was fortunate since she understood what was actually said, and also because she would be the last one to perform. Scooter wondered if this was intentional because Gabby was a rookie. *Show 'em how it's done, Baboo.*

Wayne nodded to Vennie. She motioned the first lab to her. As the sprinting dog neared the blanket, Vennie held her hand out, palm open. When the dog neared the blanket, she rotated her hand in a tight circle, lowering it as she bent over. The lab hit the blanket, sniffed for fifteen to twenty seconds, and then plopped down.

The next two pooches also spent time checking out the fragrance on the blanket. Scooter doubted they were supposed to do that and hoped Gabby would ignore the smell and plop down quickly. Vennie raised her hand. Gabby's ears shot straight up. When the signal was given, Gabby leaped from her frozen position, front paws digging deep into the sand, and sprinted to the blanket. Her focus was glued to Vennie's hand, following each signal. She bounced up on the blanket, quickly performed her three-spin routine, and plopped down, head on paws. Vennie clapped and rubbed her head. "Good, Gabby," she said, handing her a treat.

Jan looked at Scooter. "She's a smart one, Scooter."

Flash's tail slapped Scooter's calf like a drumstick setting a quick tempo. Scooter nudged Jan and pointed down. "Looks like Flash agrees." They both laughed.

"Wonder what they'll do next, Jan?"

"I figure Wayne will give the dogs a bit of a rest and some fresh water. Vennie stresses the importance of allowing the animals to calm down and recoup. She believes after so many challenges and commands they become hyper."

Using a hand motion, Vennie directed the dogs to a far corner of the area where four bowls filled with cool water were set out. Bobbi joined them, discussing something with Vennie. Scooter noticed Wayne jotting notes on his clipboard. Upon completion, he walked over to the little gate and opened it, then stepped back. A red-haired little girl entered the fenced area, moving smoothly on aluminum leg braces and shiny crutches. She wore a pair of white shorts, a blue T-shirt, and a broad smile. Scooter estimated her age to be around nine. "Look, Jan. Does the little girl have something to do with the audition?"

Jan nodded. "Since there will be scenes where Gabby entertains the special needs children that come to your beach, Wayne wanted one of the young actors in the movie to make an appearance to see how the dogs react. Pretty good idea, I think."

"It sure is. If Gabby's been nervous, this should calm her. She's very comfortable with the children." He reached down and scratched Flash's head. "And so is my little sidekick."

Wayne escorted the little girl to a plastic chair several feet back from the tide line. She sat down and laid her crutches on a towel. Wayne dropped to one knee beside her and placed a red Frisbee on her lap, talking and laughing with her and pointed to the water.

Jan said, "I told you Wayne was a stickler for detail. The screenwriters did a fantastic job writing the scenes showing children interacting with Gabby."

Scooter released a sigh. "I'm sure fetching a Frisbee is child's play for these labs, but Gabby loves performing for children. If she's not too nervous, you will see a real show-off." A rush of pride filled his chest. *Let it rip, Gabby.*

"I have no doubt, Scooter."

When the dogs' break ended, Vennie and Bobbi huddled around them, pointing to the little girl. Bobbi showed them a Frisbee like the one held by the young actress. After the pups' pep talk, both animal specialists led them over to the chair. Vennie introduced them to Janelle. "Okay, sweetie, when I drop my hand, you toss the Frisbee as far as you can into the water."

"I'll do my best, Miss Vennie," replied Janelle in a soft voice.

Vennie walked into the cold water up to her knees. She motioned to Bobbie to ready the first dog. Janelle gripped the Frisbee and took a deep breath. Vennie quick-stepped in place in a futile attempt to warm her feet, then raised her hand. When it dropped, Janelle whipped the Frisbee high into the air. The first black lab took off for the water. No sooner than the red disc landed on the frothy white water, the lab snatched it up, raced back, and dropped it on the ground in front of Janelle. Then the pooch completed a full body shake.

Scooter said, "I don't blame the dog for shaking. Gabby and I went out in the water this morning. I'm still thawing."

Jan giggled. "You did not."

Scooter nodded. "Didn't we, Flash?"

The beagle yipped.

Jan again stared at him. Before she spoke, Scooter said, "See, I used his name."

Jan cut hazel eyes at him and nodded slowly as a tiny smile curled the sides of her mouth.

The other labs performed exactly as the first one had. Scooter inhaled a deep breath of warm, salty air. *Gabby, time to get creative. Remember how you jumped for the ball I tossed at the shelter. Give the folks something to clap for.*

Gabby settled beside Janelle's chair and focused on Vennie, who was still high-stepping to keep warm. When her hand dropped, Janelle flung the Frisbee lower and farther this time. Gabby barked, took off like a black bullet, outrunning the spinning disc as she kept her eyes on the sky. As if she knew where it would land, she leaped over the rolling wave, turned her agile body, and grabbed the Frisbee before it touched the water. Then she quickly dog-paddled into shallow water, paused, and shook. With her head high, Gabby trotted up and gently placed the Frisbee on Janelle's bare knee. She sat, ears perked, and panting.

The applause started with Wayne Zurl, followed quickly by Vennie and Bobbi. Within seconds, the entire throng of people joined in, including Janelle. A happy tear fell from Scooter's eye. Flash barked twice. Gabby heard her beagle buddy and stared in their direction. She yipped once. Scooter looked at Jan. "That's our Gabby."

Jan excitedly patted him on the back. "In my opinion, that was the clincher, Scooter. But we'll have to wait for Wayne's decision tomorrow morning."

"Whether she's selected or not, I'm darn proud of her. You agree, little dude?"

Flash barked twice.

Jan smiled. "He answers to 'dude', too?"

Scooter nodded. Wayne announced the audition was over and thanked the spectators for remaining quiet and allowing the dogs to concentrate on their commands.

"Why don't you and Flash go in and congratulate Gabby? I'll wait for you here," said Jan.

The words were barely spoken before Flash and Scooter were plowing through the sand toward the gate. When they entered, the Disney director greeted them. "Scooter, Gabby is one intelligent dog. I've never seen a dog, untrained by professionals, follow commands like she does. And, I'm blown away with how, at the right time, she ad-libs and brings life to the scene."

"Thank you, Wayne. Coming from you, that means a lot."

Squatting beside Flash, Wayne rubbed the beagle's head. "Scooter, you are aware we're planning to end the movie with a rescued Flash at the beach with you and Gabby. After Paul and Ruthie complete the first draft of the ending, I'll eyeball it. If our selection works out in Gabby's favor, I'll get you all back here for a shooting. Flash's part will not be as detailed as Gabby's. I'm sure he can fetch, and you said last night he was exceptional around the children."

Scooter felt oxygen rush from his lungs. "Yes, he quickly bonded with them. However, at this point, Flash hasn't had much swim time. The ocean is still new to him. But he does fetch and will do what I ask. His real talent is his nose." Scooter chuckled.

Wayne nodded. "I think he would be ideal for the message Disney wants to convey about how good-hearted people step up and rescue unwanted animals." Wayne extended his hand, and they shook. "Now, let's get Gabby away from Vennie and Bobbi, her new fans, so you two can congratulate her." Wayne clapped his hands. When they looked up, he waved. "Gabby! Someone is here to see you." Gabby sprinted toward them. "I'll get up with you in the morning with my decision. Have a relaxing evening, Scooter."

"Thank you, Wayne. It's been a pleasure meeting you. I hope we have the chance to work together."

In a flurry of white sand, Gabby came to a quick stop in front of them. Wayne chuckled and bent down to rub her head. "Good chance we will, Scooter." He waved to Vennie and Bobbi as he left.

Flash yipped as Scooter knelt and pulled Gabby tight against his chest. "You did great! We're mighty proud of you."

Gabby turned her head, checking to see if anyone was within earshot. Seeing no one, she said, *I wasn't even nervous, Scooter. And you were right...I heard exactly what they wanted me to do.*

You did some neat stuff, too.

Gabby nudged Flash with her sand-covered snoot. *Aw, thanks. You know how it is...gotta give them what they don't know they need.* She yipped.

"Before we go, would you take us to meet little Janelle and her parents?"

Sure, Scoot-toot, because I know we're going to celebrate tonight. Right?

"How do you want to celebrate?"

Flash and I would love to have supper...delivered to our room.

"I knew food was part of the celebration. You are a mess. Come on, let's go meet Janelle."

Janelle greeted Flash and Scooter as if she had known them her entire short life. Her smile would put a California sunset to shame. "I love doggies. And Gabby is so polite. She didn't shake sand and water on me like the others did. And...she put the Frisbee on my leg instead of dropping it in the sand. I want Gabby in the movie."

Flash and Gabby yipped. Janelle giggled and rubbed their heads.

Scooter met Janelle's parents and shared a little about how they work with special needs children at Sandbridge. Her mother complimented him on what a great idea it was and asked a few questions about how to start something similar in California. After they talked for a while, Scooter said, "It's been a pleasure meeting you." He touched Janelle on her thin arm. "Especially you, young lady. But we've had a really long day. We need to get back to the hotel to relax and have supper."

Janelle got situated on her crutches, and they walked together toward the parking lot with Jan, Vennie, and Bobbie behind. *Life is good.*

CHAPTER 18

Scooter leaned back against the headboard of the huge bed and observed the peaceful scene before him, allowing his pride to run loose. Before him, stretched out on the foot of the bed, was an exhausted Gabby. Flash was curled tightly in a large, wing-backed chair against the wall. A grin worked its way onto Scooter's lips. "Tonight will be a night of celebration for this motley-looking trio from Sandbridge Beach." He sat straight up and clapped his hands. "Can I get some cuddly, furry friends up here beside me?" Scooter opened his arms. "I don't care where we are…it's our home when we're all together." Both pups leaped up and nestled against his warm chest. "This is priceless."

Since Gabby has been working hard today and doing everything Mr. Zurl asked her to do, I think she will get the part. We should let her choose what we have for supper.

Gabby cut her tired eyes across Scooter's stomach and looked at Flash. *That's sweet, Flash. It would be cool to play myself in the movie, but that means you and Scooter would go home, and I'd stay here all alone.* She looked at Scooter. *Right?*

The ache of leaving Gabby pierced his heart. Scooter realized there would be sacrifices in order to achieve their dreams, but he had no idea how tough they might be. Yes, it would be fun to have both pups traveling with him on his book-signing tour, but if Gabby was selected to be in the movie, that would not be possible. "It looks that way, Baboo. You don't like flying back and forth, and I've got to go from city to city signing the book you helped get published. We have a hectic schedule, and making everything fit together seems impossible. I guess we didn't think of these mixed-up schedules because our opportunities unfolded so quickly."

I understand. I'm sad to know we'll be separated, but, putting that aside for now, I suggest we have fried pork chops, mashed potatoes, and a sliver of Virginia country-fried ham. And, since I'm a 'maybe' movie star, I'd like a couple of sunny-side up eggs. Can you pull that off? Gabby sat up and tilted her head. *If so, I'll pull some strings and get you both a free limo ride to the premiere.*

Scooter laughed and kicked his feet in the air. "You beat all I've ever seen, Gabby!"

That's why I'm me…and sometimes that's not easy. She yipped, joined by Flash.

And it's not easy being a sniffing beagle, either. Gabby yipped as Flash rolled over on his back and wiggled his feet like Scooter. *It's really fun living with you two.*

"Flash, do Gabby's choices sound good to your taste buds?"

Yeah!

"Then it's a go! My talented twosome gets what they want." He pulled them close again. "You guys have added a ton of fun to my life."

Both pups yipped twice.

After a tummy-splitting supper in the calm of their room, Mr. Sandman paid each of them a visit and gently closed their tired eyes for a restful night of sleep. Maybe Mr. Sandman knew tomorrow would turn out to be a red-letter day sprinkled with a few tears.

* * * *

The seven o'clock wake-up call found the trio wrapped in a soothing sleep. Scooter slipped from the comfortable bed. He stretched, taking note of Gabby curled up on the foot of the bed. Flash was stretched out in the wingback chair with his floppy ears hanging over the side. "Time to rise and shine, furry friends. Today's a big day." Scooter entered the bathroom for his shower, looked back, and noticed neither pooch had budged. "Breakfast will get them up."

Scooter mentally prepared for what he knew could be a bittersweet day. Director Zurl, along with Producer Winton, would meet them at the studio at nine o'clock for the announcement of the dog selected to star in the movie. If Gabby won, she would remain behind on Vennie's sizeable animal farm, and, depending on schedule changes, would also stay with Paul, Ruthie, and their two rescue dogs. Scooter had no doubt these animal lovers would provide the utmost care and love to Gabby. "At least she'll be with friends and not in a kennel."

After their breakfast of scrambled eggs, bacon, and toast, along with nuggets of Puppy Chow blended in for the pups, Scooter finished packing and glanced at his watch. "Okay, we better get downstairs. The limo will be here in ten minutes. Are you excited?"

I am. Flash looked at Gabby as she licked her front paws. *Are you, Gabby?*

Without pausing, she replied, *I guess so.*

Scooter quickly picked up on her lackluster reply. Truth be told, this day would hold even more emotional challenges for her. "Flash, we could be sitting in the presence of a future Disney movie star."

I know.

"And Mr. Zurl will tell me this morning if they plan to add a few scenes with you in the ending. So you might also become a star."

Now I'm nervous.

"Well, if it happens, you'll do fine." The pooches stood patiently while Scooter leashed them. "So long, fancy room. See ya later." Scooter picked up his suitcases and opened the door, letting the pooches lead.

Scooter, when we come back, will we stay in the same room?

"Probably. I'll be sure and tell the clerk how much we enjoyed it."

Lewis parked the limo in front of the administrative offices. Scooter saw Jan talking with Vennie and Bobbi. "Looks like your fan club is here, Gabby and Flash," said Lewis, holding open the rear door. "I'll pick you up at eleven-fifteen to go to the airport."

"Thank you, Lewis," said Scooter, as the girls rushed up and greeted the pups. The limo pulled away, signing off with a honk. Scooter eased over beside Jan. "I didn't expect all of you here."

She gave him a warm hug. "We wouldn't dare miss the big announcement."

"No, we wouldn't," added Bobbi.

"And for your information, Scooter, we were also consulted during the selection process," Vennie said with a smile.

Scooter nodded. "Before things get busy around here, I want to tell you how much we've appreciated your hospitality and expertise. All of you have made our experience enjoyable," said Scooter. "And, Vennie, if Gabby's chosen, I am truly thankful to you and Paul and Ruthie for tending to her."

Vennie smiled. "You're welcome. I consider it an honor. Don't you fret one bit." Vennie looked down at the pups. "Just promise me I'll be forgiven if I spoil her even more than she already is."

"Since I'm sure you will, I'll forgive you now. But Gabby says it's not spoiling…it's loving."

Shortly, two vehicles pulled up. Scooter felt his butterflies come to life when Tom and Wayne stepped out of a black Suburban. Then Paul and Ruthie pulled up in a lime green antique '68 Mustang. Gabby and Flash trotted over to greet them.

Tom placed his hand on Scooter's shoulder. "Nervous?"

"Not really. I know you and Wayne are professionals and will do what's best for Disney and your audience. Truthfully, we're honored to even be considered. We're thrilled to have a movie about Gabby."

Wayne nodded. "Since we're all here, let's make this official." He motioned for the others to come closer. "As you all know, selecting actors for any movie involves the consideration of many variables, especially the ability of actors. However, the task is made easier when all of the applicants are multi-talented, as was the case with this project. Tom and I have viewed all of the footage shot during the tryouts, discussed the pros and cons of each pup, and we've agreed that Gabby should play herself." He knelt and rubbed her head. The group applauded and congratulated Scooter and waited their turn for Gabby. Flash yipped once, prompting the others to laugh.

Tom held up his hand. "Also, we've read over the new ending submitted by Paul and Ruthie." He gave the screenwriters a thumb up and looked down at the floppy-eared beagle. "We've decided to conclude the movie with Flash and Gabby doing their thing on the beach as they provide the special needs children with a wonderful day on the coastline. We're talking about a win-win conclusion that will tie up this heartwarming story to highlight the importance of caring folks adopting unwanted animals." The area exploded with cheers, whistles, and applause. "Thanks to Scooter's rescues with these talented, loving doggies."

While Gabby and Flash received deserved congratulations from the others, Tom motioned Scooter and Wayne over to the Suburban. He went over the scheduled shootings and whether they were set to be on the coast or inside the studio. Scooter thought his head might pop trying to comprehend the events until Tom chuckled and handed him a folder. "Just wanted to let you know we waste no time, Scooter. Right, Wayne?"

"After joining Disney, I was pleased to find there were only twenty-six hours in a day. Law enforcement on Long Island had taught me there were thirty," replied Wayne, with a laugh and slap on Scooter's back.

Tom added, "Once we've discovered a quality production and have all of the actors and walk-ons in place, we 'roll'." He pointed to the folder Scooter gripped between tight fingers. "I've highlighted the two approximate dates we need you and Flash back here. Of course, no matter where you are on your book tour, our jet will meet you at the nearest airport. We'll pick you up and return you to your next scheduled stop. You won't miss any of your events, Scooter."

Wayne nodded. "I've carefully put together Flash's scenes and compiled them into one, long day, shoot, but I set up another date just in case we need a re-shoot."

"Any questions, Scooter?" Tom asked, quickly shoving his hands in and out of his navy Dockers pockets.

"Naw, I think I'm good. I know you guys will do a great job, and the people keeping Gabby will also be fine. If your skills could help minimize the sadness of leaving our Gabby, I'd certainly ask."

"I know this is the hard part, Scooter. But remember, Gabby will be busy, and she'll be pooped each night. As will you and Flash while you zip around the country. And the night of the premiere in Virginia Beach will be one fantastic event," said Wayne.

As the limo pulled up, Scooter's stomach tightened, knowing the time had finally arrived to say good-bye to Gabby. He spotted her wagging tail in the crowd as Vennie knelt beside her and talked to Bobbi. "Looks like it's time to go, guys. Please give us a minute," whispered Scooter.

Wayne gave Scooter a pat on his back. "Take your time."

The trio walked in silence down the street between the various studios. They pulled up beneath a tall oak. Scooter sat on the green grass with both pooches settled onto his lap. As he rubbed their heads, a piece of his heart slipped away on the warm breeze. He bowed his head and ran trembling fingers over his forehead. He sucked in a deep breath. "Here we are. Gabby's starring in a movie for Disney." He drew in another vital gulp of air. "In a few minutes, Flash and I will get on a plane, return home for a few days, and then head to West Virginia and other states to sign books." Scooter bit his lip. He looked into Gabby's eyes. "I remember leaving my parents and family the day I left to go into the Army. It hurt. But my first visit back home was so awesome." He smiled and hugged them. "Seeing my family when I came off of the plane totally erased that sad day I left. That's how it's gonna be with us when Flash and I come back here, Gabby."

I know, Scooter. But since the day you got me from that cold, uncomfortable cage, we've not been apart.

"That's true, Baboo."

Do you think you and Flash can travel around and sign books in strange cities without me there to watch over you?

Flash yipped and Scooter chuckled. "It's going to be hard, but we'll have to manage. We know you'll be in good hands with Vennie and Paul and Ruthie."

Gabby licked Scooter on the arm. *Flash, you watch over Scoot. You know how he acts a little childish and tries to be the funny guy. Keep him in line.* She leaned over and placed her black paw on the beagle's head. *And please try to eat a little faster. Oh, and I suggest you practice swimming, because you might be asked to fetch a Frisbee for a kid in the movie. Scoot-toot will help you.*

I don't know about the eating part, Gabby, but I'll try the water. And I can't wait to see you in the movie.

You'll be in it, too, Flash! Get with the program, little floppy-eared pal. She dropped her head. *I will miss you both.*

Wayne's deep voice split the quiet. "Time, Scooter."

Scooter waved. He whispered to Gabby, "We'll miss you, too, but I'll call and check on you every day. We'll have lots of stories to share when we get back together."

I'll miss you, Gabby.

Take care of Scooter, Flash.

After a long hug and the shedding of a few tears, the trio joined the group. Scooter leashed Flash and looked back at Gabby sitting between Vennie and Bobbi. They all waved as the beach guy and his floppy-eared friend disappeared into the limo.

CHAPTER 19

Sandbridge Beach welcomed Flash and Scooter with a coastal thunderstorm and a sharp bolt of loneliness. The absence of Gabby and her normal comments upon arriving back at her beach did not go unnoticed by the two dudes. *It's so quiet, Scooter. I miss Gabby already.*

Scooter chuckled, attempting a move to a lighter note. "Yeah, so do I. Enjoy the quiet. It won't be long before we're all back together." Scooter released an exhaustive sigh. "We've had a long day. I think some vittles and sleep is in order. This storm should blow out, and tomorrow we'll have sunshine and a warm breeze. We need some ocean time."

While preparing their late supper, Scooter thought back to their uneventful flight home. Captain Blow and Lt. Wilson were pleased to hear Gabby was selected for the movie, but they sensed his and Flash's sadness in traveling without her.

"At least we had good weather for the flight," Scooter said, placing Flash's bowl of Puppy Chow on the floor.

Flash sniffed his meal, paused, and looked up at Scooter. *I like flying. It'll be fun to go back and see Gabby.*

"Since we'll be busy traveling on the book tour, the time will fly until we see her again."

They devoured their supper in silence. Scooter mentally inventoried what needed attention before they hit the road in two days on the book tour. On top of his list; spend some time with Darla Kay and share their experiences from the West Coast. Another duty included scheduling and delivery of their rental car, along with mapping out their first leg of stops that would take one week. They would begin in Bluefield, West Virginia, then to Pennsylvania, and move into Ohio, and finally work back down the East Coast. Goldberg Publishing handled all expenses, had already shipped copies of his book to each bookstore, and scheduled the dates and times. Scooter's main job was to arrive on time for each appearance, meet the customers and sign books, and then head out for the next stop. There was no doubt the tour would be demanding, but the excitement of his accomplishment of having his first published work would supply sufficient energy to keep the two of them going. He looked forward to having Flash as his sidekick, knowing Gabby would also be busy doing her thing. *Time will pass quickly, and in three weeks, Christmas will be here and we'll all be together.*

The following morning unfolded exactly as Scooter hoped. As the orange sun balanced on the horizon, glassy, knee-high waves swelled and rolled onto shore. If the upcoming schedule didn't have them leaving the beach in two days, Scooter would turn his jet-lagged body over and return to a dreamless sleep. However, a morning on the waves offered the perfect sanctuary to mentally adjust to a new facet of his future. He looked over and found Flash sitting up and peering out the window. "Good morning, partner. Did you sleep well?"

Yeah. I didn't even dream. I wonder what Gabby's doing?

Scooter looked at the digital clock on the nightstand. "Well, their time is three hours behind ours, so that means it's four o'clock in California. I'd say Miss Movie Star is sound asleep."

I wonder if she's dreaming about Sandbridge and us.

Scooter slipped from the comfortable bed. "Knowing her, it could be about anything. Are you up for some beach time?"

Flash stretched and yawned. *I want to get into the water and get used to the waves. Will you help me?*

"Sure I will. What prompted this?"

I was thinking about the movie. Mr. Zurl might want me to fetch one of the children's Frisbees that goes into the water. I'd be embarrassed if I couldn't.

Scooter put on his surf baggies and a T-shirt. "I agree, it's better to be prepared. We'll take care of your swimming lessons today. You'll do fine."

In thirty minutes, Flash was dog-paddling up and over the swells. The first couple of shore breaks completely swamped him and rolled him onto the damp sand like a little fur ball. The feisty beagle clamored to his feet, shook his head, and charged back into the water. After his initiation, Flash pawed through the water like a lab or retriever. "Nice work!" The floppy-eared pup yipped and paddled up near Scooter's surfboard.

Swimming is fun. Now I can swim like Gabby.

Scooter smiled. "Now I have two water-loving pooches. Come over a little closer, I've got a good idea." Flash raked his big paws through the water and up to Scooter's board. *What are we going to do?*

Scooter pulled Flash up and settled him on the board between his legs. "We're going to ride a wave."

With perfect balance, Flash turned the upper part of his body around and looked into Scooter's eyes. *I can't surf.*

"That's because you haven't tried. I'll be riding with you. Remember, we make a good team." Scooter spotted a small swell approaching. "Now, I'll get on my knees and paddle. You sit right there. No big deal."

I'll try.

The wave slowly picked them up and propelled them forward. Scooter balanced, placing his hands on Flash's back. "That's it. We're surfing."

Wow! This is fun.

Thirty seconds later, the board's fin scraped the ocean's floor. "Perfect, Flash. You're now a surfer."

Flash jumped from the board and splashed up beside Scooter. ***That was easy. I wish Gabby could have seen me. Maybe Mr. Zurl will want me to surf.***

"He might. Now I have another idea." Scooter trotted through the ankle-deep white water and went up on the sand and grabbed his towel. He joined Flash in the water and spread the towel over the board. Then he picked up Flash and placed him on the towel. "I'm going to walk you out. When the wave picks you up, you can sit or stand. I'll be beside you while you ride in. Okay?"

I'll try. If I fall off, at least I can swim.

"That's right. And the correct surfing term for falling off is 'wiping out'. But with your big paws and good balance, you won't wipe-out." Scooter turned the board around and slowly pushed it and the beagle out to the chest-deep sandbar. "Okay. I see a nice one coming. I'll aim you for shore, and when it gets here, I'll give you an easy shove. Off you'll go, surfer dog."

At the right moment, Scooter pushed the board and watched as the wave lifted it, carrying them forward. "You've got it, Flash. Stand up on all fours if you want."

Flash yipped twice. He pushed to his paws, wobbled from side to side, and then re-gained his balance. ***I got it, Scoot-toot! I'm surfing by myself!***

A broad smile filled Scooter's face. "Cowabunga, dude!" He watched Flash's ears slowly flapping as the speed increased. When the wave broke, Flash once again shifted his paws, settled, and rode smoothly into shore. "Great ride, Flash!"

The board came to an abrupt stop in the shallow water, and Flash leaped off. He barked twice and shook his head. ***Now both of us are surfers!***

An hour later, the duo walked back to the cottage for breakfast. Scooter gave his pup a pat on his wet head. "You're one brave beagle. I'm proud of you."

The towel was a good idea because my feet didn't slip. I like surfing.

The day proved productive. Scooter made several phone calls, jotted notes for directions to his destinations, then started packing all three suitcases. Darla Kay would join them for supper and Scooter's famous New York strips and baked potatoes on the grill. His enthusiasm continued when the rental company confirmed his selection of a new '95 Ford Bronco Eddie Bauer Edition. "If we're covering this much territory, we should go in comfort and class. No cramped small car for me and the Flashter." Flash spent his day relaxing and catching up on much-needed sleep, no doubt dreaming of riding big waves.

After a delicious supper, Scooter and Darla Kay relaxed in the small den and discussed the past trip, along with the upcoming venture from state to state. Since Darla Kay was more of a movie buff than Scooter, she was ecstatic about Meg Ryan playing her in the movie. Of course, she oohed and awed about Kevin Costner in the role of Scooter. "This is so cool. I sure hope I have the opportunity to meet them. I've seen all of their movies. Will they attend the premiere here in Virginia Beach?"

"I haven't heard, but when I do, you'll be the first to know. You sound pretty excited."

She gave him a hug. "I am! And I'm also looking forward to the special needs children who will play our local children. That's so nice of Disney to include them. A lot of production companies would probably write out that part."

Scooter nodded. "From all I've seen, everyone associated with Disney, including the limo driver, has been first-class. They are a fine group to work with."

Darla Kay leaned down and rubbed Flash's ears. "I know you and Scooter will stay in touch with the people who are caring for Gabby. I'll bet you already miss her." Flash yipped.

Scooter told her about Flash's surfing accomplishment and how Gabby will be surprised to see him riding a wave. "I hope the director will give serious thought to having him ride a couple of waves in the movie. Of course, their waves are a mite bigger than ours. We'll see."

When the hour became late, Darla Kay stood. "I'm going to miss you. We have a conference in Richmond all day tomorrow, so I won't see you until you get back for Christmas. You will call me, right?"

As they walked to her car, Scooter put his arm around her shoulders and pulled her tight. "You bet we'll check in with you. And I'm looking forward to spending Christmas with you."

Beside her car, Darla Kay stood on tiptoes and kissed Scooter on the lips. She leaned back and smiled. "Please be safe, Scooter." She looked down at Flash. "And you take care of him, too. I hope you have a wonderful trip." After another kiss, she said, "I'm proud of you, Scooter. Your hard work has finally paid off."

Flash and Scooter watched the darkness swallow the VW's red taillights. "Well, surfer dude, the day after tomorrow, we'll hit the road."

I'm excited, Scoot. I like seeing new things with you. But I'll still miss Gabby.

"So will I, but we'll call Vennie every day to check on her. Now let's get some sleep. I still have a few things to do tomorrow. Then we're off to West Virginia."

There's no ocean in West Virginia, is there?

Scooter chuckled. "Nothing but rivers and mountains, but life's still good there."

Flash yipped twice and headed for his comfy chair in the bedroom.

"See you in the morning, dude." Flash's reply came in the form of heavy breathing. "He's one pooped pup." Scooter eased his head onto the cool pillow and whispered a silent prayer for Gabby.

CHAPTER 20

Seven hours after leaving Sandbridge Beach, Scooter and Flash pulled the silver and black Bronco into the beautiful town of Bluefield, West Virginia. Bright November sunshine worked to warm 'The Air Conditioned City', and, compared to the beach, it failed. "We're here, Flash," said Scooter, reaching over and stroking the head of his relaxed passenger.

That was fast.

"I guess so. You slept most of the way. If you have a winter coat, put it on. It's a bit nippily up here in the mountains."

Flash sat up, eyeing him with big browns. *I don't have a winter coat.*

Scooter chuckled and picked up his map. "Now, if I can find East Cumberland Road, there's a pet-friendly motel where we'll spend the next two nights. It's called…let me see, oh yeah, Knights Inn." Scooter stopped for a red light and read the street signs. "Before we ride around lost, like the tourists do coming into Sandbridge, I'll stop and ask how to get there." When the light turned green, Scooter pulled forward on the nearly vacant road and checked out the signs.

After a couple of minutes, and nearing frustration, Scooter spotted the desired street. "Here it is. East Cumberland." He took a right and moved slowly past several small businesses. Up ahead, he saw the royal blue sign atop a red-roofed two-story motel. "We're here!"

Good. I've got to visit math class.

"That makes two of us, pal." Scooter pulled into the lot and parked. "Your math class is held in this vacant field," he said, pointing. "I'll take you over before I check in." After leashing Flash, Scooter walked him across the brown grass at the end of the motel. Upon completion, they walked into the office. Automatically, Flash began to frantically sniff the tan indoor/outdoor carpet and legs of the chairs. "Easy, boy. Lots of pets come in here."

The wiry, white-haired man checked them in, wearing a smile beneath a pencil-thin, also white, moustache. "Okay, that's all the information we need, sir. Enjoy your stay at Knights Inn. If you need anything else, don't hesitate to stop by or call me. Also, we offer free coffee and homemade doughnuts each morning from seven to ten o'clock." He handed Scooter the brass key attached to the green plastic thingy with the room number printed on it.

"Thank you," replied Scooter as they returned outside into the chilly early afternoon.

Once they were in their room, Scooter freshened up and changed into a light blue oxford shirt and navy slacks. "Okay, little partner. We're going to meet the two nice ladies who own Hearthside Books. We'll grab a bite to eat, and, hopefully, sign books for three hours. Are you ready?"

I'm nervous.

"No need to be, we're together. It's my first time doing this, and I'm not nervous. When we come back this evening, we'll call and check on Gabby."

Okay. But I'm going to stay close to you.

Scooter chuckled as they climbed into the smooth-riding Bronco, and he fired it up. "According to the map, we're only about five minutes away." He pulled out and turned left. They drove slowly, enjoying the quietness of the city and watching people strolling the sidewalk. "This is the city where I set my novel. Only a couple of miles outside of town is the Bluefield Golf Course. That's where my two main characters get summer jobs as caddies. I'd really like my novel to be well received here." Scooter suddenly felt his resident butterflies awaken. He honestly believed if the locals appreciated his novel, then he had succeeded. "I'm glad you're with me. When we return next year to introduce the sequel, Gabby will be with us, and you'll be guiding her."

That will be neat. And when we go see the movie, Gabby and I will be guiding you. Flash yipped.

"Right you are, surfer pup." Scooter spotted the homey-looking bookstore just ahead on the right. He glanced at his legal pad of notes. "The owners are Anne and Wilma. Let's act like we've been away from the beach before," Scooter joked.

Scooter shut down the big truck, attached Flash's leash, and they walked into the store. The fragrance of fresh flowers and new books wafted through the neatly decorated showroom. Six-foot-high wooden shelves, packed with books, created several aisles, also leaving a wider aisle in the middle for easy access to an old, polished wooden counter. Two or three displays featuring newly-released books by various authors accented the area. Suddenly, Scooter saw a large cardboard picture of himself holding a copy of 'If Bullfrogs Had Wings'. He froze, trying to swallow, but his mouth felt like dry sand. He pointed and whispered to Flash, "Look."

Flash stopped his sniffing and looked. *That's you.*

Scooter released a nervous sigh and stepped forward and picked up a copy. A tiny smile tightened his lips. *Thank you, Gabby. It's really true.* He flipped through the pages, trying to comprehend the words that came from his imagination. Suddenly, a soft, feminine voice said, "May I help you with something?" Scooter jumped, startled. He looked up into the warm, brown eyes of a tall, thin lady in her early thirties. "Ah, well, I was showing my pup my book." He held it up, feeling his hand tremble.

The attractive lady gave him a friendly smile. "Okay. Your puppy reads, and this is your book, right?" She giggled.

"Ah, no, Flash doesn't read, but he knows about my book." Scooter stepped beside the large picture and nodded toward it. "See, that's me. I wrote this book." Sweat bubbled on his forehead.

The lady did a double-take, paused, and started laughing as she offered her hand. "I'm so sorry. I didn't realize you were Mr. Bissell." She released his hand. "Please, forgive me. I'm Anne, one of the owners." She called to the back, "Wilma, could you come up front, please?"

"Oh, that's no problem. I'm not famous or anything. Besides, this is my first stop on the book tour. It's nice to meet you, Anne. Please, call me Scooter."

A shorter lady approached from a back room. "What is it, Anne?" She asked, giving Scooter and Flash a quick glance.

"This is Mr. Bissell, the author of the new novel set here in Bluefield." She giggled. "It seems I surprised him, and then he returned the favor. Scooter, this is the other owner, Wilma."

Wilma shook Scooter's hand. "Nice to meet you. Did you say Scooter?"

"Yes, that's my nickname." He looked down at his little beagle. "And this is Flash. I hope you don't mind him being in here for the signing."

Both ladies shook their heads. Anne replied, "Oh, no. We love pets. We even allow our customers to bring theirs." She quickly moved behind the counter and returned with a Milk Bone. She handed it to Flash. "You are one cute fellow." Flash yipped. Scooter said, "He's never met a stranger."

"So, you're doing a signing today from four until seven, and tomorrow from noon to four, right?" Wilma asked.

Scooter nodded. "Yes. I hope you received copies of the book."

"We did. I think they sent three hundred. We've advertised it in our local paper and on three radio stations. We're looking for a big turnout. We've already sold twenty or more copies," said Anne.

"I've got my copy, Scooter, and already finished it. I loved it, especially Keith and Flea. It's such a realistic story with good storylines and a few both happy and sad tears. The ending is fabulous. I would like your autograph before you leave."

A wave of pride warmed Scooter, since this was the first true review he'd ever heard besides the editors' and Jason's. "Thank you, Wilma. I'm happy you liked it. And I'd be pleased to sign it for you." He swiped sweat from his brow. "So, we've got about an hour before the signing. Can you recommend somewhere my little buddy and I can grab a snack?"

Anne said, "What are you looking for?"

"Maybe pizza or a sub," answered Scooter.

Pointing to her left, Anne said, "One block this way and you'll see a small convenience store named Papa's Pop In. They have the best pizza, and their meatball subs are to die for. Right, Wilma?"

Wilma nodded. "And they still sell the small glass bottles of Coke. You know, the best-tasting Coke."

"Well, you just solved our vittles problem. We'll zip on down there and be back here before four o'clock. Anything else I need to know? Remember, this is my first signing."

The ladies shook their heads. "Just be ready to write and answer questions from our locals," said Anne. "You'll probably hear enough secrets and stories about our little town to write five more novels." She giggled and nudged Wilma.

"She's not joking."

Scooter thanked them and led Flash into a serene Bluefield afternoon. "I hope you're hungry, because I'm starving."

I'm real hungry. Hey, I think those ladies were nice, and we're going to have fun here.

"I like your attitude." Scooter chuckled as he checked out the different shops and businesses lining the street. They hadn't gone far before the aroma of pizza slipped past. Flash yipped. "I'll bet the place is not far."

Good. Can I have a whole piece?

"You bet."

They passed a small shop named 'Jenny's Junque Shoppe'. A display table out front offered antique kitchen implements such as frying pans, pots, bowls, and utensils. Scooter rolled his eyes when he noticed their condition. "Well, part of the store's name is right." Two shops later, they came up on a small parking lot with three vehicles parked beside a double-windowed building. The hand painted, bright orange letters told everyone this was 'Papa's Pop In'. "We found it, Flash."

As the duo walked behind two pick-ups and a blue van, Flash raised his snoot into the air, jerking Scooter in the direction of the older van. "Hey, what's going on?"

Flash continued to use every ounce of strength to pull Scooter up to the back doors of the van. Once they were within a couple of feet, Flash said, *I smell something bad.*

A light breeze Scooter tagged as the same one delivering the pizza aroma suddenly hit him with the unadulterated stench of hog manure. The corners of his mouth curled as he recalled the large hog farm next door to the family farm he was raised on. Whenever the wind blew from the east, this identical odor blew across their place. "I smell it, too. It's hog poop, buddy. It's coming from the van."

Flash ran his white muzzle inches from the double-doors. *No, Scoot. I smell something different than a poop smell. It's real strong.*

Scooter looked around, hoping no one saw him allowing his beagle to sniff someone's vehicle. *That would not be the proper way to meet locals.* Not seeing anyone, he whispered, "Whatever it is, does not come under the head of our business. In other words, leave it be."

Scoot, it burns my nose.

Scooter released a tension-building sigh. "Okay. What does it smell like?"

Flash backed from the van and looked up at him. *It smells exactly like your grill after you turn it on, just before you light it. You know what I mean?*

Scooter continued to try and act normal, casually looking down the street while he thought about Flash's statement. Then it hit him like a brickbat upside the head. "Propane gas?"

I don't know what it's called. But your grill smells like this, before you light it.

"I think propane is odorless. And all I smell is hog manure. Listen, come over here and wait by the door while I go inside. Maybe someone in there will know." He tugged several times to get Flash moving. "Now, wait here."

Okay. Hurry back.

Scooter opened the glass door and entered the small, product-crammed store. It appeared every known snack, cake, cookie, and canned good ever made filled the shelves that ran length-wise through the store. The far wall was lined with built-in coolers with glass doors packed with different drinks and beers. Scooter glanced toward the counter, spotting a small grill and oven on the back wall. *That's where the pizza and subs are made.* He hustled over to the drink cooler and pulled out a bottle of water and two of the six-and-a-half ounce bottles of Coke Wilma had mentioned. When Scooter stepped up to the counter, he was behind a young man in his mid-twenties. The fellow wore blue jeans, a denim shirt, hiking boots, and a camo ball cap. Without trying, Scooter overheard the conversation between the young guy and the older man on the register.

Young man: *'I need a Bic lighter to go along with these five cigars, too. I don't smoke, but I'm celebrating the birth of our first son.'*

Cashier: *'Well, congratulations, young feller. That's mighty fine, and worth celebratin' with a good stogie. I still remember my first day as a Papa. Yeah, seems like yesterday.'*

Young man: *'Got me a hundred pound dressed hog in the van. Gonna get home and put it on the cooker. Yep, tomorrow, all our friends are comin' over for a cookout.'*

Cashier: *'Okay, your total is only four bucks and one dime. Y'all have a good outin'. Congratulations again.'*

Scooter watched the new father strut out the door. *Well, now I know where the hog stench came from.* The cashier asked Scooter if he wanted anything besides the drinks. "How about three slices of your Pepperoni pizza to go?"

"Okie-dokie. It'll only take me a few minutes."

Scooter wondered about the other odor in the van, and since he knew who the owner was, he figured it wouldn't hurt to check into it. One thing was for certain: when Flash smelled something he thought was like their grill gas, there was likely something to it. "Sir, I'll be right back. I'm going outside to check on my puppy."

"Fine. I'll keep the slices warm for ya."

Scooter hurried from the small store and found Flash again sniffing the back doors of the van. Beside him was the young father. Placing a friendly smile on his face, Scooter walked up and picked up Flash's leash. "I'm sorry about him, buddy. Sometimes his nose takes control over him. You know how beagles are."

The man nodded as he removed the cellophane from the cigar. "Sure do, cause I had one when I was a little tike. They can smell a gnat's fart in a windstorm. What's his name?"

Scooter chuckled at the fellow's description of a beagle's keen sniffer. "Flash."

The grinning man replied, "And I know what he's smellin'. Yep, got me a dressed hog inside that's gonna make some mighty fine bar-b-que." He fiddled with the Bic lighter, unable to get it to stay lit in the breeze. "And my nasty knee-boots is back there, too. They's covered with fresh hog crap." He let out a deep belly laugh. "Bet'cha can smell that, can't ya, Flash?"

Scooter needed to approach the question about the gas fumes in a nonchalant way so as not to appear nosey. "Love home-cooked hog. Do you all cook over wood or charcoal?"

"Naw, not for something this big. We use propane cause it's easier, and I can't tell much difference if we keep it moist with our special vinegar sauce. Sauce makes the bar-b-que. We're celebrating the birth of our first child…a little boy."

Scooter extended his hand, and they shook. "Congratulations, man. You look like a proud father." Flash barked. "Easy, boy."

"Well, I best get on down the road. Gotta get this hog on the spit. We got a long night of cookin' ahead. Nice meeting you both." He shoved the cigar in his mouth and flicked the Bic. It lit, then went out.

Transporting propane tanks was no big deal, but if Flash was right, even a small leak would fill the van, and one spark from the lighter could possibly be the last thing this fellow ever did. "Excuse me, buddy, I know you're in a hurry, but my pup keeps sniffing around the doors. I don't know what he's smelling. It's probably the hog or the manure, so since he's never seen a pig, would you mind letting him see it? Maybe that will calm him. He won't lick or bite it." Flash yipped twice.

The young man chuckled and shoved the Bic into his pocket. "Sure. No problem." He stepped over and opened both doors and pointed to the hog. "Ain't it a beaut?"

Scooter's eyes landed on two large, torpedo-shaped tanks. With the van's doors open, even he got a slight whiff of gas. "Yeah, that's some hunk of hog." Scooter reached over and felt the 'off-on' knob on one of the tanks and noticed it was not fully shut off. He tightened it and then checked the other, finding it tight. "Not being nosey, but did you just get these filled?"

"Sure did, down yonder at Harry's feed store. He's got the best gas price around. Nice guy, too. Why? You needin' some?"

"No, but I noticed this tank wasn't fully shut off, so I tightened it for you. The other is fine. By chance, did you smell gas inside the van?"

The young man shook his head. "Buddy, my nose ain't never worked right. I think it's only on my face to hold up my sunglasses. No, sirree, I can barely smell the hog dung."

"I'm pretty sure that's what Flash was smelling. Glad we found it."

Suddenly the man's eyes widened, and he snatched off his ball cap. "Oh, God!" He sat down on the bumper and bowed his head. "And I was gonna be the proud daddy and light up to celebrate little Bobby's birth." He looked up at Scooter with tear-filled eyes. Then he slipped from the van and knelt beside Flash and draped his arm over him. "Flash, you probably saved my life." He pulled the little beagle close. "I'll never forget you and your buddy. This could've been my last day on earth." After taking a deep breath and exhaling, he stood. He shook Scooter's hand. "Thank you. I can't tell you how glad I am to have run into you both. I promise you this – when Bobby is old enough for a pup, I'm getting him a beagle, and we're gonna name him Flash Junior." He snatched a handkerchief from his hip pocket and blew his nose.

Scooter placed a hand on the fellow's shoulder. "Well, my mama always said, 'All's well that ends well'. I would suggest you wait until you're standing in your back yard before lighting that cigar."

The thankful man smiled at them. "Thanks." Then he closed the back doors and walked slowly to the driver's door and crawled in. Scooter and Flash watched him pull from the lot, waving. Scooter returned the wave and knelt beside his beagle. "You did good, boy. I think you just saved that man's life." Scooter felt his throat tighten. "I'm proud of you."

I didn't do a lot, Scoot. It was the strange smell. Thanks for checking it out. The man was happy you found the leak.

"You're one humble hound. Okay, I'm going back inside to get our vittles. We've got a book signing to attend."

I'll sit right beside you.

"I like it when you're beside me, Flash." Scooter strutted inside feeling as proud as the young father. *Life's good.*

CHAPTER 21

Scooter and Flash reclined on their uncomfortable bed at Knights Inn, tuckered out after three busy hours of signing books. If asked to rate their afternoon's events, Scooter would place a blue ribbon on Flash's life-saving discovery of leaking propane, a very successful book signing, and the hospitality shown by Anne and Wilma. Thinking back on the many months of struggling to write his novel, Scooter recalled periods of despair and doubt when his thoughts and creativity hit the proverbial brick wall. Then his muse, Gabby, entered his life with 'fresh eyes' and helpful suggestions. After the miraculous saving of little Kay, prompting the chance meeting of Jason Goldberg, each step was key in placing him before the friendly and appreciative folks of Bluefield. "Flash, we had a great time today."

Flash lifted his head from Scooter's leg and yawned. *We were nervous for nothing. These people are so nice. I wish Gabby could've been here today.*

Scooter lightly stroked the beagle's snoot. "Yeah, she would have certainly enjoyed herself around them, just like you did. We'll tell her all about it, and when we return to promote the sequel, she'll be with us."

Are you going to call and check on her?

"Yep. But since their time is different, I'll wait until ten o'clock our time." Scooter paused and chuckled. "It's a shame we can't talk to her."

I was thinking about that, but Miss Vennie might be able to hear her.

"We don't want to take that chance. You were a first-class partner today. The people, especially the kids, sure made over you. You were as much of a hit as my book."

Thanks, Scoot. I like being your partner. Oh, and one little girl gave me a piece of her candy.

Scooter chuckled. "I noticed. We sold just over a hundred books. That surprised me. Maybe we'll sell out during the four hours tomorrow."

I hope so. You and Gabby worked hard on that book. Where do we go from here?

"We go to Columbus, Ohio, for two stops, and then to Pennsylvania for several stops. After leaving Pennsylvania, we head east down the coast. At least we're staying busy and having fun. Right?"

Flash stretched, made two turns, and plopped down. *I am.*

"Good. Now I'm going to take a nap. I've set the alarm clock for ten o'clock to call Vennie and check on our movie star. Rest up. Tomorrow at noon, we're back to signing."

Okay. Wake me up when you call.

"I will."

Saturday morning in the quaint town of Bluefield was American life at its best. Scooter and Flash sat on a bench beside the same bus stop mentioned in "If Bullfrogs Had Wings" where Keith and Flea would get on and off to travel to and from their homes in McComas. Scooter smiled at the thought of creating memorable characters in this little town. "We've got another beautiful day ahead of us, Flash. Gabby's doing just fine with her movie, and we slept well and just finished a delicious breakfast. In one hour, we'll be back at the table, pen in hand, talking to the folks. I'd say life's good."

Flash yipped. *I'm excited. And Miss Anne will give me a couple of Milk Bones, too. Yes, life is good.*

Scooter chuckled and continued to watch people walking past, shopping and talking. He was thankful to be where he was, doing what he was doing. He was proud to have one talented pooch doing her thing in California and another talented pup sitting beside him. "I'm one lucky man," he whispered.

A middle-aged couple across the street waved, and the lady said, "Hey! I started your book last night, and it's great! Thank you!" As they continued along, Scooter waved back. "Thank you!"

The approaching noon sun warmed Scooter as he stood. "Time to go, Flash."

Flash pushed up and shook. *I'm ready.*

When four-thirty rolled around and the last book and customer were gone, Scooter signed Anne and Wilma's copies. He thanked them for their generous assistance and kindness and led Flash outside. "Well, Flash, if the rest of our signings go this well, I'll be thrilled."

They will, Scoot.

"You're not only humble, you're positive, too."

CHAPTER 22

Late Sunday afternoon, the traveling duo pulled into Columbus, Ohio, exhausted and hungry. Traffic had been hectic, not to mention Scooter made a couple of wrong turns, which wasted at least an hour. Storm clouds were building, threatening a heavy downpour as they checked into their motel. Flash was restless. Scooter blamed the low pressure. After Scooter returned with their supper from a nearby Kentucky Fried Chicken, they devoured the meal and hit the sack, recharging their batteries for tomorrow evening's three-hour signing at Barnes & Noble.

The number of customers and sales dipped below Bluefield's, but everyone was friendly and helpful. Flash remained popular with the customers, no matter their age, as he sat calmly beside Scooter's feet. They thanked the staff, signed their personal copies of "If Bullfrogs Had Wings", and walked from the store into the rain and cold temperature. "I'm pooped, Flash. How're you feeling?"

I want a bowl of Puppy Chow, fresh water, and sleep. Don't forget to call Miss Vennie and check on Gabby.

"You bet I will. Then after a shower and a burger and fries, I'm getting a good night's sleep. We head to Pennsylvania in the morning."

The news from California was excellent. Vennie said Gabby was performing like a professional. She did notice a tad of homesickness which appeared in the form of Gabby not eating as much, along with a few nights of restless sleep. Scooter asked Vennie to tell Gabby things were going well with them and it wouldn't be long before they would see her. He hung up the phone and relayed the news to one tired beagle. "Okay, sleep tight, Flash. Like Willie Nelson's song, tomorrow we're 'On the Road Again'. Scooter chuckled and turned off the light, tried but failed to fluff un-fluffy pillows, and laid down.

The Ohio dawn welcomed the twosome with beaming sunshine and slightly warmer temperatures. After a quick breakfast from the window of a Hardees's drive-thru, Scooter sipped his black coffee and pulled the Bronco onto the road. "Here we go. Next stop is New Kensington, Pennsylvania.

Flash performed his typical three spins in the large bucket seat and plopped down. *How long before we get there?*

"About four hours." He laughed. "That's if I don't get lost." Scooter took another long sip of 'go juice', pushed the powerful engine to sixty, and set the cruise control. "Remember, each day that passes is one day closer to seeing Gabby."

That's how I've been looking at our trip.

"You're one smart canine."

So are you, Scooter.

Scooter thought about the innocence of his statement and chuckled. "I'm learning a lot from you and Gabby."

They arrived at their destination on time. Sunshine escorted them the entire trip while traffic was minimal. Scooter felt energized and ready for another signing and meeting new people who wanted to read his scribblings. "Flash, what would you like for lunch? My breakfast is gone, and I'm hungry."

Whatever you want. When you stopped to get gas, I hopped in the back and nibbled some Puppy Chow.

Scooter laughed. "Next time, share with me." He turned onto Tarentum Bridge Road. "Our hotel should be up here on the right. After we check in, let's take a walk and loosen up our stiff muscles. It's a pretty day. I'll find a place to get us something to eat. We're scheduled at the Barnes & Noble for six o'clock."

How long do we sign books?

Scooter pulled into the Clarion Hotel and parked in front of the lobby. "Four hours. One hour longer tonight."

Flash stretched. *We'll do fine. I'm getting used to our busy schedule.*

"Good. So am I. You wait here while I go check in." Within ten minutes, he had unloaded his suitcase. "Okay, Flash, let me take a quick shower, and then we'll head out into this nice day and see how the people live around here."

I'll take a quick nap.

The two beach buddies settled down behind the polished table at the Barnes & Noble on 7th Street in New Kensington and were amazed at how many customers lined up, holding copies of the book. Scooter's smile remained for the entire four hours, while his left hand throbbed from requested inscriptions and his signature. These folks reminded him of the Bluefield people, laid back and down-to-earth. He heard a few coalmining stories about their ancestors, as well as several golf stories from the men. Of course, Flash was the perfect under-the-table host, his tail continually slapping Scooter's leg each time someone reached down and gave him a pat.

At the conclusion of the signing, the kind manager told Scooter they had sold two hundred and fifty books. "Man, the last time we moved that many copies, the author was already well-known and it was his third book."

Scooter shook his head. "Wow! I have no clue why. But I will say all of tonight's customers were very friendly. And you and the staff have been hospitable and helpful."

After Scooter signed a complimentary copy for the young manager, he led his pooch outside into the chilly night. "We nailed it tonight, Flash. Wha'cha think?"

It was fun. Those people loved petting on me.

"That's cause you look so intelligent and professional." Scooter laughed. "Just imagine how they'd act if they knew you were a surfer?"

They returned to the hotel. Scooter walked the tired beagle to a grassy area for math class, and then they entered their room. Flash perched on the bed as Scooter called Vennie. After they shared the latest news, Scooter asked her to put the phone to Gabby's ear. "Okay, wait a minute." A few seconds passed, and Vennie said, "Here's the star."

Scooter quickly said, "A yip will do just fine. Hey, Baboo! Flash and I miss you, but it won't be long before you'll be coming to Sandbridge for the holidays. Here's Flash."

Flash yipped and looked at Scooter. "Go ahead, talk to her."

I miss you, Gabby! We're glad you're doing good in your movie. I can't wait to see you, and the movie. Scooter's selling a lot of books. Night, sleep tight. I love you, Baboo.

Gabby yipped twice and then barked.

Scooter said, "Okay, Baboo, let me talk to Vennie." Gabby yipped again, and then Vennie said, "You should've seen those beautiful brown eyes, Scooter. They were wide-open and twinkling. Now she's lying on her back and wiggling her feet in the air. I don't know what you said, but she's happier than I've seen her."

"I don't know why I didn't think about letting you put the phone to her ear. From now on, we'll do that. Okay, you have a nice evening and tell everyone we said 'hi'. Talk to you tomorrow." Scooter placed the receiver in the cradle and laughed.

I'll bet Gabby liked hearing our voices.

Scooter told him what Vennie said about Gabby acting very happy and rolling around on the floor. "From now on, we'll talk to her every night."

Then I'll sleep better.

"Me too, partner. Oh, and we're sleeping in tomorrow. We don't need to be in Philadelphia for two days, and I have a super idea to pass the time. I'll tell you in the morning. Sleep tight."

Scooter, I like your ideas. See you in the morning.

Bright sunshine poured through the narrow opening between the heavy curtains, zapping Scooter squarely in the eyes. He rolled over, flipped the pillow on his face, and grabbed another thirty minutes of dreamless sleep. Flash released a double-yip, evidently reacting to something going on in his dream. Scooter stirred and peeped at the clock on the nightstand. "Nine-thirty."

Scooter decided to call Darla Kay and catch her up on their activities and successful sales in some of the stores. After that, a call to Jason would be made to detail the high points of the signings and sales. Then, Scooter and Flash would spend a couple of days in the country, hiking and exploring. Flash could roam and sniff to his heart's content. The little fellow deserved some free time in the open air since he had behaved so well in the bookstores, not to mention his discovery of the leaking gas. "A break will do us both good before we hit the big cities on the final leg of this tour." Scooter slid from the bed and tip-toed into the bathroom for a much-needed hot shower.

Two hours later, the phone calls were completed, Flash had devoured his Puppy Chow and visited math class, and Scooter had checked out. As he fired up the Bronco, he scanned his map. According to the directions, in about forty minutes they would be out in the country, surrounded by streams and vast woods. Even as a lover of the beach, Scooter was excited about spending time in a different region. "On the road again, Flash! No more books to sign for two days. And I know you're going to have fun."

Flash stood in the seat, his tail flapping and eyes twinkling. *What are we going to do?*

After a chuckle, Scooter replied, "You're going to be surprised, that's what."

I like surprises.

"You're one easy pooch to please."

Scooter put the Bronco on Route 28N, also called the Allegheny Valley Expressway, and locked the cruise control on fifty. Brilliant sunshine reflected off the coal-black hood as passing trees displayed leaves of multiple colors. "This is one beautiful stretch of road, Flash. If I couldn't live on the coast, I'd live out here."

Not many houses out here.

"Welcome to the country. All we need is a small motel out in the boonies with a small restaurant close by."

When they neared Kittanning, Scooter started looking for signs advertising motels. About five miles later, he spotted a small hand-painted sign shaped like a big finger pointing to the right. Beneath it read, The

Shady Seven Motel next right. "That sounds exactly what we're looking for."

Flash pushed up on his paws and looked out the windshield. *A motel?*

"Yep," Scooter answered, turning onto Raccoon Road. "Down here just a bit."

Scooter slowed the Bronco as he spied a cinderblock, flat-top motel sitting in the midst of tall pines with seven attached rooms and a wooden chair beside each bright blue door. "There it is, the Shady Seven Motel. Now, this is what I had in mind." Scooter whipped into the gravel driveway and parked in front of the center door marked 'Office'. "Only one pick-up truck here. They should have a room for us."

I like it out here, Scoot. I'll bet there are lots of wild animals living around here.

Scooter nodded and shut off the truck. "You can bet on it."

Neither of them knew exactly which wild animal Flash would come face to face with, but one would soon be the focus of the beagle's most unforgettable experiences.

CHAPTER 23

Terry Zimmerman scratched his white beard and eyeballed the shiny Bronco as it rolled up the driveway. He turned and hollered through the office's screen door, "Gloria, we've got a customer. Looks like a city slicker. I told ya today would be lucky." He took a seat in a rustic Adirondack chair, picked up a piece of wood, whipped his trusty Barlow knife from his bib overalls, and began to whittle. "She never believes a word I say," he mumbled.

Scooter leashed his excited companion and slipped from the seat. "Let's go check in."

I already smell a lot of good stuff, Scoot.

"Okay, but be easy around the man. In case they're not pet friendly, we need to make a good first impression."

I will.

"Good morning," Scooter said as they walked up. "A beautiful day."

Zimmerman continued to whittle and nodded. "Every day's beautiful when a body wakes up. What can we do for ya?"

"Wondering if you have a room available for a couple of nights?"

Zimmerman looked up from his wooden masterpiece and glanced from his left to right and chuckled. "Judgin' by the empty lot, we shore ain't full. Yeah, we can handle ya."

Scooter and Flash stopped in front of the man. "Are you all pet friendly, sir?"

The razor-sharp Barlow froze in mid-whittle. "I'm friendly to all animals 'cept the ones that ain't friendly to me." He looked at Flash, who was sitting quietly, tail sweeping the ground. "Got yerself a fine-lookin' rabbit dog."

Scooter pushed out a small smile. "Yeah, he's my little buddy. Name's Flash."

"Had one years ago. Little fellow'd rather follow his nose than eat. Got on a mama bear's scent one evening." Zimmerman took a deep breath, gazed into the woods, and sighed. "Still miss him, shore do."

A knot formed in Scooter's stomach. "I'm sorry." Before he could ask about getting checked in and for information on fishing or canoeing, an attractive lady Scooter figured for the man's wife opened the screen door. "Welcome."

"Little beagle looks like Sniffy, don't ya think, Gloria?"

She looked down at Flash and nodded. "Could be his twin."

"His name's Flash," said Scooter. "Nice to meet you, ma'am."

She pushed her fingers through dark hair. "I'm Gloria, and this here's my husband Terry. He ain't gonna fret much on names unless they're attached to an animal. And your name?"

"I go by Scooter. Scooter Bissell."

Terry slowly looked up with wary eyes. "Scooter?"

"Yes, sir. My nickname."

Gloria shot her husband a stare. "Leave the nice man alone, Terry. You've been tagged with a few nicknames yourself over the years. Now, if this man and his pup want to stay here, I'll be glad to check 'em in." She giggled. "Scooter, if'n you was to stand here all day, Terry would sit and talk. Follow me, please," she said, entering the office.

Terry's personality might rub some people raw, but Scooter felt welcome here. Country folks were different, not unlike some beach people – set in their ways. He appreciated the straightforward approach in lieu of phony. He smiled. "Terry, you mind if I leave Flash out here with you while I check-in?"

Terry gave his leg a pat. "Come here, Flash." The beagle eased up, still wagging his tail. "Let your buddy tend to business while I tell you a story 'bout Sniffy."

Hearing the word 'business', Flash looked up at Scooter and yipped.

"Thanks, Terry. Oh, whenever Flash yips that means he's happy." Scooter handed Terry the leash and entered the office.

Twenty minutes later, Scooter and Gloria walked outside into the sunshine. "Terry, you're not going to believe where Scooter and Flash live."

Terry continued to stroke Flash's head and looked up. "I would, unless you said Mars or something crazy like that."

Gloria waved her hand in the air and shook her head. "They live at your favorite vacation place."

Terry glanced up at Scooter. "You live at Sandbridge in Virginia?"

Scooter nodded. "Yep. Gloria said you all come down for a week every summer to fish and relax."

Terry extended his calloused hand. They shook. "Well, ain't it a small world? You bet we go there; in fact, I could live down there. Good place to fish."

"Yes, it is. You will have to look us up next summer. I know a few good places to catch a mess of spot and drum, and maybe some flounder."

Gloria told Terry about Scooter's novel and that they were on a book tour. "They have a couple of days off and wanted to get out and relax in the country and fish or canoe." She laughed. "I told him they came to the right place."

161

"Dang right! We got you covered, Scooter. I can put you in a canoe *and* on fish, too."

Gloria held up her hand. "Terry, tell the truth and let the Lord love ya. You put him in the canoe, but I'll put him over the fish, honey."

Terry nodded. "Yeah, she ain't lying. And her daughter and son-in-law own a bait and rental place just up the road on Mill Run. You aimin' to get on the water today?"

"We sure are, Terry. It's too nice of a day not to. Let me get my suitcase unloaded and change clothes." He knelt beside Flash. "Hear that, little buddy? We're going out in a canoe and catch some fish." Flash yipped twice.

Terry and Gloria laughed. "You can get everything you need from Matt and Mikael's place. When you're ready, you can follow me," said Terry, jumping to his feet like a teenager. He looked at Gloria. "See, woman, told you today would be a good 'un."

"He'll never let me live this down."

One hour later, Scooter and Flash were standing in M&M's Bait & Rental being assisted by Matt and Mikael. They told Scooter some smallmouth bass were being caught, along with a few other freshwater species. Scooter showed Mikael a drawing of the stream that Gloria had given him with a few Xs where she usually caught fish. "Are these places hard to find? Remember, I'm a rookie on a new stream."

"Not at all. My mother knows this place as good as she does her kitchen. The water's moving slow now, so you'll drift along, but when you catch one, drop the small anchor and work the area," said Mikael.

Matt added, "Save the nice ones, Scooter. Clean them when you get back to the motel, and Gloria will be happy to fry them for you."

"I sure appreciate your help, folks. When you come to Sandbridge next summer, I'll return the favor."

Terry said, "I'd start paddling back around three o'clock. Stop and work the places where you caught some for ten or fifteen minutes, and then move on. Don't let the darkness fall on ya out there. Gets a mite nippy at night."

They walked Scooter and Flash out to the canoe and helped load up. Matt handed Scooter two containers of red wigglers and one of crickets. "You're set, buddy. Oh, and if by chance you tip the canoe, don't fret. The water's wet and cold, but only waist deep." He grinned and slapped Scooter on the shoulder.

Scooter put Flash on the seat. "I'd rather skip wading and fish from the comfort of the canoe. Thanks again."

Matt pushed them off the bank and into the middle of Mill Run beneath a noonday sun. "Have fun!" Scooter and his eager hound straightened out the canoe and moved slowly downstream.

Once they were a hundred yards downstream, Flash yipped. *Scoot, this is so neat. Everything smells so good and clean. And I've never seen anyone catch a fish, so please catch one.*

"I'll do my best, little dude. I've fished since I was a kid, but not too often in streams. We've got a little map where they hang out, we've got the bait they eat, and we're having fun in the wide open country. Right?"

I wish Gabby was with us. She'd probably go swimming.

Scooter slowly got the hang of using the paddle to steer the canoe, allowing the slow-moving water to push him. Every so often, he spotted a calm area, usually behind a large rock. "The next smooth area, I'll drop anchor and get baited up and check it out."

Flash sat comfortably on his haunches on the front seat, his front paws on the bow. His head and floppy ears rotated from side to side, refusing to miss a sight or smell. Up ahead, Scooter saw another large boulder. He placed the paddle down, picked up the lightweight anchor, and eased it over the side. When it grabbed hold on the bottom, Scooter fed out enough rope to carry them just past the rock, then tied it to a cleat. "We'll try a worm first and see what we get." Using the paddle, he checked the depth. "It's about three feet deep." After adjusting the cork, he baited the hook and flipped his line into the calm water. "Okay, buddy. We're fishin'."

Flash leaned forward, staring at the red and white bobber on the surface. *How do you know when a fish bites?*

"The bobber will bounce up and down and then disappear under the water. Then I tighten the line, set the hook, and reel him in." Scooter inhaled a lungful of fresh air and felt his muscles relax. "It's sure nice out here, isn't it?"

Yeah, replied Flash, his brown eyes still glued to the bobber. *And there's so many different smells floating around here, too.*

Before Scooter could reply, Flash barked. *Scooter, the little ball went under the water!*

Returning his eyes to the water, Scooter saw no cork. He reeled the slack from the line and felt a light resistance. He set the hook. As the fight ensued, he announced, "Got one!"

Flash leaned farther over the bow. *Get it, Scoot-toot.*

The calm surface erupted as the bass came to the top, pulling and gliding from side to side. Scooter gently reeled him in close to the canoe, leaned over, and slipped his thumb into the two-pound bass's mouth. "It's a smallmouth bass, Flash."

The beagle hopped from the seat and pulled up beside Scooter, nose over the edge, sniffing his first fish. *Wow! We got one. Wait until I tell Gabby about this.*

Scooter removed the hook from the bass' mouth and put him on the stringer. "These are delicious to eat."

Miss Gloria will cook it for us?

"Yeah, if we catch enough for a meal. Maybe we'll catch enough for all of us."

Oh, goodie! They are very nice people.

"They certainly are. And the next time they come to Sandbridge, maybe we'll have them over for a cookout."

That will be fun.

Scooter baited his hook and cast back into the water. "Okay, keep your eye on the bobber."

Scooter relaxed as the pleasant sounds of chirping birds in nearby trees blended with the water rushing around the boulder surrounded him. The previous days of traveling and book signings were enjoyable, but he believed time should always be taken to unwind and get outdoors. And, they had found the perfect place to do just that. Several peaceful minutes passed, and then Flash yipped. *Bobber's gone again!*

Repeating the hooking process, Scooter reeled in another bass, a little bigger than the last one. "I think we've found one of Gloria's hot spots." He put the fish on the stringer, re-baited, and cast back out. "This fun to you, Flash?"

You bet!

After six more fish were on the stringer, the action slowed. "Let's move up and find another spot."

Good idea, Scoot. When you're not catching one, I get sleepy.

Scooter chuckled as he pulled up the anchor, allowing the canoe to move with the current. "Out here is the perfect place to nap, too."

Once they found another spot, Scooter set up and cast his line. No sooner than the bait hit the surface, the water exploded. "Whoa! Now this is a whopper!" Flash hopped back up to the bow and leaned forward. *Wow! I can see it under the water. It's big!*

Using smooth movements, Scooter worked the fish away from the bank and into deeper water, not wanting it to get tangled on anything underwater. "Come to papa." The rod tip bent downward as the line sliced through the water with a 'zing'. "This baby will feed three of us, Flash!"

Maybe it was the excitement of the moment or just plain curiosity, but little Flash wanted to be as close to the action as possible. It was at that moment, while leaning over the bow, he lost his balance and fell headfirst into the cold water. Scooter watched Flash's tri-colored tail disappear over the canoe's side. "I'll get you. Paddle!" He held the rod with one hand and moved forward and leaned over. Flash bobbed on the surface and worked his front paws up and down. Scooter felt the large fish continuing to fight and pull. There was no way he could bring Flash into the canoe with only one hand. The decision was made. He quickly tucked the rod under the seat, reached over and pulled Flash to him. As he leaned over the side to get his hands under the beagle, he felt the canoe tip…and tip…and then, Scooter went headfirst into the cold water. He righted himself in chest-deep water and scooped Flash under his arm and pushed the canoe back upright, thankful to see the rod still locked beneath the seat. He placed the soaked pooch on the seat and walked the canoe to the shallow shoreline. Once he was back in the canoe, he laughed so hard his belly ached. Between loud guffaws, he said, "Gabby will love…hearing…this story!"

Flash hopped down on the canoe's floor and completed a full body shake. *I'm sorry. Did the big fish get away?*

Realizing he had completely forgotten about the fish, Scooter picked up the rod and cranked. "Gone. But that's okay. If we'd had him for supper, in time we would've forgotten how good it was. But now, we will never forget this adventure, buddy." Flash yipped and Scooter laughed.

The sunshine did little to warm the two. After winding in the line, Scooter pulled the stringer of fish into the canoe, then the anchor. He started paddling back up the stream. "We've had enough fun for one day. Let's go in and let me get into some warm clothes. Then I'll clean these fish for supper."

It was all my fault. I leaned over too far.

Scooter chuckled. "I leaned too far, too."

While they moved against the easy-moving current, Scooter knew their escapade would produce laughs from their new friends. *Well, we had fun, and we're not the first ones over the side of a canoe.*

Mikael and Matt went easy on the drenched duo, but they did compliment Scooter on the nice bass. "Don't worry, Scooter. You'll forget this little mishap while you're eating. Mom can fry some fish," bragged Mikael.

"Even so, you two will never forget today." Matt laughed almost as hard as Scooter had on the water.

"We added another memory to our long list. Thank you for all your help. We'll look forward to seeing you at Sandbridge next summer."

The friends shook hands. Matt drew a little map for Scooter to get them back to the motel. As they pulled out of the parking lot, Scooter said to Flash, "It's been a good day and life's still good."

Life's good, even if we're wet and cold.

Unbeknownst to the damp duo, they were not finished compiling memories or stories.

CHAPTER 24

The new friends and Flash relaxed in comfortable chairs outside the quaint motel. Terry gazed into the star-filled sky and puffed his fragrant pipe. Gloria slowly worked her knitting needles, adding stitches to what would be a colorful sweater for Mikael's Christmas gift. Scooter inhaled deep breaths of fresh, pine-scented air and relished the serenity of the evening. For him, the day could not have been any better unless Gabby had been with them.

"Gloria, that was one delicious supper. Mikael was right about you having the knack of frying fish. And the sauerkraut in place of cole slaw was awesome! Thank you."

"You're more than welcome. The sauerkraut was made by Mikael…her specialty. I'll be sure and tell her you enjoyed it. It's not often we have such exceptional guests out here in the boonies. Right, Terry?"

"I told you today would be a good 'un."

"Today has been a good 'un." She winked at Scooter. "Now that I've agreed with him, that'll be the end of it."

Scooter rubbed Flash's head and yawned. "Little buddy, I think your math class is in the woods. You go visit it, then we'll turn in." Flash yipped and trotted toward the tall pines. "It's okay if you sniff around a little. I've seen your nose twitching all evening."

Terry threw a match to his pipe. "Did you say 'math class', Scooter?"

"That's what we call doing his business."

A cloud of smoke circled Terry's head. "You've lost me, friend."

Scooter chuckled. "Well, he does a number one and then a number two, and he gets a three."

The Zimmermans exploded into full-blown laughter. Terry choked on his previous puff, and Gloria missed a stitch. "I've never heard it put quite that way," Terry finally said after getting control of his hacking.

"I'll bet you two have had a blast traveling around and meeting new people," added Gloria.

Scooter stretched his arms over his head at the precise moment a loud bark poured from the woods followed by a hair-raising howl. "What in the world? Flash?" Scooter was quickly on his feet, sensing the seriousness of the sound of distress. "Flash? Come here, boy!"

In a calm voice, Terry said, "Looks like Flash done met 'The Boss'."

"The Boss? Who's that? A bear? A wildcat?"

Terry chuckled, as did Gloria. "Naw, nothing that dangerous. I'm talking 'bout the boss of the forest. You'll see when Flash returns. Won't take but a minute. Might as well sit and wait, cause your night is jest beginning."

"I hope Dewberry's is still open, Terry," said Gloria, soft as cotton.

Terry squinted at his watch. "Ah, it's only eight. He's usually there till ten playin' cards with the boys. I'll ride with Scooter."

Scooter felt the hair on his arms rise when another long howl filled the serene area. "What are you talking about?" No sooner than the words were out of his mouth, he heard several whimpers at the edge of the pines. "Flash?"

What he saw next broke his heart. His normally perky beagle staggered into the clearing, whimpering and stopping every step or two to paw his eyes. Scooter started toward him until Terry said, "I wouldn't do that yet, Scooter. Let him tend to this for a few minutes. You've got to stay 'stink free'...at least until we get the stuff."

"Stink? The stuff?"

"Yeah. Works every time," replied Terry.

Flash continued to stagger in circles, pawing and whining. From the way the pup was moving, he appeared to be blind. Suddenly, in the midst of pawing his snoot, Flash dropped to the ground and rolled over, frantically wiggling his back in the dirt. Scooter's emotions were in overdrive, and he couldn't hold back. He trotted over to his bewildered beagle. As he got within a few feet, he said, "Flash..." Before Scooter could form another word, he stepped back several steps and threw his hands over his face. "Oh, no!"

Terry and Gloria exploded with laughter as Flash's whines and whimpers continued. "Little buddy," Scooter said, continuing to back up, "we've got one very stinky mess on our hands."

"The stink ain't on your hands yet, Scooter, but it soon will be. Gloria's going to keep an eye on Flash while he keeps tryin' to clean himself up, but that won't happen fully until we get back from Dewberry's Store. It 'taint far. This job can only be done correctly with tomato juice and ketchup. Now, you best get back over here cause old man Dewberry ain't lettin' you inside his store smellin' like no skunk." Terry chuckled and stood.

"Did you say ketchup and tomato juice?" Scooter asked as he pulled up in front of Terry.

"Yep. We'll tell you how to use it." Terry chuckled. "Didn't figure on learnin' this kind of info while you were here, did ya?"

Scooter shook his head and looked back to his pup, still rolling on the ground and pawing his eyes. "Poor thing."

Terry kissed Gloria on the cheek. "We won't be long, honey. Don't let Flash inside. You remember the night Sniffy got sprayed and ran into the office and through the back and into our living area?"

"Won't ever forget. I'll get the brush and washtub from the storage room and gather the other ingredients and have them ready."

Scooter looked from Gloria to Terry, wide-eyed and confused as to what he was hearing.

Terry moseyed over and climbed into the new Bronco. "Ain't never ridden in one of these."

Scooter hopped in and started the truck. He leaned out the window. "Flash. I'll be right back, and we'll get you cleaned up." When the Bronco hit the narrow country road, Scooter chuckled. "In your words, Terry, today's a good 'un." Both men laughed as the headlights pierced the darkness on their way to Dewberry's Store. *Life's good, even if sometimes it stinks a little.*

CHAPTER 25

Scooter continued to smile as he and Terry walked out of Dewberry's Country Store carrying the large burlap bag over his shoulder. "Dewberry is hilarious. How old is he?" Scooter asked.

Re-lighting his pipe, Terry smiled. "Nobody knows for sure. I'd say he's pushing ninety-five, but you'd never know it the way he gets around. And the rascal's got a memory like a lock box."

Scooter loaded the bag containing five half-gallons of tomato juice and two large bottles of Heinz ketchup into the back of the Bronco and rolled up the window. "I could sit around that country store for a week and come up with a ton of funny short stories." Scooter climbed behind the wheel. "And the stock and smells in the old store are classic. The shelves hold utensils and household products I thought were long gone. Amazing place. It's like stepping back in time." Scooter fired up the big engine.

"You're right. If those walls could talk…my, my, my. And, unless you want to throw your money away, do not play poker with those old codgers. No, sirree. I learned that years ago…the hard way."

Scooter's concern about Flash's encounter with the skunk and his stinky condition had diminished a little after the older men had joked with him about his beagle meeting 'The Boss'. However, the reason for bathing in tomato juice blended with ketchup was never revealed. "So, Terry, does Flash have to drink some of this tomato juice, too? Cause I don't think he cares for tomatoes." Scooter chuckled. "Help this beach fellow out, because he's clueless."

Terry scratched his beard. "You'll give Flash an old-fashioned scrubbing in the juice and ketchup, then rinse him off. No drinkin' required." Terry tamped down the tobacco and struck a wooden match and lit his pipe. "And you'll be stinkin' just like him after the bath."

"Now I'm really confused. If the juice gets rid of the odor, seems we wouldn't smell after the bath. Right?"

Terry took a few puffs. "Wrong."

Scooter laughed. "Is this whole process an initiation for city folks inducted into the secret club of 'The Boss'? Sort of like the old country joke about snipe hunting?"

Terry's laughter shot smoke out of his nose. "Naw, nothin' like that. See, it's complicated, but since you seem to be a smart guy, I'll try to explain it to you. Okay?"

"Please do."

"The oilish stuff the skunk shoots at predators comes from around his, as you say, his number two shoot. With me so far?"

Scooter nodded.

"It's very, very strong and contains sulfur chemicals, which are very difficult to remove. But if a person or animal smells this stink for a period of time their olfactory senses, better known as the nose, become acclimated to the stench. I figure one gets sick and tired of smelling it, so the nose shuts down that particular scent."

"That makes sense."

"Now, the juice bath will replace the nasty smell, and the nose will then pick up that smell, but the sprayed victim will continue to stink to anyone who hasn't been exposed yet. In other words, Gloria and I will be able to smell 'The Boss' on Flash and you after the bath. That's why you'll be doing the bathing." Terry chuckled.

"Then why bother with the bath?"

Terry slapped Scooter on the shoulder and chuckled. "I figured you'd ask that question. Well, after the juice bath, *you* will give Flash another washing using a unique tested and tried mixture. The final scrubbing will break down the sulfur chemicals from all fur or skin that's been affected by meeting 'The Boss'. You with me?"

Scooter released a deep sigh. "Then why don't we skip the juice bath and go with this magic potion?"

"Have you ever smelled something real nasty?"

"Of course. Nothing is worse than a rotten egg, dead fish, and rotten potatoes."

"You'll soon be adding 'skunk funk' to your list." Terry broke into uncontrolled laughter. When he was able to speak, he added, "Even after you're away from those nasty smells, you can still smell them, right?"

"Yeah, for a while."

"Wouldn't it be nice to get rid of the lingerin' smell quickly?"

"Sure."

"The tomato juice bath replaces the skunk funk in the nose, and then we break down the sulfur chemicals with the, as you call it, magic potion. And believe me, Scooter, you'll be thankful for the magic potion because you're going to be stinking as bad as Flash."

Scooter chuckled. "This day is still a good 'un." Both men were still laughing when Scooter pulled up to the Shady Seven Motel.

Flash remained in the clearing but had regained some of his composure; however, his brown eyes portrayed his pain. Gloria greeted the men with a smile. "Everything's ready." She pointed, like Vanna White, to an area between them and Flash. "Behold, one washtub, one stiff-bristled brush, two clean towels, previously used for stink removal, and two pairs of latex gloves."

Terry gave her a hug. "Thank you, honey. You've got the magic potion ingredients ready?" He looked at Scooter shouldering the burlap bag.

She looked at them with a puzzled look in her brown eyes. "Magic potion?"

"That's what Scooter calls the final bath." Terry lit his pipe. "And I haven't told him what the secret chemicals are." Husband and wife laughed.

"Let's get this party started," said Scooter, setting the bag on the ground. "Just tell me what to do."

Flash yipped twice and pawed his muzzle.

"Scooter, the first thing is to dig out a pair of pants or, better yet, shorts, if you brought any that you don't mind throwing away."

"I've got an old pair of shorts."

"Good. Go change and forget the shirt," said Terry. "It's gonna be a bit nippily out here, but a hot shower will thaw you out afterwards."

Scooter chuckled. "I'll be right back." He looked over at his pitiful pooch sitting on his haunches, listening intently. "It won't be long now, Flash."

The juice bath proved to be an experience, one Scooter knew Gabby would enjoy hearing about. Flash behaved like a champ because Scooter had explained this procedure needed to be performed if he wanted the nasty smell to go away. Since Gloria and Terry were sitting across the lot beside the office door, Flash had quietly replied, *Scoot, I'll do anything to quit stinking. This is so bad. I wish my nose didn't work so good.*

Once the ketchup and tomato juice mixture was rinsed from Flash's furry body, Scooter emptied the tub in the woods and refilled it with buckets of warm water brought out by Terry. Now it was time to mix the magic ingredients, and Scooter was as ready for this step as Flash.

"Scooter, over here you'll find the three *magic* ingredients." Terry pointed to a cardboard box. "Pour the entire quart bottle of Peroxide into the water. Then add one-quarter cup of baking soda and two tablespoons of the dish detergent. The measuring devices are also in the box. Now stir and watch the suds grow. Then give Flash another good scrubbing like the first one, except don't get it in his eyes. For his face, use the washcloth. Have fun." Terry chuckled.

Gloria added, "After you're done, Scooter, wash yourself with the washcloth. Terry was probably hoping you'd use the stiff-bristled brush. He's like that, as you now know."

"I can't thank you enough for helping get Flash, *and me*, clean from this very stinky situation. 'The Boss' has earned our respect, that's for sure."

Once the whole bathing process was completed, Scooter took a hot shower and put on clean clothes and a hefty application of Cool Water cologne. He then joined Terry, Gloria, and Flash outside. "In the words of my new friends, 'today has been a good 'un'." Scooter took a sip of hot coffee. "The only way something like this could happen at the beach is if you get in the middle of a pack of stinging nettles. I have a classic remedy for those stings."

Terry asked, "So, what's on your list of fun stuff for tomorrow?"

"Don't be so nosey, Terry. It's none of our business what they do. You don't ask that of our other guests."

Terry lit his pipe. "I'm not being nosey, Gloria. Our other guests are just that, *guests*. Scooter and Flash are our friends. Right, Flash?" Flash yipped twice and extended his paw to shake with Terry. As they shook, Terry said, "Yep. Right as rain."

Scooter said, "I was thinking of taking Flash on a hike. From what Terry has taught me and what I've learned about the nose, I believe a few hours in the woods would clean Flash's sniffer from the nasty smell." Scooter laughed. "What'cha think, Flash? You want us to take a long walk through the woods?" Flash barked three times. "I thought so."

Gloria giggled. "About a mile from here is the perfect place to hike. I'll draw you a map. You'll have pine forests, small streams, and open natural areas. I'll even fix you guys a picnic lunch."

"Thank you, but we don't want to put you out for a lunch. You've done plenty for us."

Terry nudged Gloria. "She hasn't told you, but your payback for the lunch will be a cookout at your place in Sandbridge. Right, Gloria?"

"Exactly."

Scooter stood. "Consider it done, friends. Now, we've kept you up long enough. And I'm sure my furry friend is as pooped as I am. Again, thank you." Flash yipped. "See you in the morning." Scooter and Flash headed to their room at the Shady Seven Motel, looking forward to a restful sleep.

CHAPTER 26

Abundant sunshine spilled across vast acres of meadow and scrub pines beneath white, puffy clouds lazily floating through Carolina Blue skies. Scooter sat, leaning against a warm, sun-kissed boulder, watching his little beagle's tail swishing through the knee-high grass while he sniffed to his heart's content. "If the past four hours haven't flushed the skunk odor from his snoot, nothing will." Thoughts of sharing their experiences with Gabby in a few days put a tiny grin on his face. "Not one to be left out, she'll demand that we come back here for the sequel."

I smell a rabbit, Scoot!

"Go get him! We've got all day." Flash released several barks Scooter had never heard before. "Yeah, he's on a rabbit scent. This has to be the perfect picture of a contented pooch." Scooter closed his eyes and inhaled pine fragrances. *Life's good when you're relaxing with your pooch.*

Thirty minutes had passed when Flash finally returned, exhausted, and pulled Scooter from a nap. Scooter picked cockle berries from the pup's fur. "Did you lose the rabbit's scent?"

Scoot, do rabbits swim?

"Ah, I'm not sure, but maybe they can for a short distance, if they had to. Why?"

Well, the scent kept getting stronger, and then I came to a little stream, and it disappeared.

Scooter pictured the description for a few seconds. "Was the stream wide?"

No. Flash looked across the field. *About as wide as that little tree is from us.*

"That's about eight feet. My guess is, the rabbit knew you were on his trail, and he jumped the stream."

Flash looked up at Scooter. *They can jump that far?*

"Sure can, especially when they know a beagle, one of the best sniffers around, is tracking them. See, we all learn something new every day."

The pup's head slowly lowered to his front paws. *We've learned a lot on this trip.*

Scooter gently stroked his companion's head. "We sure have, and we'll never finish learning, either. Speaking of gathering new information, I figured, after your skunk ordeal and those two baths last night, that you weren't in the mood to tell me everything that happened between you and the skunk. Do you mind sharing it?"

The little pup remained in the prone position and took a deep breath. *I don't like skunks.*

"You don't? Why?"

They're sneaky and mean.

"Sneaky?"

Scoot, before a dog or cat attacks, they give a signal. You know, like a bark or growl for a dog, or a hiss for a cat. Well, a skunk acts friendly, and then sprays something really stinky. That's mean and sneaky. See?

Scooter was glad Flash kept his head on his big paws. The initial encounter was humorous, and Scooter could not make his grin disappear. "I think so. But I've not had any dealings with skunks. I guess they have their own technique to make a possible predator go away."

They need to come up with a better way. Anyway, I came on the skunk after I did my math. I was sniffing around the woods when a different scent caught my attention. So I sniffed along with my head down, and the scent was getting real strong. I knew I was gaining on whatever it was. Suddenly, I heard leaves crunching and looked up. I saw what looked like a black and white cat standing beside a tree. Flash paused and shook his head. *Whenever I picture that scoundrel, I'm afraid the smell will come back. So, for a long while, we just looked at each other and remained quiet. When I took a little step toward what I figured was a cat, its tail shot straight up in the air.* Flash looked up at Scooter. Thankfully, Scooter's grin was gone. *This animal had the fluffiest tail I've ever seen. Anyway, then it gets up on its toes and dances around. It was real neat to watch, Scoot. They've got good balance. Well, this cat-like sneak bounces and struts around for a while, so I figured it wanted to play. I took another step, and suddenly it turns its rear end toward me and freezes.* Flash placed his head back on his paws.

Scooter waited for a few seconds and finally said, "And?"

That's when it happened. You know how dogs sniff other dogs' rear ends?

After a quick chuckle, Scooter replied, "Ah, yeah."

It's part of our nature. I thought this 'thing' wanted me to sniff for identification, but that's how it tricked me.

"Tricked you?"

Yeah. I stepped forward to sniff, and then this sneaky skunk squirted a mist from its rear end, and the stuff hit me in the face. My eyes burned like they were on fire, and I couldn't open them. That odor took my breath away, Scooter. I've never smelled anything like it before. It's a wonder it didn't burn up my sniff glands. Flash rolled over and eyed Scooter. *And so I tried to make my eyes quit burning while trying to get away from the stink, but I couldn't see where I was going. And now you know how it happened. I never want to meet another skunk...ever.*

"I'm so sorry, Flash. That does sound like a bad experience. What happened to the skunk?"

I don't know. I guess the nasty-smelling thing ran off. I'm glad it didn't stay there and keep squirting me.

"Thank you for telling me what happened. I was mighty worried about your condition, but then Terry and Gloria told me a couple of special baths would make things better. Why don't you take a nap? I know you're tired after chasing the rabbit."

Flash's reply to Scooter's suggestion came in the form of twitching paws. "Pup's pooped," whispered Scooter as he, too, closed his eyes.

When the exhausted hiking duo returned to the motel, the sun was perched on the western mountains. Scooter looked at his watch to find it was nearing four-thirty. As he placed the picnic basket beside the office door, he noticed a note. It read: *Scooter, we've gone for supper at Mikael and Matt's. Should be back late. Hope you two had a great day. See you in the morning. Gloria.*

"Well, little dude, looks like it's me and you tonight. I'm in the mood for an Italian sub. We passed a Subway a few miles out on the main road. Let me shower and change clothes, and we'll take a ride."

I'm not very hungry after that delicious picnic lunch, but I'll eat some Puppy Chow. I'll sleep good tonight.

"That makes two of us. Tomorrow morning, we have to get out of here early. Next stop is Philadelphia. We'll call Gabby tonight before we turn in."

I miss her.

"So do I, buddy."

The following morning greeted Scooter and Flash with a cold breeze and light showers. After packing and sharing a cup of coffee with Terry and Gloria, they said 'goodbyes' and Scooter gave them his phone number. "We look forward to your visit next summer. Thank you both for a fun and memorable stay." The pooch and Scooter crawled into the Bronco and headed for Philadelphia and another book signing. "Back to work, Flash."

We're one day closer to seeing Gabby.

"As Terry says, 'Right as rain'."

I don't understand that.

"Nor do I, but it sounds cool."

The travelers' trip to Philadelphia was uneventful, but things would not remain that way.

CHAPTER 27

In Scooter's opinion, congested traffic rated somewhere between a toothache and the flu, so while they putt-putted along Walnut Street in downtown Philadelphia, Scooter felt the need to visit both a doctor *and* a dentist. "Flash, you were lucky to be able to nap through this mess."

I would've helped if I could.

Suddenly, a small foreign car zipped in front of him. Scooter jammed the brake pedal and came to a quick stop. "Guess those models don't come with a turn signal," he growled.

The Barnes & Noble, according to Scooter's directions, should be up ahead about three blocks. The goal of finding a pet-friendly place to relax, shower, and spend the night did not look promising. If worse came to worst, since the rain had blown out, they could sightsee for three hours until the six o'clock signing. After the signing, they would get out of the city and try to find a motel on the outskirts. "We should've visited for three more hours with Gloria and Terry."

At five-forty-five, Scooter and Flash walked on tired legs into the Barnes & Noble. Even though Scooter felt like an old, dirty blanket, at least his face was clean from the hot water and paper towel wash-up he performed in the restaurant's restroom. Flash waited outside with a nice, pooch-loving lady who kept an eye on him. Scooter popped a stick of Juicy Fruit into his mouth and put a smile on his face. "Okay, buddy, let's do this thing for the next four hours."

I'm ready, Scoot. Remember, we're getting closer to seeing Gabby.

"And, that's a good thing. Thanks for keeping me focused."

The bookstore's manager, Ken, appeared to be in his mid-thirties and was a bit nerdy-looking. But Ken was very hospitable and offered to get Scooter a mug of freshly brewed coffee and Flash a bowl of cool water.

When Ken returned with their much-desired fluids, Scooter thanked him and asked where the signing would take place. "Follow me, sir. We received four cases of your novel yesterday, but I have a feeling we'll go through all of them with no problem." They walked down a long center aisle and came out into a sizeable sitting room with comfortable-looking chairs and sofas. "Your table's over there, sir." Ken pointed to a long, polished oak table with a ladder-backed chair. The table was stacked with four piles of his book. "I've put three new pens and a legal pad for notes behind the books. If you need anything else, let me know. I'll check on you from time to time."

Scooter shook his hand and thanked him again. "This is first-class, Ken. We haven't had this nice of a set-up anywhere." The manager nodded and headed back to the front of the store.

The Philly folks could not have been any nicer to Scooter and Flash. Several people brought in previously purchased copies of 'If Bullfrogs Had Wings' for a signature and the opportunity to express how much they enjoyed the story featuring Keith and Flea. A burst of pride replaced Scooter's fatigue as he signed the books and thanked his fans for their encouragement.

Ken joined Scooter and Flash at ten o'clock after the last customer walked out. "This was a real success, Scooter," announced Ken, grinning from ear to ear. "We are totally out of your books. Even though the rain returned, the people turned out."

Scooter stood and stretched. "You do have a great clientele. You certainly deserve a lot of the credit. You've gone the extra mile with me and Flash. Thank you." Scooter removed a copy of his novel from his tattered briefcase, signed it, and added a personal inscription for Ken. "Here's the last copy of my novel, friend, at least until the next shipment arrives. I hope you enjoy it."

Ken's grin became a full-fledged smile. "Thank you, Scooter." He looked down at the beagle. "And you, too, Flash. You have been the nicest author to visit here in the three years that I've been open. It's been a pleasure."

As they walked toward the front door, Scooter asked if there was a pet-friendly hotel or motel close by. Ken shook his head. "Not that I'm aware of. Your best bet is a little town about fifteen miles to the east."

Scooter thanked him again and led Flash out into the dark night filled with drizzle and a chilly wind. "Okay, partner, looks like we've got a short drive ahead of us, but at least the traffic is gone."

Good. We had a neat time.

"Yeah, makes this long afternoon and night worth it." Scooter turned left and walked along the front of the large brick building. The streets and the sidewalks were deserted. Once they reached the end of the building and turned left, they entered a narrow alley to get behind the bookstore to the small employee parking lot. Mid-way into the dimly lit alley, Flash growled lowly and froze. "What's the matter?"

The reply to Scooter's question came from a strange, deep voice in front of them. "You's pushin' your luck to be out this late…all alone…in a dark alley. This be a bad part of town, man."

Flash moved up tight to Scooter's leg. "I can't do anything about the time. We just left the bookstore, and I'm going to get my truck, then we're heading home."

Suddenly a younger man stepped up beside the first man. They moved two steps closer. The new arrival laughed and nudged his partner, which prompted the older fellow to say, "You ain't getting nothin' till you pay us." An evil laugh filled the alley. "Me and my brother own the lot you parked your ride in, man. Now give me your money!" He snatched his hand from the pocket of a baggy coat and waved a large switchblade in Scooter's face. *Now we've got a situation to deal with.*

Scooter needed time to analyze their predicament. In a fake, whiny voice he said, "I'm sorry. I'm flat broke." Scooter nodded down to Flash. "Spent all my money on his dog food." At present, nothing looked good. Thankfully, Scooter knew how to protect himself and disarm enemies after three hard years in the Army as a proud member of the Green Berets. So, mentally, he ran over his options. The main one was to get hold of the knife, turn the tables, and pray neither man possessed a gun and was drugged up enough to use it.

The knifeless man said, "What's in da briefcase?"

"Books. No bucks. You want to read one?"

"Naw, we don't read. If you ain't got no money, then sell the dog food, cause your mutt goes with us," said Mr. Knife. They both laughed and slapped high fives. "Yeah, if you can't pay…your dog will play…with my very mean Pit Bull. Your dog will warm him up before he fights for big money." He sneered, revealing a gold tooth. "And that puppy ain't gonna stand nary a chance, boy."

Scooter figured the time was at hand to force one of them to make a move, but he would need to set the stage for his advantage. He said to the knife man, "Okay, you can check my wallet. You won't find any money." Scooter slowly pulled his wallet from his back pocket with his free hand. When he extended it toward the man's hand, he let it slip. As it slapped the wet pavement, the man's eyes followed. He snickered and stared up into Scooter's eyes, slowly squatting and reaching for the wallet.

Before the man's hand made contact with the wallet, Flash leaped forward and chomped down on the man's bare wrist. A deep growl filled the night's silence as Flash's head thrashed wildly from side to side. The mugger released an earsplitting scream. Scooter made his move.

While the man continued to scream and struggled to free his arm, Scooter reared back and, as hard as possible, put his leather-soled Weejun squarely into the mugger's face. Mr. Knife's head snapped back in a brutal backlash. The switchblade hit the pavement with a clank. In a split second, Scooter snatched it up, then powerfully stomped the man's outstretched hand. He heard several bones snap, and another blood-curdling scream echoed through the alley.

Scooter looked up as the other man made a move toward him. With glaring eyes, Scooter took his stance and pointed the knife at the man. "Play the fool, and I'll gladly use this."

The man froze as his eyes opened wide. He spun around and mumbled, "I'm outta here." He scooted like a wet cat down the alley.

The situation had changed dramatically in Scooter's favor, and he worked to control his growing anger at the entire ordeal. He reached down and grabbed the man's coat collar and told Flash to back up. The still-growling beagle obeyed and sat on his haunches beside Scooter.

Scooter snatched the boney thug to his feet, flipped the knife over, and placed the dull edge tight beneath the man's jaw. "One sudden move, and I'll slice you like a piece of moldy cheese."

"Ain't gonna move, man," squeaked the failed thief.

After retrieving his wallet, Scooter and Flash proudly walked their captive back to the front door of the bookstore. "Nice work, Flash." Flash barked, causing the mugger to flinch. Scooter laughed and rapped on the glass door. "Flash, guess you showed this punk what a bad judge of pooches he was." Scooter was grinning when Ken appeared and peeked through the glass, his eyes as big as golf balls.

Ken quickly unlocked and opened the door, then re-locked it after Scooter forcefully shoved the man through the door. "What happened, Scooter?" Ken asked with a trembling voice.

"Just a little misunderstanding," replied Scooter.

"Huh?"

"Yeah, this guy misunderstands the correct way to obtain money. The dummy thinks all you have to do is talk tough, threaten innocent pups, and wave a knife. He knows how to scare people with a knife, but look where it got him." Scooter chuckled. "His partner in crime took off like a scalded cat."

"I'll call the police."

"Better hurry, Ken. I'm getting madder by the minute."

"But you've got him now."

Scooter shook the thug like a ragdoll. "Yeah, but even though I can take a lot from low-lifes, when they threaten harm to my dogs…I want to do more than turn them over to the law. Go call, Ken…and hurry." The mugger released a high-pitched whine.

Two hours later, the criminal had been arrested for attempted robbery with a deadly weapon and hauled off to jail. Detective Dave Keith was satisfied with Scooter's statement and asked where he was staying. "In case we need to get in touch with you for more questions."

Scooter explained he was on a book tour and that they had yet to find a place to spend the night because he required a pet-friendly hotel or motel. He looked down at his quiet pooch. "Until this happened, we were planning to depart the city and find something on the outskirts before heading east in the morning." Scooter gave him a home phone number and offered to keep tabs by phone.

Detective Keith smiled. "I see no problem. You said you'd be home in a few days, so there's no reason for you to call me. However, the city of Philadelphia is sorry for your inconvenience, Mr. Bissell. Since you helped us get another criminal off of our streets, the least I can do at this late hour is offer you and your brave pup a place to spend the night."

Scooter said to Flash, "Hey, buddy, the nice policeman will give us a place to sleep for the night." Flash yipped.

Detective Keith chuckled. "Hope you don't mind a room at the station where our officers grab a few winks. Three comfortable beds, bathroom and shower, and we'll provide you with a hot breakfast from a local restaurant. What'cha think?"

Scooter shook Detective Keith's hand, and then Ken's. "I don't care what folks say about Philly, we've met two nice guys and a lot of supportive readers. And since we're pooped, your offer is gratefully accepted, Detective."

"Good. Follow me."

Scooter stopped on the sidewalk and pulled his beagle close. "You're one brave dude. Thank you, Flash. Your heroic actions got us out of a big mess. I love you."

I love you too, Scooter. I wasn't going to let that man take your wallet.

CHAPTER 28

Five days later, Scooter opened the Bronco's passenger door and put Flash on the seat. After tossing his ragged briefcase on the backseat, he walked around and crawled behind the wheel. "Well, little buddy, that was our last bookstore on this trip. We visited stores in West Virginia, Ohio, Pennsylvania, New York, New Jersey, Maryland, and Delaware. And we met a bunch of nice people. How do you think it went?" Scooter started the big vehicle to warm up.

Most of it was fun. But not everything. The two bad men and the skunk weren't fun. But a lot of people bought your books. That was good.

"Will you go with me when we go to Florida after the first of the year?"

Flash looked at him and wagged his tri-colored tail. *You bet! We still make a good team.*

Scooter reached over and scratched the beagle's head. "That we do, Flash." Scooter looked at his watch and noticed it was two o'clock on a sunny Saturday afternoon. The quaint bookstore on the Eastern Shore had a surprising turn-out for a morning signing. *Now it's time to give Flash a wonderful surprise.*

They pulled out on the country road and headed toward the Chesapeake Bay Bridge Tunnel. Before they reached the time-saving bridge, they would pass the Pony Diner, owned and operated by Miss Celie. This kind lady was responsible for keeping little Flash alive with scraps and fresh water until the day Scooter and Gabby stopped by on their way to New York for a meeting with the publisher about the novel. Scooter wanted to show Miss Celie how Flash had bounced back from his pitiful condition. And the truth was, Scooter also wanted to see the big-hearted lady with the genuine smile who loved God.

"I'm getting a bit hungry, Flash. How about we stop and get some delicious fried chicken and a homemade biscuit?"

Flash's head shot straight up. *Yeah, Scoot! I love chicken.*

A smile tugged at the corners of Scooter's mouth. "I know just the place, and the lady can really cook. We'll be there in a few minutes."

Good. My stomach has been making noise.

Ahead on the left, Scooter spotted the Pony Diner. A special feeling filled his heart, anticipating a joyful, yet happy, tearful reunion. When he pulled into the small oyster-shell parking lot, his throat tightened. *I hope*

Miss Celie's still winning her battle against cancer. If not, this might not turn out to be such a good surprise.

Scooter parked beside a battered pick-up truck and shut down the Bronco. "I'll bet you remember this place, Flash." Scooter watched the little beagle sit up, place his big paws on the dashboard, and look out the windshield. The pup's tail slowly wagged, and he released a soft, high-pitched yip. He looked at Scooter. *This is Miss Celie's diner.*

Scooter nodded. "Yep." He pulled Flash into his lap and opened his door. "Let's go see her. I hope she's working today," Scooter added, just in case God had called her home.

Scooter, I remember the smell. This is the best part of our trip.

"That it is." They walked across the lot and up to the front door. Scooter said, "You wait out here, and I'll go see if Miss Celie's inside."

Okay. She'll be here, Scoot, cause she never missed a day when I lived in the woods. I'm going to walk over to the bush where Gabby found me. Sometimes I have happy dreams about that day you two found me.

"That's nice, Flash. It was a great day."

The four-paned wooden door squeaked as Scooter opened it and entered. Two older men dressed in bib overalls and flannel shirts sat at one of the small round tables covered with a red and white checkered tablecloth. *Hardworking farmers enjoying a home-cooked lunch.*

From the kitchen came the sound of a woman's voice singing a peppy hymn along with a choir on the radio. *Thank you, God. She's still with us.* He blinked back a few happy tears and stepped up to the wood counter. As if Miss Celie sensed someone behind her, she turned and looked through the opening. Instantly, a smile filled her dark face and lit up her eyes. She grabbed a small white towel and swiped her frail hands as she scooted through the swinging kitchen door. "It's you!" She looked up. "Thank you, dear Lord. Thank you!" Miss Celie came around the counter, opened her thin arms wide, and hugged Scooter. "How's my special friend and his puppies?"

Scooter gently gave her a gentle pat on the back. "We're fine, Miss Celie. I only brought one pup with me today, but you'll be surprised how good he looks." Scooter leaned back and looked into moisture-filled brown eyes. "Our little Flash is outside and wants to see the sweet lady who kept him alive."

Tears trickled down her leathery cheeks. "Oh, Lordy. Let's git out and see Flash," she whispered, turning Scooter loose and making a beeline for the door. "Thank you, Jesus," she said, pulling the door open and hopping down the steps like a five-year-old. Scooter nodded at the two farmers as he passed them on his way out.

When Scooter stepped outside, the sight before him freed a few tears. Neither age nor feeble health prevented Miss Celie from kneeling in the dust on boney knees and cradling a tail-flapping Flash tight to her chest and nuzzling her head in his fur. "Lordy, how I've missed ya, Flash. Ever night I prays for ya. An God's answerin', too." Flash released the quietest yip Scooter had ever heard. "You's looks so clean and healthy. I told ya God would put ya with someone who loved ya." Another quiet yip.

Miss Celie looked up at Scooter, still holding Flash tight...as if she eased up, he would disappear. "How's little Gabby?"

"She's just fine, Miss Celie. Disney's doing a movie about her saving a little girl from drowning, and they're filming in California." He pointed to Flash. "And we really miss her, but she's coming home for Christmas in a few days."

"My, my," cooed the sweet lady. "You's got some sweet pups, Scooter, shore do."

Scooter chuckled. "And little Flash is very talented. He's smart, and no matter what he does, brave or kind, he's always humble."

Miss Celie nuzzled the beagle's head. "That's cause he knows God don't love pride seekers. Ain't that right, Flash?" Another soft yip.

The three of them spent fifteen minutes in the sunshine catching up on some highlights of Flash's activities, leaving out the mugger story to keep Miss Celie from worrying. When two customers pulled up and entered the diner, Scooter mentioned another reason for stopping was for her fried chicken and biscuits. A smile that would shame a sunrise filled the lady's face. "Well, then, git your mess inside, and I'll fry you some breasts and wings. My biscuits is ready to go in the oven." She slowly pushed up to her feet. "Come on in, and that means you, too, Flash. Miss Celie makes the rules around the Pony Diner, right?" Flash's normal yip was his reply.

Two hours later the diner was empty, and Scooter and Flash were full. "Miss Celie, you fry a mean chicken," Scooter said. "I wish you lived closer to Sandbridge."

Her angelic smile appeared. "Does a cook's heart good to hear compliments on their vittles. You come back whenever you git a hankerin' for my chicken." She knelt and scratched Flash's back. "And you keep helpin' Scooter and Gabby when you can. I know you brought a lotta love to them, jest like you did to me." She pulled him tight and hugged him. "I'll keep on prayin' for all of you, ever night."

Scooter stood and gave her a gentle hug. "It's so good to see you again. We're always thinking of you, Miss Celie. Your care for this little pup is treasured by all of us."

"I knowed the Lord had a purpose for this little angel, shore did. This old lady rests well ever night knowin' Flash is with those who love him." Scooter heard her voice crack. "I hope the Lord leaves me around til you come back and visit me. If not, well, you'll know I departed a happy servant of His."

Scooter nodded. "We hope so, too, Miss Celie. Please remember to tell our vet friend how well Flash is doing. We're expecting to see him and his family next summer when they come to the beach for vacation. You take care, Miss Celie. And thank you for all you've done for us."

When Scooter pulled from the lot, Miss Celie stood on the steps, waving with one hand and wiping happy tears with the other. Flash watched through the window until she was out of sight. He yipped once and sighed. *Thank you for stopping by to see Miss Celie. I'll never forget her.*

"You're very welcome, Flash. I won't forget her either." Scooter took a deep breath and exhaled. "Our next stop is Sandbridge Beach, and in three days we go to the airport and pick up Gabby. We're going to have a wonderful Christmas."

We've got a lot to tell her.

"That we do. Now take a nap, and I'll wake you up when we get close to the beach."

Flash curled up in the seat and placed his head on his big paws.

CHAPTER 29

Scooter wrapped the multi-colored lights around his Gordon & Smith seven-foot surfboard, then spaced pieces of clear tape over the coated wire to hold them in place. Flash was pooped from his earlier beach walk and remained stretched out on the floor, stubby legs in the air, watching Scooter's every move. Scooter explained he wanted to have the cottage decorated for Christmas when they brought Gabby back from the airport. "Since I was a little boy, I've liked Christmas, Flash. It's a special time of the year. We will enjoy some delicious food, too. I'm cooking a turkey, mashed potatoes, dressing and gravy, and my favorite, collards." Flash yipped and yawned. "And I have presents for you and Gabby." Scooter stepped back, checking out the twinkling lights strung around his white board. "There aren't many locals down here during the winter, but I'm sure we're the only ones with a surfboard tree."

Scooter, when do you go sign more books?

Scooter reached up and taped a big golden bow on the pointed nose of the surfboard. "In two weeks, a few days after the New Year. We will drive down to Florida and work our way back here. Why? Are you excited about getting back on the road?"

Yeah! We meet a lot of nice people, and I like riding in a car and seeing new things. Flash rolled over and stood. *But I'm really looking forward to seeing Gabby. I miss her.*

Scooter drained his sweet tea and knelt beside Flash. "That makes two of us. It's been five weeks without her. And I'll bet she's ready to come home for a couple of weeks."

To show her that I've missed her, I'm going to share my treats and food with her.

"That's mighty nice." A rush of love and pride raced over Scooter. "That's what Christmas is all about, Flash…sharing with others. Speaking of sharing, you know Gabby is going to share a lot of her stories with us."

That will be neat.

"Yes, it will. Whenever I talk to Vennie or Paul and Ruthie, they tell me how polite and kind Gabby's been with the other dogs and animals. And Mr. Zurl, the movie director, said she's doing a fantastic job with her parts." Scooter rubbed the beagle's back. "The three of us are going to have a great time. And because of you, Gabby and I will have a very special Christmas."

Me?

"You bet! Having you come live with us is the best present we could receive."

Flash looked into Scooter's eyes. *But you said Christmas was about giving and sharing with others.*

"Right."

Well, Scooter, it was you and Gabby who shared with me. You shared your home. I didn't have anything to share with you.

"Oh, yes, you did. You've made our lives happier. See, when people share because of love, then everyone feels good. It's like this, we shared our lives with you, and you shared with us. See, now we're all happy. Understand?"

I guess so. But living here with you is so much better than living alone in the woods, unloved, hungry and sick.

"Okay, here's a thought for you. If it wasn't for you, Darla Kay wouldn't have her bracelet back."

Oh. I forgot that. Flash pawed his eyes. *Scooter?*

"Yeah."

You know I've missed Gabby a lot. And today she's coming home for a few days, right?

"That's right."

Sometimes when I'm walking the beach, I think about how lonely it is without Gabby. And then I remember my sister. Gabby can come home, but my sister can't. That makes me feel sad. I wish my sister could have lived here with us.

Scooter pulled Flash close. "I know, buddy. When we lose someone we love, there's always an empty place in our hearts. You know your sister is in paradise with all the other animals, but you still miss her." Scooter took a deep breath and released a silent sigh. "I'll tell you something. The day we brought you home with us, Gabby and I decided that no matter what the future held for us, we would always try to do good things for people and animals that are less fortunate. So, since we've been blessed with a novel and a movie, we have a lot more money than I ever imagined. You've given me a good idea on what we can do with some of it. Once Gabby's home and we're sitting around, I'll tell you. I'm sure Gabby will approve of it. And we'll do it in the memory of your sister. How's that?"

Flash dropped his head. *I don't really understand what you mean, but if it's about my sister, that's real nice.*

Scooter took a deep breath. "You better go tend to your business. It's time for us to go pick up Gabby from the airport."

Flash hopped up, tail flapping and floppy ears attempting to stand straight. *Oh boy, Scoot-toot! I'll be right back.* The short-legged pup squeezed through the opening in the sliding door and disappeared down the deck stairs.

"There goes one compassionate canine." As Scooter entered the bedroom to change clothes, he pictured Gabby sprinting from the Disney G5. "Life's good!"

Flash moved through the Norfolk International Airport terminal like his hind end was on fire. The leash remained taut, even though Scooter quick-stepped across the tile floor. They finally made it to the private jet counter and were greeted by the friendly, grey-haired lady. "Merry Christmas to my favorite clients." She hustled around the podium and shook Scooter's hand, then bent over to give Flash a gentle pat on the head. "I know you are here for Miss Gabby. I'll bet you've missed her."

Scooter nodded. "And a very Merry Christmas to you, too. And, yes, it seems more like five months instead of five weeks. Right, Flash?" The pup yipped once.

The efficient lady returned to her counter and picked up a pink slip of paper. "The flight is on time," she glanced at the clock on the wall, "and should land in fifteen minutes."

"That's great." Before Scooter could say more, a well-dressed man carrying a leather briefcase stepped up, nodded to him, and cut his red-rimmed eyes at Flash. Scooter and Flash backed away from the counter, unsure from the man's stern look whether he was an animal lover or not. They took a seat while the woman assisted him.

The customer's attitude and gruff words told Scooter this fellow would not make the lady's list of 'favorite clients'. Scooter figured he lacked courtesy and the Christmas spirit. *I guess it takes all kinds.*

The customer and lady were still discussing a late flight when she excused herself. "Please excuse me for a minute, sir." She stepped over beside Scooter and rolled her eyes. "You two may go out to the waiting area on the tarmac. The Disney jet has landed and is rolling up. I'll see you when you come in with Gabby." She smiled and returned to straighten out the situation with Mr. Unhappy.

Scooter and Flash stood outside in the unseasonably warm sunshine. "There's the plane. You think Gabby is excited?"

Yeah, Scoot! I think she's looking out the window right now.

"I'll bet so. And she'll run like the wind to greet us."

I would.

The G5 turned at the end of the runway and pulled up, nose toward the building, and stopped about fifty yards away. Through the windshield, Scooter saw Captain Brian Blow throw up his hand. After shutting down the powerful engines, the door slowly opened and folded down. "Here we go, Flash!" The beagle howled and tugged against his leash. "Let's go over and greet our Gabby." Scooter thought his arm would be yanked from the socket when Flash rocketed forward. "Easy, dude."

Lieutenant Wilson appeared in the doorway. "Howdy, Scooter and Flash! We brought someone to see you." He turned and said something, then disappeared aside. Unleashed, Gabby bolted down the blue-carpeted steps like a black shadow.

Scooter clapped his hands. Flash barked. An excited Gabby hollered, *I'm back!* She leaped into Scooter's arms and he lost his balance and toppled onto his backside. "Hey, girl! We've missed you a bunch." Breaking one of Scooter's rules, she licked his face like it was a scoop of ice cream. *I missed you both! I'm so glad to be home!* She crawled from Scooter's chest and bounced over and nudged and pawed Flash. *Hey, little buddy! Glad you took care of Scoot-toot!*

I missed you, Gabby! Wait until you see our Christmas surfboard.
Gabby backed up. *Our what?*
Scooter put lights on one of his surfboards.

Wilson and Blow came down the G5's steps. Scooter cautioned, "Easy on the talking, pups. We have company." He pushed up from the asphalt, wiped off his pants, and moved to greet his pilot friends. They shook hands as Scooter said, "It's good to see you again. I hope Gabby was no problem flying alone."

Captain Blow shook his head. "Not one bit, Scooter. In fact, she was a different dog." He chuckled. "I think it had something to do with coming to see you."

Gabby nuzzled up beside Scooter, her tail whipping his leg. "Lt. Wilson, did Gabby eat during the flight?"

"Does a bear poop in the woods?" The men laughed as Scooter rubbed Gabby's ears. "She did sleep for most of the flight," added Wilson.

They talked for a few minutes before Blow said they needed to refuel and head back. They were scheduled to pick Gabby up on January 3rd. "Are you going back with her, Scooter?" asked Wilson.

"No, I'm still doing the book tour. But we're scheduled to be in Burbank around the middle of January for a meeting and shooting a few closing scenes featuring Gabby and our beagle buddy."

They wished each other Merry Christmas and a Happy New Year, and the Sandbridge trio watched as the pilots disappeared into the shiny G5.

"Gabby, are you ready to hit your beach?"
I'm ready! And I can't imagine why you decorated a surfboard. Oh, and I've got a few stories to tell you.
Scooter said you would have stories.

"Let's go inside and see the nice lady at the counter. She's also excited to see you, Gabby. Then we'll hop in the Datsun and head to Sandbridge."

I never thought the word Sandbridge would sound so good to my ears. Come on, let's go!

CHAPTER 30

Gabby sat high and proud in the passenger seat as Scooter zipped the 240Z down the country road toward Sandbridge. Her head swiveled from front to back as she shared humorous experiences not only from the studio, but also from Vennie's animal farm and Paul and Ruthie's house. Flash's reflection filled the rearview mirror, his brown eyes big as saucers as he hung on to Gabby's every word. Scooter grinned as he heard his two pooches getting reacquainted. *They really did miss each other.*

When there was a short break in the storytelling, Scooter said, "Does Vennie have a lot of neat animals?"

Gabby looked at Scooter and then turned to Flash. *Little buddy, you would wear out your sniffer on her farm. She has monkeys, ferrets, rabbits, and lots of dogs and cats, and some other animals I've never seen or heard of. Oh, and she has two big birds that talk, and they live inside her big house, too.*

Are the animals wild?

Yeah. Well, sort of. See, they live in huge cages with trees and rocks and water ponds, like they were free.

Did you talk to the birds?

No, because Vennie was always with me. Gabby looked at Scooter.

Scooter gave her a pat on the head. "Very good, Baboo."

When they reached Pungo, a few miles west of Sandbridge, Scooter turned into the small country store. "I need to fill up with gas. You two relax. I'll be right back." He slipped from the sports car and closed the door.

"Merry Christmas, Scooter!"

Scooter instantly recognized the charming, feminine voice behind him. "And the same to you, Kaycee!" He turned around, greeted by her authentic smile that was seen by many locals at nine o'clock each morning on her talk show, Sunshine & Rainbows. "Nice to see you again, dear."

Kaycee stepped up and gave him a warm hug, and a fragrance of mild vanilla filled the air. She glanced into the Z's back glass. "Wow! You have another doggie." She stuck her head into the open driver's window. "Hey, Gabby! Who's your new friend? He's a real cutie."

Scooter explained how they found the flea-infested and emaciated little Flash living in the woods on the Eastern Shore. After a kind vet in Maryland treated him for several days, they brought him home. "He's doing fine now."

"Aww, that's so cruel when wretched people abuse and throw animals out like they're trash. The good part of this story is now Flash has a loving home at the beach. Were you and Gabby visiting friends on the Eastern Shore or on vacation?"

Not wanting to toot a personal horn, Scooter casually mentioned the publication of his debut novel by a New York company. "Honestly, Gabby played the major role in getting me face time with the publisher because she bravely rescued his little daughter from some rough waves and undertow. If not for her actions, their vacation could've quickly turned tragic."

Wide-eyed, Kaycee stood motionless, listening intently to the story. Scooter imagined her skilled interviewer wheels spinning. "Oh, my," she whispered, looking back inside the car at Gabby. "You're amazing, girl."

"Now I have two pooches to keep me straight."

Kaycee shook her brown, shoulder-length hair from her eyes. "Please don't think I'm bugging you or being self-promoting, Scooter, but would you consider bringing the pups on my show and sharing this wonderful story?"

Clicking off and removing the nozzle from the Z's gas tank, Scooter returned it to the slot on the pump. "I don't know, Kaycee. I mean, your show is highly rated and respected, but..."

Not being one to allow a good story to slip away, Kaycee produced another award-winning smile. "If you think the publisher would have a problem with us putting his personal story out, even though New York's outside of our market, I'll simply leave out his name."

Scooter scratched his head and wondered if Disney would have concerns about it since they had not even finished the movie about Gabby's rescue. Unsure of the legalities, the last thing he needed was to overstep his bounds and break some fine-printed promotion clause. He also knew if he told Kaycee about Disney's project, she would be drooling to announce the 'big scoop'. However, if Disney approved, he would love for his friend to have the first opportunity to feature Gabby. "Kaycee, if it were up to me, we would gladly appear on your program. But there's a little more to Gabby's story, and I should make a phone call before committing. Can I call you with an answer tomorrow?"

A puzzled look filled her twinkling green eyes. "Oh, sure. If it's a go, I'd like to have you on the day after tomorrow. This heartwarming story is ideal for the Christmas season. And, as you know, Sunshine & Rainbows only features happy, uplifting stories." She pulled a colorful business card from the huge pocketbook decorated with seashells and handed it to him. "I really appreciate this, Scooter."

"The day after tomorrow is the day before Christmas Eve."

Kaycee's priceless smile returned. "Yep. And if the segment goes as I expect it will, I'll request the station run it again on Christmas Eve morning. Maybe animal lovers will choose to adopt an unwanted pooch or kitty for Christmas."

Scooter placed her card in his pocket. "That's a good idea. Thank you for understanding. If we're permitted to do this, you'll get the full story." He smiled. "And I'm sure Gabby will enjoy being on television. Flash could be a mite timid because everything's still new to him. However, he's been accompanying me on the book-signing tour, so he's getting 'on the job' training about humans and their habits."

Kaycee giggled. After she said good bye to the pups, they walked together into the store so Scooter could pay. "I'll call you tomorrow, Kaycee. And thanks for your patience and understanding. I hope everything works out for both of us."

As Scooter returned to the car, he decided not to mention Kaycee's offer until he had the green light. *Gabby's excitement might be for naught...and she wouldn't take kindly to that.*

"Home again, home again, jiggety jog," announced Scooter as he shut down the Z. Gabby bounced like a rubber ball in the seat. *Let us out, Scoot! I've gotta get on my beach and into some warmer water.*

Scooter opened his door, and exactly like Gabby did on the day he brought her from the shelter, she flew past him like a black flash. As he laughed out loud, Flash scrambled between the bucket seats, climbed over his lap, and shot out the door. Gabby sprinted up the dune like a crab on fire. Flash quickly pumped his stubby lets up and down, still falling behind. *Have fun.*

By the time Scooter stepped out onto his deck with a glass of water, Gabby was doggie paddling over the knee-high breakers, dipping her head in and out of the blue-green water. "I'm as happy to have you back home as you are to be here, Gabby." After watching for a few minutes, he hustled inside and pulled their gifts from the hall closet. "With presents around the lighted surfboard, Gabby will go easy with her taunts."

No sooner than he had arranged the colorful boxes, Scooter heard the pooches plodding up the deck steps. He grabbed a towel from the bathroom and met the soaked Gabby at the sliding door. "Let me give you a quick wipe before you drip on the carpet."

Hurry up, Scooter. Flash wants my opinion on your surfboard tree.

I think it's neat. Flash entered and stood beside the tree. ***Scooter, what are all of these fancy boxes around it?***

Gabby's ears perked when Scooter replied, "They are gifts for you and Gabby from me."

Okay, I'm dry, Scoot-toot. Gabby wiggled free from his grasp and slipped through the door. On damp paws, she slid across the kitchen floor and came to a stop in front of the twinkling surfboard. Her eyes slowly looked it up and down. *It doesn't look as bad as I imagined. Which presents are mine, Scoot?*

Scooter laughed. "You two are very talented, but as yet, you can't read, and each gift has a tag with a name on it. So you have to wait until Christmas morning. And don't start bugging me with questions. Be patient."

Come on, Scooter-tooter, please.

"No. Now who's hungry for a treat?"

I am.

I'm starving.

Scooter opened a new box of Milk Bones. "No surprise there."

The pups gobbled the treats as Scooter fished Jan's card from his wallet. "Hope she hasn't left work yet." After dialing the number, he waited and watched the pups devouring their treats. Jan's upbeat voice greeted him. "This is Jan Robbins. May I help you?"

"Hey, Jan. It's Scooter in Virginia Beach. How are you?"

"What a pleasant surprise. I'll bet our soon-to-be-famous puppy is right beside you."

Scooter looked over at Gabby as she pawed her muzzle. "Yep. She's relaxing with her buddy, Flash. We got home from the airport an hour ago. She's already been in the Atlantic and devoured a treat. The pilots said she did great on the flight."

"That doesn't surprise me. She's very intelligent. So, to what do I owe this special phone call?"

"Excuse me for a second, Jan." He looked at his furry companions. "How about you two go out on the deck while I talk business?" He waited while they trotted outside, then he walked over and closed the door.

Scooter picked up the phone and explained the situation concerning Kaycee's request. He waited while Jan made an inner-office call. She clicked back on the line. "I buzzed Blaine. He says there's nothing in the contract preventing it. And we agreed it's a good way to create interest in your community for the upcoming movie. I hope the station will make a tape of the interview, and you can bring us a copy on your next visit. I'd love to see you all on television."

"That's good news, Jan. Kaycee is a highly-rated host and lives in Sandbridge. I'm sure she will make you a tape. Hey, it would be neat if you pulled some strings and had your local station air it. That would be great exposure for Disney and Kaycee."

"I'll do my best." In the background, another ringing phone sliced into Jan's words. "I'm sorry, Scooter, I've got another call. Give both doggies a hug for me. See ya."

"Thanks, Jan."

Scooter dialed Darla Kay's number to tell her Gabby was back home and see if she wanted to join them for supper, featuring his Sandbridge burgers. When she answered, he informed her the trio was now happily in Sandbridge. Her reply to his invitation was an immediate 'yes'. "Great. We'll see you around six o'clock. Don't bring anything, except your smiling face. And I have a really cool announcement to make after supper."

"Ooh, now you're teasing me, Scooter. I'll see you at six."

Scooter hung up the phone, settled on the sofa, and motioned the pups to sit at his feet. "We need to have a 'family' meeting."

With a puzzled stare, Gabby asked, *Family meeting? We've never had...whatever it is. What is it?*

Scooter reminded Gabby of their decision to do whatever they could to help the less fortunate animals and people. He explained that due to their good fortune with landing the novel and the movie, the money would allow them to do much more for others. To illustrate, he used the Christmas gifts as an example of giving. Both pups quickly grasped the concept.

"So I've been thinking of a way we could help unwanted pups and kittens find good homes. See what you think of this idea. I'll contact the S.P.C.A. in the three nearby cities and the Norfolk Animal Care Center and offer to pay all of the adoption fees, including shots and a donation of a bag of food and two bowls, for the first one hundred adoptions. We will call this program Adoption Assistance. Sound good?"

That's nice, Scooter, but I don't know anything about fees and shots. Me, either, Flash, but I don't like shots. Needles hurt.

Scooter chuckled. "Well, adopting an animal is not free. The shelters must charge a fee to help them pay expenses to care for the animals. Their normal charge for adoption, including everything, is between eighty and a hundred dollars. So we would pay the fees, and the people would get their puppy or kitten for free. This should be a great incentive, and Christmas is the best time to do it. And, I think we should do this in memory of Flash's sister who was killed by the truck."

Gabby looked at Flash and moved up against him. *I vote 'yes', and we should do it...every Christmas.* She placed her paw on the beagle's back.

Scooter, my sister would be so happy. I vote 'yes', too. And thank you for thinking of her.

Scooter smiled. "Hop up here with me." They both snuggled close. "This act of kindness for the lonely animals and the loving people will guarantee everyone, us included, will experience the true meaning of Christmas. I'm proud of you both." He looked down at Flash. "Your name came from the men who ate at the Pony Diner and saw how fast you could run. Your sister didn't have a name, did she?"

Flash shook his head.

We need to give her a name, Scoot.

"Right, Gabby. All animals should have a name. Flash, do you have any suggestions?"

I don't know. Will you all help me think of one?

I will, Flash. What was she like? See, my name was Gabriella when Scooter adopted me, but he changed it to Gabby. She looked at Scooter. *Would you care to give Flash the background on my name change?*

Scooter nodded. "Flash, I thought it was too fancy for a beach guy to have a dog with that name."

You're not getting off that easy.

"Okay. I shortened her name to Gabby because she was talking to me before I even found her in the cage."

That's a good name, because she does talk a lot. But I'm glad she does. I've learned a lot from her.

Thank you, Flash. Besides, I've grown to like my name.

"I'll leave it up to you two to name Flash's sister. Now, I'm going to call these four shelters and tell them about our program so they can begin their advertising. Since Darla Kay lives in town, maybe she'll help us by taking each location a check to cover twenty five adoptions."

Good idea, Scoot. You're always doing stuff to move up to the top of her list, you sly fox. Gabby yipped and was joined by Flash.

Scooter hugged them tightly. "Both of you are something. But I love you the way you are."

Gabby and Flash settled in a corner of the room and discussed possible names for Flash's sister. Scooter made the calls, amazed at how receptive each facility was. They gratefully agreed that a check would be fine, and they would make signs and begin telling potential adoptive families immediately. Scooter promised they would have the check tomorrow. He hung up the phone, feeling better than he ever imagined. "It's a go, pooches! Our program is now underway in all four shelters! I think a celebration is in order."

Gabby and little Flash yipped as they hustled into the kitchen. Scooter whispered, "Life is real good."

As expected, Scooter's beach burgers were a hit. When the canines received their bowls of burger and Puppy Chow, Darla Kay and Scooter realized Flash's slow, precise eating technique was as much a part of his personality as his ability to use his sensitive sniffer. "Like us, Scooter, we're all different," whispered Darla Kay, a tiny smile on her lips.

After the delicious meal, they all retired to the deck and watched the stars appearing in the clear night sky. The light breeze had cooled just enough to accent the Christmas season at Sandbridge. Both pooches stretched out, trance-like, as they watched cotton-topped waves roll onto shore. Scooter felt the time was perfect for his announcement. He reached over and took Darla Kay's hand. "I promised to tell you about a special offer the pups and I have been given. Want to hear about it?" He chuckled when Gabby and Flash turned to face him. "I assume that's a 'yes' from the curious canines," he said.

"I vote yes, too, Scooter."

Scooter explained about telling Kaycee how Gabby and her lifesaving of little Kay kicked off the publication of 'If Bullfrogs Had Wings' by putting him face to face with a real publisher. Then he told Kaycee how they came upon little Flash in the woods on the Eastern Shore. When Scooter finished, he took a deep breath. "I know that sounds confusing, but that's how it unfolded, because Kaycee first asked how we acquired little Flash. But here's the cool news."

Gabby yipped. Flash followed suit. Darla Kay waited anxiously.

"On Thursday, the three of us will be guests on Kaycee's show Sunshine & Rainbows at nine o'clock!" Scooter kissed Darla Kay on the cheek, then moved from his chair and knelt beside his companions. "Won't we be a sight for sore eyes?"

Darla Kay applauded. "I think it's great! And that's a heartwarming show, too."

"Kaycee said she will request the station run the segment again on Christmas Eve morning. She hopes people see how special adopted dogs and cats are, and some may choose to visit a shelter and give one a loving home." Scooter pulled Gabby and Flash tight against his thigh. "I know my Christmas will be much better because of these two." Gabby and Flash yipped again. Scooter put his arm around Darla Kay. "And also because of you." They kissed, and Gabby yipped twice.

"And I feel the same way." Darla Kay laid her head on his shoulder.

Then Scooter proudly shared the news of their new Adoption Assistance program with her. "We want to make this Christmas special for unwanted animals and kind-hearted animal lovers. We've decided to do it every Christmas." Scooter received a hug and another kiss from a teary-eyed Darla Kay and a yip from Gabby. "I'm honored to deliver the checks and be a part of something so wonderful."

After Darla Kay left for home, Scooter and his furry friends hit the sack, exhausted. "Are you two excited about going on television with Kaycee?"

Gabby stretched out on her back on the foot of the bed. *I am, but it's not quite as exciting for me, since I'll be in a movie. At least I won't be nervous.*

I'm nervous. But we don't have to talk like you will, Scoot.

"Both of you are correct. And, Flash, I'm glad you mentioned talking. Please don't let a word slip out…please. Oh, and I'll also ask Kaycee to announce our adoption program to her viewers. That will be excellent advertising." He turned out the light.

Scoot?

"Yes."

It feels so good to be back in my own bed.

"I'm sure it does, Baboo. Good night and sleep tight and sweet dreams. Maybe a name for Flash's sister will come to you while you're dreaming."

I'll be dreaming about our Christmas meal, Scoot. We'll tackle the name tomorrow while we walk on the beach.

I'll dream about our gifts and helping unwanted animals find a good home, like mine.

"We're very blessed. Good night."

CHAPTER 31

The following morning lacked the orange orb rising from the Atlantic due to low-hanging, moisture-laden clouds. Scattered raindrops hit, paused, and trickled down the windows like runaway diamonds. Scooter situated his pillow against the headboard and propped up, pleased to see both dogs still wrapped comfortably in slumber. "I hope they'll enjoy being on Kaycee's show tomorrow," he whispered.

As his 'to-do' list appeared in his head, he quickly realized his day would be chock-full. First thing, call Kaycee before she left for the station to give her as much lead time as possible. Next, he needed to carefully go over the script to add specific details to the first draft of the new ending featuring Flash. Upon completion, he would call Paul with the additions and suggestions. Then a quick visit to the grocery store for Christmas vittles, which would include a turkey, ham, and traditional sides. The afternoon required he call Jason for the times and addresses on the next leg of his book tour. "No more laid-back beach life," he said, slipping from the warm bed and into the bathroom for a hot shower.

Scooter stood in the kitchen, stirring his coffee and punching out Kaycee's home phone number. She answered on the second ring, out of breath. "Good morning."

"Good news, Kaycee." Scooter knew she was hustling around preparing to leave for the station, so he condensed his conversation with Jan and chose to unveil the adoption program when he saw her.

"I'm thrilled, Scooter! And, yes, you'll receive a taped copy of the show before you leave the studio. So we'll meet at eight-thirty in the morning. The receptionist will be expecting you and show you to my office. I can't wait! Oh, and I'm giving the audience a 'tease' as I close today's show. I want to pique our viewers' curiosity. Okay, I've got to run. See you in the morning."

As Scooter hung up, Gabby and Flash moseyed into the kitchen. Flash's mouth was wide open in the midst of a yawn. "Well, look what the cat drug in," Scooter said.

Nix on the cat jokes, Scoot. Breakfast, please. This movie star is starving.

"Well, excuse me, Gabby. I'll get right on it. Wouldn't want our star to be hungry." He picked up their bowls. "Are you hungry, Flash?"

Yes.

The furry companions dined on their breakfast. "I talked to Kaycee. We're to be at the television studio in Norfolk tomorrow morning at eight-thirty."

Is it okay if we yip when you say something about us?

I don't want to yip, Gabby. I'm nervous, and we're not even there.

Stick with me. I'll show you how to be cool in front of a camera.

"The interview is going to be about you both. I don't mind a yip or two, but not every time you're mentioned. That would drive the viewers nuts."

You're a lot stricter than Wayne, and he's a professional director. He likes me to, ah...he calls it...ad-lib. So I'll use my expertise and pick the two best places to yip. Okay?

"Fine. Now, I've got a lot to do today, so before it rains any harder, you go tend to business. Oh, and if you're nice, Gabby, I'll tell you what happened to us in Philadelphia and how Flash prevented a robbery or maybe something worse."

Gabby's stare flipped over to Flash. *What? Somebody tried to hurt you? Forget my run to the pier. I want to hear this.*

Scooter felt a jolt of pride to see Gabby's interest in her new companion's actions. "Flash might not be big, but he's twenty pounds of pure bravery."

Come on, let's tend to business, Flash. I like exciting stories.

It's not exciting.

I'll be the judge of that. Remember, I know excitement.

They disappeared down the back steps, as quick as if they were being chased by hornets. Scooter opened his briefcase and pulled out the script to make additions to the movie ending. "Okay, the focus is on little Flash and his timid actions until he became more comfortable with those who love and care for him. And how well he behaves with the special needs children. I'll throw in his strict eating technique in case Paul and Ruthie might want to use it."

Scooter was hanging up the phone after giving Paul the additions for the script when the pooches returned, damp from chilly drizzle delivered by the north wind. Scooter grabbed the 'wipe-down' towel and gave them a quick once-over. "Okay, get comfortable, it's story time." Scooter took a seat on the sofa and leaned back. Gabby and Flash settled at his feet, heads on paws and eyes glued on him.

"We had a book signing at a large bookstore in Philadelphia. When we left it was ten o'clock at night, very cold and raining, like it is now. Our rental Bronco was parked behind the building in a small lot. So Flash and I walk the dimly-lit sidewalk and turn left and enter a narrow alley, with one measly light, toward the lot. Suddenly, two young men dressed in baggy jeans and coats step in front of us. Their hands remained deep in their pockets. I couldn't see their faces too good because they wore dark stocking caps pulled down low, barely above their eyes." Scooter paused and sipped his sweet tea.

Gabby extended her paw and tapped Scooter's foot. *Come on, Scoot. I'm the only one here that does not know what happened...the suspense is getting to me.*

"Okay. So one of the guys says, 'It's real late to be in this bad part of town, man.' I felt Flash move up against my leg. I held his leash tight and said, 'We're just going to our car and then home.' Both men moved up closer and one says, 'You gotta pay me to get your car. Now give me your money!' Then he pulls his hand from a pocket, and he's holding a big knife." Scooter sips again.

Scooter!

"I needed to buy some time, so I said, 'I'm broke, man.' I looked down at Flash and said, 'I spent all my money on his dog food.' You didn't know this, but I was in the Army for three years, and a member of the Green Berets, and I learned how to protect myself and disarm enemies. So I wanted to check out my options. The only way out was to get hold of the knife, and I didn't know if the other guy had a weapon. I told him, 'I don't have any money.'

Were you scared?

I was.

When Scooter finished the whole story, Gabby's eyes bulged from her head and her mouth gaped open. *Flash really bit the man? Wow!* She looked at the little beagle and shook her head. *I didn't know you had it in you, Flash. You're brave.*

I'm not brave. Nobody was going to take Scooter's wallet.

Gabby looked from Flash to Scooter, still wide-eyed. *I'm serious, you are brave. I'm glad nothing bad happened to you two. If I'd been there, the man who ran would've had me hot on his heels.* She leaned against Flash. *Thank you for protecting our Scooter. I'm proud of you.*

You're welcome, but I know you would have done the same thing. Saving the little girl from drowning was brave. I couldn't have done that.

"Well, let's hope we never have to face that kind of threat again. And I know we all would do whatever was needed to protect each other."

Scooter knelt on the floor between two very special dogs and cuddled them against his chest. "You both are amazing. I'm a lucky guy to have you, and we do make one unbeatable team. I love you. Now, we have time for one more 'road' story. This one's funny, Gabby. You know how Flash likes to sniff out wild animals?"

Like the fox? Yeah, he'd rather sniff than eat.

"Maybe Flash should tell you about meeting a wild animal in Pennsylvania." He tapped Flash on the back. "Tell Gabby about your new friend. Don't forget the baths." Scooter chuckled. Gabby's eyes again widened.

Tell me, Flash. Did you meet a fox face to face?

Flash shook his head, and, like any good storyteller, he started at the beginning. With accurate detail, he unfolded his skunk story with 'first person' excitement. Even Scooter enjoyed hearing it again.

One minute Gabby was perked up with anticipation and concern about her little buddy, and then once the spraying was clearly described in detail, she instantly switched to laughter, mingled with several 'PU's' and 'oh, no's'. Finally, when Flash detailed the two baths, Gabby became overwhelmed with 'why's and wonders'. *That'll teach you about sniffing things you don't know about. You should focus on foods like burgers and steaks, they don't stink...and they're delicious to eat.*

I don't ever want to meet another skunk.

"Okay, Gabby, enough stories for tonight. We want to hear about your experiences in California, but we have to wait until tomorrow. It's been a long, relaxing day and we've got a busy one tomorrow. It's time to hit the hay. You go to math class and hurry back."

None of my stories come close to these. Gabby yipped. *My story is in a movie.*

I can't wait to see it.

You're going to be in it.

Oh, that's right.

"Time for math class," said Scooter, around a yawn.

The pooches slipped out onto the wet deck and down the steps while Scooter held the door and waited. Everyone settled down for the night. Gabby said, *And I thought my movie was exciting. You two are real heroes. Good night.*

So are you and Scooter. 'Night.

Scooter turned off the light and fluffed his pillows. "Sleep tight. We'll see what tomorrow holds for the terrific trio. Remember, together we can overcome anything."

CHAPTER 32

Kaycee McCoy greeted Scooter and the pooches outside her office wearing a smile and smartly dressed for her TV show. Brown, sun-kissed hair flowed naturally, neatly framing an attractive face. "Good morning! Welcome to Sunshine & Rainbows." She shook hands with Scooter, then leaned down and made over Gabby and Flash. "You are the first animals to visit my show. Make yourselves at home."

"Don't give them that much freedom, Kaycee." Scooter handed her a copy of his new novel. "This is from all of us. I hope you enjoy it."

"Oh," she cooed. "Thank you!" She slowly read the title, "If Bullfrogs Had Wings. What a catchy title." She opened the front cover. "And you signed it from all of you. This is so sweet. I'll mention it on the air."

"It's our Christmas gift to you."

"You are the best." She glanced at her dainty gold watch. "Time to enter Kaycee's land of bright lights. Follow me."

A large, colorfully-decorated Christmas tree sat off to one side of the roomy, curved beige sofa. The show's producer situated Scooter and Kaycee so they would comfortably face each other without having to turn. Gabby and Flash were freed from their leashes and placed between Scooter and Kaycee's feet. The oak coffee table was moved a few feet to Scooter's right so the pups could be viewed by thousands of people in Hampton Roads and Southeastern North Carolina. Kaycee placed the tan-colored index card, containing a short outline, beside her leg. "I'll ask a question and you answer, and don't feel rushed. When our producer holds up two fingers, that means we have two minutes before a commercial break. Then he will hold up five fingers, meaning we're off in five seconds. He will then count them down. Once we're off air, he'll say, 'Clear'. After the break, he'll count us back 'on air' using a five-finger countdown . Got it?"

Scooter cleared his throat and nodded. "Oh, when I say something special about one of my four-legged friends, you might hear a little yip. They shouldn't do it more than a couple of times. Is that okay?" Using his knees, he nudged each of them, a reminder he would be counting. Gabby yipped once. "See, that's what I mean."

Kaycee giggled. "Of course! It's perfect. It'll add a splash of humor to our show."

The producer stepped forward. "Two minutes, Kaycee. We'll break after eight minutes."

"Thank you, Dean."

The show's theme music was one of Scooter's favorites. An instrumental of The Rascals' 'It's a Beautiful Morning' slipped through unseen speakers as Dean positioned himself beside the large camera on wheels. Bright, hot lights filled the set. Everyone, including Flash and Gabby, watched as Dean's fingers, one at a time, began to fold into his palm. Once he made a tight fist, he stepped back and nodded. Scooter took a deep breath as butterflies swarmed inside his stomach.

Kaycee introduced Scooter as Dooley 'Scooter' Bissell, and then she reached over and touched each puppy on the head and said their names. She gave a short summary about the three of them living at Sandbridge Beach. Then she opened the interview with a question about how Scooter adopted Gabby first, and then how, together, they rescued Flash, who was abandoned on the Eastern Shore.

Kaycee asked Scooter what prompted him to visit the SPCA to adopt a puppy. "One morning, I saw a couple strolling down the beach with a young puppy. They looked so happy and content watching their pup playing in the water. It'd been years since I had a dog, so I decided it was time to help an unwanted puppy. So I made a visit to the local SPCA." He smiled. "And the truth is...Gabby adopted me." Scooter waited for Kaycee to finish laughing while she stroked Gabby's head. "Fortunately, we found Flash when we were on our way to New York to see the publisher about my debut novel. We stopped at a small country diner. Gabby got a whiff of something in the woods. It turned out to be little Flash. She coaxed him out using a piece of chicken, and within a few minutes, she had the scared beagle settled. Flash was in real bad physical shape, so we took him to a vet in Salisbury to be fixed up while we made the trip to New York. The rest is history." He looked down at both of his companions. "Now we are three."

Kaycee's green eyes were moist. "That's such a sweet story, Scooter. I sense you do not regret bringing them into your life. There are so many unwanted animals out there who need a loving home, but...I'm getting ahead of myself."

The producer signaled for two minutes.

"Scooter, you told me about Gabby jumping into the rough ocean one day and pulling a little girl to safety."

"Yes, Kaycee. When Gabby first came to the beach, she had never been in the water. She was swamped by her first wave, and she immediately shied away from entering the water again. On this particular morning, I was surfing and saw the little girl bobbing on the surface and being pulled out by the current. Thankfully, she was wearing a life vest. Helpless, I watched Gabby dive in, paddle through the waves, grab the vest, and swim the girl to the beach." Gabby looked up at him and yipped. "It turns out the girl's father was a publisher in New York. Over burgers the next evening, I told him about my novel, and he wanted to read it. And he liked it. So, technically, Gabby opened the door to get my novel in front of a publisher. The rest is history." Gabby yipped twice.

The producer counted down as Kaycee said, "She's a special puppy. When we come back, we'll hear about her starring in a Disney movie. Stay tuned, folks."

After the producer took them off air for the first commercial break, Kaycee said, "Perfect, just perfect, Scooter. You're a professional interviewee."

"Thank you. You can't see the butterflies doing the jitterbug in my stomach." Gabby yipped. Scooter knew she was poking fun at his noticeable tension.

"Now, this next segment will be about Gabby and the Disney movie. Do you know when it will be in theatres?"

"They said if all goes as expected, probably in May," replied Scooter.

"Good. Say it exactly like that. I'll mention to the viewers to keep an eye out for it."

When they were back on the air, Kaycee asked leading questions about how the movie deal came to be. Scooter's answers remained tight and to the point, as pride for his pups filled his eyes. Nearing the end of the segment, Kaycee asked, "I'll bet you'll treat these special pups to several steak dinners with the Disney check, right?"

Scooter swallowed, not knowing why, because his mouth was desert-dry. He forced a smile. "Yeah. I guess so." Both dogs yipped. Scooter added, "I do plan to expand our Sandbridge Surf School to more schools that serve special needs children. We will cut back on the price so smaller schools can participate. Many of them don't have budgets for outside activities." He reached down and rubbed the pups' heads. "We are very fortunate to be able to provide these children with unforgettable memories of their trips to the beach. And Gabby and Flash love showing off and fetching balls and Frisbees for them."

"That's so heartwarming, Scooter." Kaycee saw the producer give the two minute countdown to off-air. "It's so rewarding to feature people like you. Everyone loves happy, upbeat stories, especially during this time of the year. And speaking of 'happy', Scooter and his furry friends brought me a Christmas present." She held up the novel. "The title is so intriguing, 'If Bullfrogs Had Wings'. You said it's a Young Adult and Baby Boomer novel, so I'll certainly read it, because I still qualify as a young adult. If any of our viewers are looking for last minute gifts, go to a bookstore and get a copy. I guarantee it will make a great gift."

"Thank you, Kaycee."

Kaycee placed the book on the table and clapped her hands once. "I have another gift from Scooter and his cute companions for one hundred of you. In an effort to help unwanted puppies and kittens find a loving home, they have initiated a wonderful Christmas program in memory of Flash's little sister. Sadly, she was run over by a truck several days after she and Flash were thrown out on the side of the road. So, their Adoption Assistance Program will benefit the first one hundred animal lovers who want to adopt a puppy or kitty. Contact the local shelters and ask about it. If you're willing to provide loving care and a good home to an unwanted animal, this program will pay every cent of the adoption fee. Remember, giving is what Christmas is truly about. And don't forget to keep your eyes open next summer for the Disney movie starring Gabby. If everything remains on schedule, it should be in theatres this May." She reached over and shook Scooter's hand. "Thank you, Scooter and pups, for being my special guests today. And to all of my viewing friends for watching Sunshine & Rainbows! Merry Christmas! Tell your friends who might have missed today's fantastic show, we're airing this feature on Scooter, Gabby, and Flash again tomorrow."

"We're clear!" announced Dean. "Great show! I know my wife and I are going to take advantage of your new program, Scooter. He shook Scooter's hand and pet Gabby and Flash on the head.

Kaycee bubbled with excitement as she praised the trio for allowing her the opportunity to feature them on her show. "This one goes down as my best ever, Scooter. I hope your adoption program is a big hit, and one-hundred puppies and kitties will find a loving home. You are the perfect example of a happy pet owner." When they neared the front door, a young man approached, holding a video tape. "Ms. McCoy, here's the show copy you requested."

"Thank you, Robert." She handed it to Scooter.

Scooter said, "I talked to Disney about airing this in California and they also plan to run it in Florida. You're going to be famous, Kaycee." He gave her a gentle hug. "Thank you for having us. I hope kind-hearted people will decide to adopt some homeless pets. As you correctly said, my life has been more worthwhile since they've been a part of it." He smiled. "And, I'm not talking about the novel or the movie."

"I know you aren't, Scooter. That was only the icing on the cake. I'll let you go back to the beach and relax. Merry Christmas and Happy New Year. And thank you for the novel. I'll see you on the beach."

A high-pitched yip from both pooches prompted Scooter and Kaycee to laugh. "They are the most intelligent doggies I've ever seen."

As Scooter opened the front door of the studio, he looked over his shoulder. "You have no idea, friend. Merry Christmas, and keep smilin'."

The long drive back to Sandbridge was made shorter with Gabby's humorous critique of Scooter's obvious nervousness and responses to Kaycee's questions. Flash remained silent, looking side to side from Gabby to Scooter like she was viewing a tennis match.

They entered the cottage as rain began to fall. "I think you both deserve a treat!"

So do you, Scoot-toot. I was only teasing, Flash and I think you did great.

Yes, you did. I was more nervous than the night I bit the bad man.

Scooter laughed and Gabby yipped. After their treats, all three relaxed on the sofa and listened to the rain ping against the windows. "We're going to have a super cool Christmas and New Year."

And a lot of dogs and cats will, too, Scooter. I'm glad we could help. It makes me feel good.

* * * *

Unfortunately, at the same time, two not-so-nice viewers of Kaycee's show began to devise a sinister plot for Scooter and his pups' New Year.

CHAPTER 33

Christmas Day on the coast of Sandbridge Beach unfolded with laughter and love. With no set schedule, the morning began for the pups with Puppy Chow sprinkled with scrambled eggs and bits of ham and cheese. Scooter went easy on his meal, deciding not to spoil his appetite for the holiday feast.

Once the breakfast dishes were washed, Scooter passed out the presents to his wide-eyed companions. "No rules on how to open them. Rip, tear, and scratch the wrapping paper off to see what I got for you." He kicked back on the sofa and sipped coffee, enjoying the flurry of colorful paper and his loved ones' comments once their gifts were accessible.

Oh, Scooter, this is a big rawhide bone! It'll take me all year to eat this. Thank you!

Flash opened his three presents in the same manner he eats. With two of her gifts open, Gabby looked at Scooter and shook her head. *I hope Disney doesn't decide to do a scene with Flash eating or opening presents.*

"Why not, Gabby? I mentioned his polite style of dining to the screenwriters."

Scooter, think about it...the scene would take so long, people would fall asleep.

Suddenly, Flash snatched off the paper and found a bag of Pup Jerky Treats. He slowly sniffed the package. ***Oh, boy! I knew it was something to eat. Thank you, Scooter.*** He looked at Gabby. ***And I'll share them with you because I've missed you.***

Gabby put her paw on the beagle's head. *Thank you. I thought about you and Scoot-toot every day.*

After their gifts were opened and they thanked Scooter, he said, "There's one more surprise with both of your names on it." He picked up a large box wrapped in red and white paper. "I'll open it for you." On purpose, he moved slowly, knowing Gabby would make a statement.

You're slower than Flash.

"I'm getting to it. Believe me, it's worth waiting for." After tearing apart the cardboard, Scooter lifted out a twenty-eight inch oscillating fan. "You will enjoy this on those hot summer days."

What is it, Scoot?

Yeah. I'm clueless. Tell us what we're going to enjoy this summer.

"It's a fan! When it's hot and there's no breeze, I'll plug this in and it will keep you cool while you're stretched out napping. We can use it inside or out on the deck. Cool, huh?"

Flash moved over and sniffed. *How does it work?*

"The plastic blades spin around very fast and push air out. It also moves slowly from side to side. Watch." Scooter plugged it into the wall socket, and the blades began to rotate. "Come over here, Flash. Put your face in front of it."

Flash cautiously moved in front of the spinning blue blades. Scooter cranked the speed to 'high'. Gabby and Scooter watched as the breeze lifted Flash's floppy ears. "How's it feel, dude?"

Wow! That's neat, Scooter. Come over and see, Gabby.

I'm good right here. I feel it.

Scooter shut off the fan. "It's your personal air conditioner."

We won't need it today.

"You're right." Scooter stood up. "If we get snow, I can use it to blow the deck off."

Sometimes I worry about you, Scooter.

Scooter loaded the strewn paper and bows into the empty fan box. "So, what do you want to do? Beach walk? Sleep? It's your choice."

I want to walk on the beach with you and Gabby.

Yeah. That's a good idea. I need to stay in shape. The movie biz is physically demanding. I'm always running and going here and there for Mr. Zurl.

"Then walking the coastline is what the Terrific Trio will do."

The what?

"A trio means 'three', like us, and we are terrific!" Scooter headed for the sliding door, quickly joined by the pitter-patter of paws.

An hour later, they climbed up the deck stairs and entered the comfy cottage. Dark clouds formed in the north as the wind picked up, dropping the temperature into the mid-thirties. "Looks like tonight or tomorrow we could get rain. If the temperature continues to drop, we might get a dusting of snow. Have either of you ever seen snow?"

Their silence told Scooter they had not. He sensed they were tired and ready for a snooze. "While you rest, I'll start prepping for our big lunch."

Is Darla Kay eating with us?

I hope so. I like her a lot.

"No. She's spending the day with her family in North Carolina. But she's coming over tomorrow."

Good. Did you get her a gift?

Flash, don't be so nosey. Gabby yipped. *Hey, get it? Flash being nosey?*

"Remember, Gabby, tracking is a natural trait for him. I'm beginning to think yours is eating."

Flash yipped. Gabby curled into her sleeping pose. *Wake me in time for lunch.*

I'm going into the bedroom and sleep in my chair.

When four o'clock rolled around, the three had finished a delicious meal and were stretched out, stuffed. Scooter fought to keep his eyes open as he jotted down notes on his sequel 'Out of the Rough'. Both pooches appeared comfortable and content in their world of dreams, alternating yips and twitches. Finally, Scooter gave in and laid the pad on the coffee table and closed his eyes.

After a long nap and a few nibbles for supper, the pups took care of business and retired to the bedroom for a much-needed night of sleep. Scooter turned out the light. "It's been a wonderful Christmas. Sleep tight."

Not far down the beach, while the Terrific Trio slept peacefully, two cold-hearted individuals discussed a strategy for their next move. "When they passed you this morning, are you positive you got a good enough look to know she's the one?" growled the man.

The lady snatched off the long blonde wig and threw it on the table. "Yeah."

"How far away is their place from here?"

She lit a filter-less cigarette. "Ten cottages. When does this thing go down?"

The man scratched his four-day stubble and gazed out the picture window into the black night. "When the time is right. The sooner, the better. That man walk with his mutts every time?"

"No. Yesterday he only went in the morning. Also, the one we want always comes farther down this way than the big-eared one."

A notch above a whisper, the unkempt man said, "Tomorrow, when the dogs are alone, we make our move. Everything on our end ready?"

The haggard lady snuffed out the cigarette and sneered. "We're ready, David. The muzzle harness and leash are in your coat pocket. Our holding cottage is on the next road over. I've broken in and left the back door unlocked."

The man rubbed his calloused hands together. "Perfect."

CHAPTER 34

On December the 26th, the sunrise took place, but was not evident off the coast of Sandbridge Beach. Dark, dreary clouds draped the horizon, amid the gusting, twenty mile-per-hour north wind. Scooter stood in front of his bedroom window, hands on hips, and watched the ocean roiling wildly as if trying to eliminate an unwanted creature from its depths. The indoor/outdoor thermometer beside the window read – Outside: 34 degrees. "It certainly looks nippily," whispered Scooter. "If those clouds contain snow, the conditions are favorable for a few inches."

Scooter was busy putting the kitchen back together from yesterday's feast, knowing Darla Kay would arrive around noon for a lunch of leftovers and a relaxing afternoon. Gabby appeared in the den, pawing her muzzle. *No sunshine today, Scoot. It looks cold, too.*

"You're correct. Is Flash awake yet?"

Flash moseyed into the room. ***I'm up. After all I ate yesterday, I'm hungry again.***

Gabby looked at Scooter and shook her head. *I'd say our little floppy-eared friend is feeling more at home.*

"I'm glad. And I'm sure you could make the same statement, so I'd better fill your bowls. I'd hate to see you two pass out from hunger." He chuckled and tended to his pups' breakfast. "We'll get our beach walk finished before this weather worsens."

Neither pooch interrupted their meals to comment. Scooter slipped on his heavy coat and tennis shoes. When breakfast was finished, the trio headed down the stairs and into the chilly breeze and bleak morning.

"Here they come, David," Melody said, holding the binoculars tight to her blurry eyes. "Oh, crap! The man's with them."

David pushed up from the large leather sofa and pulled up beside her. "Give me the binoculars." Melody thrust them into his hand, grabbed her smoldering cigarette from the ashtray, and took a long drag.

"If this weather gets worse, they probably won't walk this afternoon," David growled. "Look at 'em, strolling along like it's a summer day. They're crazy! It's freezing."

Like a dragon, Melody exhaled a stream of smoke through her nostrils. "Be patient. We can outwait them. This house is for sale, and with this rotten weather, no realtor will be bringing anyone to see it."

"Yeah. You're right. Let's keep our eyes on the prize." David watched the trio walk past the cottage. "The first time that bozo lets them walk alone...the black one is ours."

"Now you're talking, baby."

Darla Kay settled on the sofa beside Scooter, pooches relaxed at their feet. "I think your interview on television was the best one I've ever seen." She looked at the pups. "I just loved their little yips. And the Adoption Assistance Program is awesome. That's so sweet, Scooter."

"Thank you. And it was successful. Yesterday I heard from the four shelters, and each one used their quota by Christmas Eve. I'm sure the announcement on Kaycee's show helped."

Darla Kay hopped up from the sofa and removed a small rectangular silver-wrapped package from her pocketbook. She returned to her seat beside Scooter. "Merry Christmas," she said, handing it to him.

Scooter took the present. "Well, thank you. I have one for you, too." He stepped over to the twinkling surfboard. "It's under the one and only surfboard tree." Gabby yipped.

"Aw, you didn't have to, Scooter." She slowly removed the red paper and lifted the top. "Oh, this is so beautiful!" She held up a silver bracelet with small dangling dolphins, sand dollars, and seahorses. "I love it." In a flash, she had it fastened around her wrist. "Thank you, Scooter, and you sweet pups." Gabby and Flash yipped.

"I'm glad you like it. That's your reminder that you always have an open invitation to visit us."

Darla Kay leaned over and gently kissed him. "I'll be sure to remember that. Now open yours."

Scooter slowly removed the paper from the box and removed a pair of black-framed Ray Ban sunglasses. "I needed these, Darla Kay. My other ones are so scratched up." He slipped them on and looked over at the canines. "Hollywood, baby...Hollywood. Thank you, dear." After another hug and kiss, Scooter said, "They fit perfectly."

"And look very good on you. I'll bet Kevin wears Ray Bans."

They both laughed. "If he doesn't, he will when he finds out that I do. Remember, he's the one trying to be like me."

Darla Kay giggled and admired her bracelet. After a minute, she leaned over and stroked Flash's head. "Now I have two very special bracelets, Flash, thanks to you. I'll take real good care of this one." The little beagle yipped. Darla Kay looked at Scooter. "If I didn't know better, I'd say your sweet companions understand what we're saying."

"They're certainly intelligent. They respond when they hear their names."

"My gift to Gabby and Flash will have to wait until my next visit." She leaned over to them. "And you won't have to unwrap it either."

Gabby yipped.

Scooter said, "Why don't we plan your visit now?"

"Fine by me."

Scooter leaned back with his hands behind his head and gazed at the ceiling. "Well, beginning January the third, our lives turn hectic again. Gabby goes back to California, and Flash and I are heading to Florida. So why don't we celebrate down here on New Year's Eve? We'll start the New Year off right. Sound good to you?"

"You read my mind. I'll bring the main entrée, and you provide the sides and the music. Okay?"

"Bingo. It's a date."

Both pups yipped twice.

"And they approve, too," Scooter said, nodding to the pups.

Darla Kay glanced at the clock on the kitchen wall. A small frown turned down her perfect lips. "As they say, all good things must come to an end. It's already four o'clock, and I have a busy day tomorrow laying out my lesson plans and approving the other teachers' plans. These next few days will be chock-a-block."

Scooter stood and looked out the window. "It looks like the bottom will drop any minute now. Gabby why don't you and Flash go tend to business while I walk Darla Kay to her car? Then we'll take a quick beach walk." He helped Darla Kay with her coat. "Gabby has several demanding shoots coming up, so we need to keep her in shape. We all have calories to work off, too." He smiled and rubbed his stomach.

"You look perfect to me. Gabby and Flash, take care of Scooter. We don't need any more close calls like the one in Philadelphia. Flash, you were one brave pooch."

Scooter held the front door open, and they entered the cold, grey afternoon. He and Darla Kay turned toward her car, and the pups headed for their preferred sand dune. Darla Kay slipped behind the wheel of her VW Bug and turned the key. Nothing happened. "Oh, no. My battery's dead."

"Cold weather pushes an old battery right over the cliff. Don't worry, I have jumper cables. You can stop by Auto Zone on the way home. They'll put a new one in for you. I'll pull my car up to yours." As he trotted over to the Z, he felt light drizzle on his face. After starting his car, he walked over the dune and spotted his pups. "Hey, guys, I have to give

Darla Kay's battery a jump. Why don't you two go on and take your walk before the rain comes?"

Gabby raced over to his feet. *Scooter, I want to run down near the pier for more exercise. I don't mind a little rain. Okay?*

"That's fine, but I want you back here before dark. You have one hour to get your exercise. Is Flash going down the coastline with you?"

No. He said he would walk a little ways, but he's pooped. I don't mind going alone.

"Tell Flash to come up the deck stairs and bark, and I'll let him in. Have fun and stay on the beach…no snooping. One hour, girl."

It's Flash who snoops. See ya.

Scooter pulled the Z over beside Darla Kay's car, and within five minutes, her car was purring like a kitten and warming up. "Have a good few days at work, dear. I can't wait until New Year's Eve."

"Me, either, Scooter. Stay warm and dry tonight." She gave him a peck on the cheek and backed out of the driveway. With a quick honk of the horn, she zipped off down the deserted beach road and out of sight.

Scooter locked up his car and headed for the warmth of the cottage and a relaxing evening with his furry companions.

CHAPTER 35

Scooter's fingers danced across the keyboard, adding rhythmic clicks to the surrounding silence. The scene unfolding in his mind became words on the computer's monitor. He was pleased with how his main character, Keith, had maintained his composure and corralled his anger after two trying years of juvenile, verbal bullying from his nemesis at the golf course. Scooter opened his sequel 'Out of the Rough' by allowing Keith to finally shut Eddie up. When the bully ended up on the manicured green grass clutching a bloody nose, Scooter cheered and leaned back in his chair. "That'll teach you to make fun of Keith's polio-stricken best friend, you spoiled rich kid." Scooter threw a fist in the air. Two loud barks snapped Scooter back to Sandbridge from West Virginia. "I'm coming, Flash."

Scooter opened the sliding door and noticed the deck was wet. "Come in where it's warm."

Flash stepped onto the mat and waited patiently while Scooter toweled him off. *It's real cold.*

Scooter finished drying the little beagle. "Okay, you're good. Curl up on the floor beside the heat vent." After he placed the towel on the counter, Scooter looked at the wall clock. "Gabby should be back in about fifteen minutes, then I'll fix us something to eat."

She was way ahead of me. It looked like two people were petting and talking to her when I turned around to come back.

Scooter chuckled. "She loves attention."

Flash took a couple of sips from his water bowl and moseyed over and curled up on the rug. Scooter returned to the computer desk and ended the chapter with Keith walking away to caddy for a customer, while the other caddies laughed at Eddie. Scooter hit the 'save' key and moved over to the sliding glass door. He raised his hands and stretched, scanning the darkening shoreline, failing to see Gabby. "Okay, Baboo, you're late." He entered the kitchen and removed a Coke from the fridge. After a long pull on the refreshing liquid, he sat at the kitchen table and looked down at his sleeping beagle. "Peaceful."

Several more minutes passed. Scooter recalled that Gabby had always returned on time, even on pretty days, but would never fail to comment about him being too strict with her. *Scoot, you act like I can't take care of myself. You know I'd come home when I got hungry.* However, tonight's weather conditions were far from pleasant, and he knew Gabby didn't care for cold weather. "I hope she isn't following a strange scent to demonstrate she's a talented sniffer like Flash," he whispered, figuring that was a stunt she might pull. "She hates to be one-upped." He drained the Coke, looked up at the clock, and stood. "Ten minutes late now."

The drizzle had become a light, steady rain as darkness placed its blanket over the beach. Flash stirred and yawned. *Has Gabby come back?*

Scooter shook his head, trying to ignore the flurry of butterflies coming to life in his stomach. "Not yet. I'm beginning to worry. She's never late."

The little beagle settled at Scooter's feet and peered through the rain-streaked glass. *Maybe she got tired from running, and she's walking.*

"I hope that's it." He dropped to one knee beside Flash. "You said two people were making over her as you turned around, right?"

Yeah. You know how people are with friendly dogs. I was a ways off, but I think it was a man and a woman.

"About how far down the beach were they?"

I don't know.

Scooter opened the door and stepped out under the eave and looked south. Darkness prevented him from seeing farther than a cottage or two. He leaned inside and flipped on the floodlights. "At least she'll be able to see our cottage now," he said to no one.

Do you want me to go down and look for her?

Scooter took a deep breath. "That's real nice, Flash. Let's give her a few more minutes. If she's not back soon, we'll both go take a look." The thought of her going into the water to practice swimming in preparation for the movie crossed his mind and sent a chill down his back. He could see the choppy waves illuminated by the cottage lights and knew the undertow would be strong. *No, she wouldn't attempt a swim in this weather.* His eyes automatically found the clock. "Thirty minutes and counting," he whispered.

Scooter, open the door, and I'll go out and bark. Maybe she'll hear me and bark back.

"Good idea." Scooter slid the door open. Flash bounded over to the edge of the deck and produced a loud, deep bark. He waited for a few seconds, then let loose with two ear-splitting howls. Scooter wondered if that was some type of signal used by dogs. They waited in silence, hearing nothing from the eerie darkness. "Let me get a raincoat. We're going to look for her. She best not be up to one of her silly games."

We'll find her. She might've found an injured animal.

Scooter snatched a flashlight and black raincoat from the closet beside the front door and put on a Ravens ball cap. "Let's go, pal."

The drizzle was now rain, but did not slow their trek on their way to the water's edge. An orb of yellow light, provided by the flashlight, danced over the sand. Large waves crashed angrily on the shore. Scooter's stomach was gripped by an iron fist. He kept telling himself this unsettling situation was just another of Gabby's silly adventures instead of something worse. Flash had pranced ahead several feet, his nose high in the cold blackness as his tail curled over his back. "Get her scent, Flash. We'll follow wherever it leads."

Flash missed not one step. *Nothing yet. The rain is not helping. Maybe I'll pick up some scents where the two people were playing with her.*

"I hope so." Scooter aimed the light just above the sand, toward the dark, vacant cottages. He inhaled a deep breath. "Gabby! Gabby!" The only reply was the crashing waves. "Baboo! Where are you?" Scooter shined the light on his watch, seeing Gabby was now an hour late. His heart raced. *Something is wrong.*

* * * *

"It didn't take 'em long, Melody," mumbled David, turning off the table lamp. "The man and his stubby-legged puppy are coming up the beach."

The ragged-looking woman pushed the curtain aside a couple of inches and peeked out. "After they pass, we'll get out of here and go over to the other cottage. That beagle will pick up the dog's scent. We don't want them snooping around while we're still here." She slipped back from the window and lit a cigarette.

"Right. When we leave, I'm gonna tie the mutt's legs and wrap her in a blanket. I'll tote her to the van so the beagle will end up sniffing himself into a dead-end until he goes cross-eyed and gives up." The scruffy man's evil laugh echoed in the large room.

"Good idea. Before you wrap her, make sure the muzzle harness is tight. We don't need her barking or biting. We've come too far to blow this, honey."

"No problem," David said, heading down the hallway to the small closet where Gabby was held captive.

* * * *

Flash now zigzagged from the water's edge, halfway up to the cottages, his nose held steady, six inches above the sand. Scooter continued shouting Gabby's name and shining the light across the area as they moved south. With each passing minute, he envisioned more negative scenarios. Each one caused his heart to pump faster and harder against his chest. "Gabby! Come, girl!"

The beagle's high-pitched yip startled Scooter. "What is it, boy?"

I'm picking up fresh scents. Flash focused on an area of fluffy, damp sand ten feet above the tide line. *It's Gabby's and humans', too.* Scooter's light found Flash glancing back in the direction of their cottage. *This could be the area where the people were with Gabby.*

Scooter eyeballed the oceanfront cottages and wondered if this couple possibly had something to do with Gabby's disappearance. He quickly put that aside, since he had never heard of dogs being snatched at Sandbridge. All of the cottages were dark and most likely vacant. He aimed the light down on the sand, hoping to see footprints. The earlier rain had smoothed out much of the sand, but maybe some deep prints would remain. He knew Gabby enjoyed prancing around when people made over her, so he looked for her paw prints, too. "Smell anything else, Flash?"

Not a lot in one spot, like if they were all here. Maybe they were a little farther down. I'll mark this area in case it rains. Scooter watched Flash use his front paws to rake out an area about a foot square, then he cocked his hind leg and let loose. A tiny grin formed on Scooter's face. "Rain won't mess up your scent?"

Nope. I'll be able to smell it. Flash yipped once.

As they moved slowly south along the coastline, the drizzle slacked off. The cold, northerly wind increased. Other than manning the flashlight, Scooter felt he was of little help to Flash. Various heart-wrenching visions of what might have happened to Gabby ran at will through his mind. If she had gotten on the scent of a fox, a feral cat, or a coyote, did it have rabies and attack Gabby, possibly injuring her? Maybe during her tracking, Gabby carelessly crossed the road; even though traffic was scarce, there was no guarantee she could not have been hit. She might be lying beside the road, injured or worse, or maybe she had crawled away to a safe place. The fact that Gabby was now two hours late told Scooter something was very wrong. Hot tears formed behind his eyes as he followed Flash's movements and observed his precise sniffing technique. He swallowed the lump forming in his throat. "Gabby! Where are you?!" The reply was silence.

"Anything, Flash ?"

The beagle stopped, sneezed twice, and turned his sand-encrusted muzzle toward Scooter. *Only seagull poop and a few places where a dead fish may have been. The best scents were back a ways.*

"Where you made your mark?"

Flash lowered his nose to the wet sand and moved forward. *Yep.*

"We should turn around when we reach the 'S' turn. On the way back, you work the beach, and I'll walk the road. You don't need the light, and I'm not much help in the sniffing department."

Flash did not even pause. *Okay.*

The 'S' turn, as it was known to locals and surfers, was one mile from Scooter's cottage. The pier was another mile and a half from there. Whether Gabby ran the entire time or if she broke it up with a walk would determine how far she may have gone. He also wondered how long the couple made over her. Scooter had decided to perform a complete search tonight, up to the 'S' turn, including the beach road. Then, if no workable scents were found, they would move forward tomorrow past the 'S' turn. The weather forecast for the following day was for sunshine, warmer temperatures, and only a light wind. He also planned to call a few friends in the morning to see if they could join the search. The thought of Gabby being somewhere out here alone overnight made him nauseous, but he and Flash needed assistance and daylight. "We'll find you, Baboo," he whispered, holding back tears as they pulled up to the slight bend on the coast. "Okay, partner. You work your way back on the beach. I'll go over to the road and do the same." He fingered sand from the puppy's muzzle. "I'm thankful you're a talented sniffer. If you find anything, bark several times, and I'll come to you. If not, I'll meet you at the cottage."

I'll do my best. Maybe when we get home, Gabby will be waiting.

"Well, that could happen, Flash. And if someone found her they can call the house because my number's on her collar. Let's think positive. Go to it, Flash."

We'll find her, Scooter. Gabby's young companion shook his head and headed back down the beach, his nose inches from the damp sand. Scooter walked across the beach and up the large access to the dark, narrow beach road. "Gabby! Gabby! Bark for me, girl!" Tears trickled down his cheeks, blurring his vision as he worked the light from side to side, moving slowly down the desolate road.

CHAPTER 36

A warm glow spilled from his cottage windows as Scooter stopped on the road. Mentally exhausted, he took a deep breath and climbed the steps, hoping to find Gabby curled up outside on the deck or beside the small storage room downstairs. He entered and moved quickly through the main room, headed to the glass slider. He shoved it open and stepped out on the deck. "Gabby? Are you here?" The silence pierced his heart like a dull knife. "Gabby! I'm home!" Scooter painfully accepted the fact she was not there. He leaned against the wood railing and gripped it so tightly his knuckles throbbed. Staring into the darkness, he recalled the many times he stood here watching Gabby and Flash playing on the beach. Now, on this cold, dreary night, Flash was scouring the beach for a scent, and Gabby was...somewhere. Scooter felt a chill in his bones that something very bad had happened. He bowed his head and released his fears in the form of hot tears.

Several minutes passed before he gathered his thoughts and returned inside the warm, empty cottage. He hung his raincoat in the closet, as the shrill, yet sweet sound of the phone filled the main room. He quickly stepped from his bedroom. "Maybe someone found her and got my number from the collar." He grabbed the receiver and placed it to his cold, numb ear. "Hello."

"Listen real good." Scooter instantly picked up on the slurred gruffness of a male voice. Before he was able to shift his mind into gear, he heard, "I have your mutt..."

"You've got Gabby? Is she alright?"

"Shut up and listen! If you want her back...alive...do exactly as I say. Got it?"

"Yeah. Is she alright?"

"She is now. But if you don't follow my orders, you'll find her on the beach...sliced wide open. Go to your mailbox! There's a letter telling you exactly what and what not to do. This ain't no game, bud. We're watching." The connection ended before Scooter could speak. He dropped the receiver in the cradle and raced out the front door and down the steps to the mailbox. With trembling hands, he reached in and snatched out a wrinkled envelope. The lack of light prevented him from reading it, but he felt something square and firm inside. In a sprint, Scooter was back up the steps and inside, ripping open the envelope as his heart thumped like a jackhammer. At that moment, Flash's loud bark sounded from the deck. Scooter stepped over and slipped the door open. "Hey, Flash. Find anything?" Scooter removed the letter and a Polaroid picture from the envelope.

I think so.

Scooter looked at the sandy, drenched beagle. "Gabby is being held by someone." He slowly eased onto a chair at the little table. "A man called and told me to get this letter out of the mailbox. Let me read it."

Flash looked at Scooter with big brown eyes. ***Can we go get her?***

Scooter's eyes fell on the fuzzy photograph. The image he saw sucked the air from his lungs and shot a chill down his back. "Oh, my. This man is sick!"

What is it, Scooter?

Scooter leaned over and held the picture for Flash. "She's lying on the floor in what appears to be a small closet. Her feet are taped together, and they've put a leather muzzle over her snout so she can't bite or bark." Scooter raised the picture and adjusted his eyes to the dark background. What he saw caused him to gasp – a large hunting knife was stuck in the floor inches from her belly. "She's got to be scared to death. Look at her eyes." He showed Flash the picture again, not mentioning the knife.

Is she hurt?

"I don't think so. At least not yet. Let me see what this sicko wants." Scooter laid the picture on the table and unfolded the letter. The words were written in pencil. The handwriting was elementary and contained several misspelled words. Scooter slowly read the note aloud: "Get her back alive. Pay 250.000 in big bills by 29 at midnite. CALL POLICE SHE DIE! Im watching you! Call you with more." Scooter silently read it again and realized this nut was not only evil, but dumb. "We're going to get our Gabby back. I'll need your expert help, buddy." Scooter dropped the note and reached down to stroke Flash. "She knows we will come get her."

Flash released a low growl and placed his damp head on Scooter's leg. *I found Darla Kay's bracelet, and getting Gabby back is even more important, Scooter. I'll find her, and then I'll bite the mean man.*

Scooter closed his eyes and visualized the three of them back together. "I'm sure glad you're helping me on this. We've got to be very careful cause he said he's watching. He used the word 'us' when he mentioned the money, so there's somebody helping him. I don't want to do anything to make him do something harmful to Gabby. It's money he wants. I'll pay to get her back, but I don't know if I can trust him to release her after he gets the money. We've got to hunt him down first." Scooter stood. "You need something to eat, partner. We need to keep our strength up. While I'm fixing your supper, tell me what you found on the beach. We need as much information as possible."

While Scooter sliced from the remaining turkey, Flash stood beside him. *The only good scent I found was the place I marked. Gabby's scent and two humans were there. So on my way back, I followed the trail up to the big house. Gabby's paw prints looked like she was digging her feet in the sand. I think the humans were dragging her. At the back door, the scents vanished. Scooter, I think they're all inside.*

Scooter nodded and added turkey pieces to Flash's bowl of Puppy Chow. "That's good." He set the bowl on the floor. "I know the cottage you're talking about. It's been for sale a long time. That would be a perfect place for the people to break in and hide out. Plus, they had a good spot to watch us go up and down the beach, and they waited until I wasn't with you." Scooter watched Flash eat, wondering why someone would do all that to get Gabby.

Flash paused his chewing. *Scooter, why did they take Gabby?*

Throwing together a turkey sandwich, Scooter realized they were on the same page. His answer should be, 'I don't know', but after taking a look back at what had happened over the past few days, the answer hit him like a boulder. "This nut probably saw us on Kaycee's television show. He figures since Disney is doing a movie about Gabby, we've got a lot of money, and we will do anything to get her back. And he also might think Disney will pay the money. But, if that's the case, why didn't he ask for more? Scooter took his sandwich and glass of sweet tea to the table.

That's why they grabbed her and not me.

Scooter followed a big bite with a gulp of tea. "Right. If they knew your sniffing talent, they should've gotten you, too." For the first time in hours, Scooter smiled. "I believe you can locate their hangout. And, then, I'll go in and rescue Gabby. Remember, Flash, we're in on this together."

Flash scratched his muzzle. *They better not hurt her.*

Scooter wiped his mouth with the back of his hand. "You're right. I can put up with a lot of people's faults and bad actions, but when they hurt or abuse children or animals, I have no patience with them." He took a deep breath, hoping to release the tension in his neck. "Let's take this one step at a time. At least we know Gabby is alive."

I better go back to the big house and do more sniffing, Scoot. If I don't...those scents will go away.

Now was the time to put together a solid plan. Scooter realized the evil 'dognappers' knew where he lived, had his phone number, and had seen his car. So, figuring this person was not the brightest light in the lamp since he had warned Scooter he would be watching, the chances were good that Gabby was being held in Sandbridge. Scooter decided it would be to their advantage to nose around beneath the cover of darkness.

Tomorrow morning, a call to his bank would be made to discuss what a withdrawal of that amount in large bills would entail. There would be no call to police or Darla Kay or friends. If Gabby could be found, it would happen with him and Flash. "You're right, Flash. It's near midnight, and the rain has stopped. I doubt the culprits will stay awake all night to keep an eye on us. They think their hiding place is safe. Let's rest for a couple of hours, and then around two-thirty or three, we'll go check out the big cottage. If you believe they are still holed up there, I'll make plans. I'm not sure how I'll handle it, but our first job is to find them. They may have used the oceanfront cottage to grab Gabby, then moved to another vacant cottage nearby. I don't think they'll be too far away, and I doubt they're locals. You want to go out and tend to business before you rest?"

Flash stood, and Scooter saw the worry in his brown eyes. ***Yes, but I don't think I will be able to sleep.***

"I understand. At least we can lie down and try to relax and put our thoughts in order. We don't want to rush into something and ruin a chance to find her." He stepped over and opened the door. Scooter watched the tense pooch scurry onto the deck and disappear down the stairs. Scooter closed his eyes, filled his lungs with salt air, and whispered a prayer for their success. *Hang tough, Baboo…we're coming.*

CHAPTER 37

To be on the safe side, Scooter had set his alarm clock for two-thirty before lying down. When 'Blackwater' by the Doobie Brothers spilled into the dark, quiet bedroom, his head sprang from the pillow. He blindly felt around and slapped the 'off' button. "Time to hunt for Gabby," he whispered, slipping from beneath the blanket.
I'm ready, Scooter.
"You're already awake?"
I've been worried about Gabby. I couldn't sleep.
Scooter flipped on the small lamp on the nightstand and saw Flash's tired eyes looking at him from the corner chair. "Now it's time to put our heads together and go to work." Scooter hustled into the main room and put on his shoes and black rubber raincoat. "Flash, you go sniff around the big cottage. Check all the doors to see if anyone has been in or out of them. With your ability, you might pick up a scent seeping from under a door. I'll sneak up the road and hide out in the yard beside the cottage behind the clump of pampas grass. If no one's inside and there's no vehicle in the driveway, I'll join you and see what you've found. Then we'll decide what to do. Remember, we must stay out of sight and be very quiet." He shoved a screwdriver, pliers, a six-inch Barlow knife, and a roll of duct tape in his coat pocket. "If we think they've been inside, but are now gone, I want to go in and check for any clues that might help us."
Flash took a long drink of water and stood beside the glass slider, tail wagging. *Okay. We've got to find Gabby…quick.*
Scooter slipped the door open. "Be careful, Flash. This is serious stuff."
I will, Scoot. Into the cold darkness of the early morning, little Flash trotted out and down the stairs.
"There goes one brave, focused pooch." Scooter glanced at the surfboard clock on the kitchen wall. "Three o'clock. We have three hours to search before daylight." Scooter stared out the glass door into the pitch black as the weight of helplessness and the ache of Gabby's situation weighed heavy on his trembling heart. "The perpetrators of this heinous crime definitely saw us on Kaycee's television show. Hateful, lazy money-grubbers lying around waiting to take advantage of innocent people…well, you've picked the wrong bunch. We don't quit. We fight back." Scooter took several calming breaths, turned off the kitchen light, and headed out the front door, fueled by love and determination.

Scooter slipped into the side yard of their target cottage, a mint green, two-story named 'Ocean Paradise'. He crouched and duck-walked up behind the large base of the five-foot Pampas grass. He parted the plumes for a good view of the side and front of the cottage. He watched Flash feverishly sniffing the slatted wood platform outside the four-paned side door. The beagle's tan and white tail swished rapidly from side to side, as if propelling his snoot forward. Scooter focused on the front yard and noticed no vehicle on the slate parking pad. "If they were here, they're gone now, or parked elsewhere." Flash slowly increased his search area down the side toward the front of the cottage.

After eyeballing the vacant cottages across the narrow road and seeing no lights or activity behind any windows, Scooter trotted up tight against the side of the cottage behind Flash. He whispered, "Anything?"

Flash halted his sniffing and sat, panting. *Three different scents come from the beach to the back door. Gabby's footprints began to dig into the sand the closer they get to the cottage. It's like she was being dragged. And there's a real strong scent from Gabby's musk glands on the wood porch in front of the door. That proves she was really scared. I know they got her inside, but I don't think they're here now.*

Scooter dropped to one knee. "Musk gland?"

It's a dog thing, Scoot. We use them for several things. You know how we always sniff other dogs at the back end?

A tiny grin tightened Scooter's mouth. "Yeah. I've never understood that."

We only do it to pick up their unique scent. To humans, it's like someone telling you their name. We remember it. In this case, Gabby was scared, so she released it so I would find it. Flash scratched his muzzle. *She knew we'd come looking for her.*

"You bet. And she knew you would be doing the tracking, too. Now check out the front area, including around the front door. I don't think anyone is here, so I'm going to pop the lock on the side door. If they've been inside, I might see something, or you might sniff out some helpful clues."

Okay.

Since Scooter was knowledgeable about beach construction, he knew most cottages were not built as securely as houses in town. Security systems had not yet found their way to Sandbridge. He wiggled the doorknob and smiled when he felt a lot of play. "My knife or credit card will become my key," he whispered, pulling out the Barlow. After he flipped the sharp blade out, he carefully pushed in on the door and slid the blade between the jamb and the catch. With a couple of twists and ups and downs, he first heard and then felt the release of tension. "We're in."

He decided to leave his knife open, just in case he encountered the culprit. Slowly, he eased the door open and peeked into the dark interior, then clicked on his flashlight.

Unlike Scooter's twenty-five-year-old cottage, the newer ones had put their storage areas inside. After a quick look-around, Scooter estimated the room to be ten by twenty feet. On the far wall, he spotted a windowless door. "That leads to the first floor living area with a central stairway to the top floor." He turned, stepped outside, and moved down the side to check on Flash.

Scooter leaned his head around the corner and spotted the busy beagle in the middle of the parking pad, his nose mere inches from the slabs of slate. Flash paused, looked up at him, and tapped his front paw twice on the ground. Scooter again eyed the surrounding cottages, saw nothing out of the way, and moved forward. "What is it?"

Scooter knelt and closely examined the fist-sized, dark spot beside Flash's paw. *What's this smelly stuff?*

"It's an oil spot." Scooter grinned. "Not to be confused with a doggie's musk spot. A vehicle was parked here, and some oil dripped from a leaky oil seal. Why?"

Could this have come from the mean people's car?

Scooter touched the edge of the spot and put it to his nose. After a quick sniff, he said, "Maybe. It hasn't been here long. You might have found something, Flash." Scooter wondered how this could be helpful in tracking Gabby's hostage-takers, but decided not to rule out any possibilities.

Does oil from other cars smell different?

"What are you getting at, Flash?"

Well, only two human scents come from the front door over here. And only one scent on each side of this spot. Watch. Flash moved about four feet away from the spot and stopped. *One human stopped here. The other one stopped near where you are. Gabby's scent is nowhere around. Maybe they left their car here and carried her out.*

Scooter nodded, the light bulb flashing in his head. "Great idea, partner. Yeah, remember in the picture, they had tied Gabby's feet? Well, maybe since they knew I had a beagle, they figured you'd be out snooping. And most humans know how well you guys can smell, so to keep you from tracking Gabby, one or both of them carried her. Very good, Flash."

Would this oil smell different from your car, Scoot?

Scooter pondered this question and realized if there was a difference, Flash's sensitive snoot would surely be able to distinguish it. "There's one way to find out, but even if there is a difference, how would it help us?"

Maybe I could walk down the road and find it, then follow it.

"Okay, we have about an hour before it gets light. I've opened the back door of the cottage. We should inspect the inside. If we're lucky, they left Gabby and went somewhere. I know they don't live here. And Gabby wouldn't be able to bark because of the muzzle they strapped on her. After we give the inside a look, we'll go home and do an oil comparison. Come on, dude." Scooter moved quickly around to the back, still amazed at the pup's talent.

As soon as they entered the ground floor of the cottage, Flash stopped. He shoved his nose straight up and sniffed. *Gabby's been in here. Her musk smell is real strong, and she did a number one, too.*

"You don't miss a thing, Flash. That's why I'm thankful you're on the case."

I feel bad, though.

Scooter closed the door. "Why?"

You said because they knew you had a beagle, they probably tied Gabby up and moved her. So that's my fault.

Scooter gently rubbed Flash's head. "You're wrong about that. It's not your fault they moved her. They only used this place to observe us and nab her. If anyone's to blame, it's me, because I wasn't walking with her. I stayed and helped Darla Kay get her car started. Let's not play the blame game."

But if I had walked with her, they might not have bothered us. I don't care what it takes, I've got to find her. It hurt real bad to lose Princess...I can't lose Gabby.

"I know that, Flash. Who's Princess?"

That's what Gabby and I named my sister. Remember? You wanted us to name her. Well, Princess was Gabby's idea. I like it because my sister was a princess. Flash bowed his head.

Scooter's heart flooded with emotion. "I like it, too." Scooter took a deep breath of early morning ocean air and swallowed a growing lump in his throat. At this point, he needed to stay focused on their mission. "Well, let's get to it. Let me know if you detect any smell that could help us."

I will.

Once they entered the first floor area, Flash took off, nose down and tail swishing. Scooter saw nothing much out of the way as he inspected a couple of bedrooms, a small den area, and a tiny kitchen. Flash was already up the stairs, applying his expertise, when Scooter appeared on the multi-windowed second floor. "Look at this place," he said, standing in the middle of the spacious room. "I know one thing, they are two nasty criminals."

Scooter! Gabby was in here. Flash stood in front of a small closet door. *And it smells bad.*

Scooter hustled across the room and down the hallway. "This must be where they kept her," he said, snatching open the white door. The sickening odor of urine, piles of poop, and damp dog fur rushed out, hitting him in the face. His red-hot anger had not been stirred since his Army days. "Poor Gabby." He closed his eyes. "Please let me get my hands on these two heartless low-lifes," he whispered.

Scooter, she must have been very scared locked up in this room. Flash backed up a few feet from the opening and looked up at him. *Do you think Gabby is still alive?*

Scooter had avoided this question. Now, hearing it from Flash brought it to the forefront of his thoughts. "Yes, Flash, I believe she's alive. Why? Do you think she's not?"

Flash bowed his head. *When Princess was killed, I went over to the side of the road where she was. She smelled just like this closet does.*

Scooter dropped to his knees and pulled the trembling beagle close against him. "I'm sure that was hard, buddy. But it was different. Princess was injured real bad, and she was dead. Gabby has been tied up and closed in this small, dark room with no fresh air. I don't see any water or food bowls, so she was probably thirsty and hungry. Let's remember how tough she is. If there's a way to survive, Gabby will find it. Besides, these common people only want money, and they promised me they would release her after I paid them. So let's stay positive, grab some clues, and get out of here before the sun comes up." Scooter took a deep breath, praying silently for both of his pups. "I will promise you this, Flash. Nothing will stop me from finding these criminals."

Me, either, Scooter. I know Gabby is counting on us. I'm going to find her, just like she found me.

"I'm going to give this joint one more look, and then we'll go home and do the oil comparison. That was a great idea, Flash. Let's hope it helps you sniff Gabby out."

The well-furnished and decorated great room was littered with empty pizza boxes, fast food bags, beer cans, ashtrays overflowing with butts, and just plain filth. Scooter checked the four bedrooms upstairs and noticed that the king-sized bed in the master bedroom remained unmade and was also covered with trash and cans. "These heartless weasels love their beer and junk food and cigarettes. When they get what they deserve, they can kiss their so-called 'good life' good-bye." Scooter felt his anger boiling again, but he knew he needed a clear head to make effective decisions to save their Gabby. "Come on, Flash, let's get out of here. I believe they've taken Gabby to a holding cottage. With your expertise and our determination, we'll find them."

I think the oil will help us, Scoot.

"I'm hoping so. When we get home, I'll explain my idea of how we might do a comparison and see what you think. We can't search outdoors again until it's dark. And I have a couple of important phone calls to make today. You need to get some rest; I need my partner fresh and alert. I'm counting on your talent more than you'll know, Flash."

I'll do my best.

As the cold, early morning dawn pushed aside the darkness, Scooter and Flash trotted down an empty road past eight vacant cottages and hustled into the welcoming warmth of their own.

CHAPTER 38

The hot shower provided Scooter with the mental and physical release of tension he needed. Events of the final hours of the previous day had unfolded into a serious ordeal. Failure of his mission to find Gabby alive guaranteed the loss of a very special part of his life.

Tears forced out by fear and helplessness blended with the water rolling off Scooter's tense body. "Gabby, we've not forgotten you. Hang on, please…we're coming." He bowed his head and slowly pulled his thoughts together. He stepped out into the steam-filled bathroom refocused, rejuvenated, and positive. "Flash will find you, and I'll free you from these people."

Scooter devoured three slices of cheese-smothered toast while Flash only nibbled a few nuggets of Puppy Chow. When Scooter asked if he would like some toast, the pup shook his head. *I'm not hungry. I'll have some with Gabby when she comes home. She'll be real hungry.*

"We'll have a feast when we get her back, Flash. Now, you need to eat to keep your strength up. If we can use your oil scent technique, you'll have to cover a lot of ground."

I can do it. I have to do it…for Gabby.

"I know you will. So, while you're eating, I'll go down and start my car. To perform a true test on the oil, it should get hot and then cool down like I'm sure it did with the vehicle from the cottage. Then I'll use the dipstick and place a few drops on our cement and let it cool to the outside temperature. That way it should be in the same consistency of the other oil. Got it?"

That sounds confusing.

"Sorry. This is my first attempt at comparing the aromas of motor oil." Scooter chuckled. "Since odors and scents are your expertise, I'll follow your lead."

Flash took a sip of water and sat on his haunches. *The temperature of the oil doesn't matter. All I need is to smell the oil from your car. See, sometimes when I pick up a scent, it's from something I haven't seen. With the oil, I've seen it and smelled it. So that smell is now locked in. It's sort of like how dogs remember different musk scents from new acquaintances.* Flash returned to his water bowl and licked.

"Well, how does seeing the oil help you? I'm only asking because you lost me with the musk thing."

My nose will tell me if there is a unique difference in the smell of oils. If there is, when I go searching, I know what an oil puddle looks like, so I'll be looking for oil on driveways or dripped on the road. If I see some, I'll sniff it. The scent in my head can only be your car's oil or the bad people's oil, because I don't have any other oil scents locked in. Got it?

Scooter reached down and scratched his pup's back. "You are one smart canine. It sounds logical to me, especially since we don't have access to a laboratory. In other words, an oil spot will look like all other spots, but after you sniff it, you'll be able to tell if it's oil you've already smelled, right?"

Right. Like your burgers...if I see two burgers sitting side by side, I know they're burgers, but when I smell them, it's easy to pick out yours. Flash yipped. *Gabby would probably say she wouldn't know until she ate them.* Flash moved toward the sliding door. *Before I check the oil, I need to visit math class.*

Scooter laughed. "Hey, I thought you didn't like the term 'math class'?"

I do now, because it's the way Gabby explained it to me my first night here.

Scooter pushed the slider open for Flash. "Yeah, that was a very good night." He cleared his throat as Flash stepped onto the deck. "You have a special gift for sniffing, and she has a knack with words and snappy comebacks."

We all have special gifts, Scoot-toot.

As Flash disappeared down the steps, Scooter gazed into the red orb perched on the ocean's surface, and its warmth lifted his spirit. "Yes, we do, and when that sun goes to bed...we're going to use them."

Scooter removed the dipstick from the Datsun 'Z''s engine and brought the tip up and eyed the golden film that covered the end. He knelt in front of Flash and steadied the stick. "Do your thing, Professor."

Flash raised his snout and snorted once, then shook his head. In slow motion, he lowered his nose to within an inch of the tip, sniffed several times, and scooted back. *Hold up, Scooter. I need one more sniff to be sure.*

"Want me to dip it into the engine again?"

No. Flash eased forward, exhaled, and repeated his sniff test. After fifteen seconds, his tail began to swish the sandy driveway. He aimed two large brown eyes up at Scooter. One yip preceded his conclusion. *You bet there's a difference! Like night and day.*

"Really? That much difference?"

The main distinction is that the bad people's oil smells exactly like the old charcoal in your little grill downstairs. Your oil doesn't. Does that make sense, Scoot?

"Yes. The other oil is old and has lost most of its properties. My oil was changed after we returned from New York. I'll bet the low-lifes who took Gabby never change their oil. They probably just add a quart or two when it gets low."

Well, I don't know anything about changing oil, but if they're still in Sandbridge, I will be able to track them down.

Scooter replaced the dipstick and closed the hood. "I'll take your word on that. That's great news. We are fortunate there are very few people down here this time of the year. I'd hate to think about tracking motor oil during tourist season." Scooter reached down and rubbed Flash's head. "And you'll remember the burned smell?"

Flash nodded. *I'll never forget it. It's nasty.*

"Let's go inside and relax. I've got phone calls to make. We can't do anything on our search until dark. You've got a lot of important work to perform tonight."

I'm excited, Scooter. We're going to find Gabby.

As the pair entered the cottage, the phone rang. Scooter hurried across the main room and snatched up the receiver. "Hello."

The gruff voice blared into Scooter's ear. "Best be getting my money, or your mutt dies. I know you got my letter, bud. Put the money in bundles and wrap in thick plastic. Put it in two big duffle bags. I'll call and tell you where to drop it, midnight on the 29th, no later! NO COPS! Ain't no game, bud!" The connection ended.

Slowly, Scooter placed the receiver in the cradle as hot needles of anger pricked his neck. "We don't need no cops, BUD!" He looked down at Flash. "Sicko was reminding us about the money."

I hope they are still here, Scoot. If they are, we're going to get them.

"I believe they are, Flash. I really believe we're dealing with two unintelligent individuals. But their ignorance won't help us unless we act with cunning." He looked at Flash and nodded. "You may not understand what I just said, but I'm sure we will get them. The man said he knew I got the ransom letter, which means he's checked the mailbox or he saw me get it." Scooter walked into the kitchen. "I need coffee. You want anything?"

Flash remained silent while he settled in front of the glass doors and looked out. Scooter prepared his antique percolator for much-needed hot, liquid caffeine as he attempted to calm his anger. *Need a cool head to outsmart this creep.*

Fifteen minutes passed. Flash remained quiet, as if in a trance. Scooter sat at the table and sipped his coffee, jotting notes on his 'to do' list. Flash suddenly barked twice and bounded over to Scooter's feet. "What is it, Flash?"

The beagle's tail swished frantically back and forth. *Scooter, you said the man knew you got his letter, right?*

Scooter nodded.

And you think he might have seen you or come by and checked the mailbox, right?

"Right."

Good! He's made his first mistake. Flash yipped.

Scooter sipped his coffee and his eyebrows scrunched together while he pondered the reason for Flash's excitement. "How's that?"

Flash jumped into the chair facing Scooter. A grin appeared on Scooter's face, since the pup had never done that before. Flash looked directly at Scooter. *I hope he checked the mailbox, but even if he saw us, we've got him, Scoot. See, if he came by and opened the mailbox, he left at least one scent, and maybe two. Right?*

Scooter's grin remained. "Yeah! If he walked up, you can pick up his scent in front of the mailbox."

Yep! And get this, Scoot. If he drove up and parked beside the mailbox and peeked in, I'll be able to smell even a tiny drop of oil. See?

"You are right, Flash! What if he only saw me go to the mailbox from close by?"

You'll have to figure that one out. Remember, I only do smells. But between us, we've got him.

Scooter pushed up to his feet. "Since you're the expert, let's go do the smell thing now."

Flash hit the floor running. *I'll do my best.*

They entered the chilly morning and Scooter paused, looking across the street at a vacant cottage, then left and right. Not seeing anything out of the norm, he moved halfway to the mailbox. "I'll wait here while you run your test."

Okay. Flash calmly stepped in front of the wood post that held a white mailbox. He dropped his muzzle to the road and worked it slowly in a three-foot square. Scooter's heartbeat increased while he watched every precise move his talented pooch made. With no reaction, Flash then stepped farther onto the road and looked down at the surface from left to right. Suddenly, his tail pointed straight up. *Got him, Scoot! He drove here, pulled up close to the mailbox, and reached out the window and opened it. He didn't get out.* Flash slowly moved several feet to the south, nose to the road. *And he went this way.*

Scooter felt a rush of pride as Flash carefully performed his investigative work. *Gabby, you should see this little fellow. He's amazing. We'll tell you all about it...soon.* "Great, Flash! Let's get in the house in case this weasel is watching us. We don't want him to get suspicious that we're on to him."

Flash trotted up the steps and into the cottage with Scooter. "Come here, little guy. You deserve a big hug!" Flash leaped into Scooter's open arms. "You are something!"

Thank you, Scoot. We're a good team. Like you and Gabby when you found me. Right?

Scooter's eyes moistened and his throat tightened. "Exactly. When we're up against the wall...we work together and overcome our obstacles. I love you, Flash."

I love you, and Gabby and Princess, too. Flash placed his head against Scooter's chest and released a big sigh.

CHAPTER 39

The determined duo's day unfolded with them being more hopeful than expected. Flash's intelligence and discovery of the oil scent had fueled them with a positive drive. Not wanting to leave anything to chance when it came to Gabby's rescue, Scooter had contacted the bank. Without divulging the reason, Scooter gave the bank president his new account numbers and set up the withdrawal. The president explained that he only required a three-hour notice to have the cash ready for pick-up. If Scooter didn't need the money, no big deal, he just wouldn't make the call. In fact, he felt positive they would have Gabby back before the ransom was due.

Once Scooter explained to Flash how exhausting the night would be as they hunted the vehicle and found Gabby's location, the beagle finally fell asleep on the floor. While the 'sniff specialist' slept, yipped, and twitched, Scooter made notes on various scenarios he might encounter during the process of recovering Gabby. He finally narrowed it down to three. Each one would depend on the actions of the two heartless humans. "What I *want* to do to them is simple, but I can't risk breaking the law, unless these dummies provide me with a justifiable reason. We'll soon find out," Scooter said, as a smile tugged the corners of his mouth.

After they enjoyed a filling lunch, Scooter set the alarm clock for eleven p.m. He and Flash turned in for a partial night of sleep before the detailed search would begin. The little beagle had remained quiet for most of the day, giving Scooter the impression that waiting was not Flash's strong suit. Truth be told, Scooter felt the same. *Hang on, Gabby...we're coming.*

Scooter woke early and watched the red digital numbers flip their way toward eleven o'clock. Two minutes before the alarm would come alive with music, he leaned over and shut it off. Flash slid from his chair and hit the floor with a 'plop'. *I'm ready.*

"Hop up here," Scooter said, patting the bed. "I want to know your plans."

Flash settled beside Scooter. *I will start at our mailbox and look for any drips of oil on the road. If I don't find anything, I will walk beside the road, and when I see a car or truck, I'll sniff under it. If I get no scent, I'll keep going. I'll go down Sandfiddler and come back on Sandpiper. I won't quit until I find Gabby.* Flash looked at Scooter with a puzzled stare. *When I find them, Scooter, what should I do?*

"I like hearing you say, 'When' I find them'. Well, 'when' you locate them, hurry back here and tell me. Then we'll sneak back, and I'll check out the situation. It depends on where they are and what style of cottage they've moved into as to how I'll handle the recovery. I'm hoping for a secluded place to hide out and watch their comings and goings. We know at least one of them goes out for food and beer. It would be best if the man goes, but it won't matter, I'll still get inside and overtake whoever is there. And then I'll surprise the other one when they return." He stroked the pup's head. "You handle the sniff and find, and I'll handle putting the bad guys out of commission. Remember, we work as a team."

Flash hopped to his feet. *Okay, Scoot. I'll hit the road and find Gabby. I'm sure she's hungry and scared.*

"You're right. I'll go crazy waiting for you, but I don't want to be seen snooping the area and give them reason to run. And, if possible, you should try to stay out of sight. They know what you look like. If you're spotted and they come after you, lead them over to the beach and then on a wild goose chase. You'll easily outrun them. Then work yourself back here and alert me with a couple of barks."

Okay, Scoot. Don't worry about me. Remember those two mean men at your book signing who wanted your money?

Scooter chuckled. "Yeah. I'll bet the guy you bit is still feeling the pain."

They walked into the main room. Scooter opened the front door and let his sniffing expert out into the cold darkness. "Do your thing, dude. I've got faith in you."

The tri-colored beagle trotted down the steps. *I'll do my best, Scoot-toot.*

Scooter observed him working around the mailbox, then he turned south, and the black night swallowed him. "Godspeed, partner." He closed the door and headed for the kitchen to put on a pot of coffee. "I hate waiting almost as much as I hate animal abusers," he said to no one.

CHAPTER 40

The hot coffee warmed Scooter while he stood on the deck gazing up at thousands of twinkling diamonds piercing the black sky. Minutes very slowly became hours; the only break in the total silence was the regular crash of a wave on damp sand. Those sounds delivered Scooter many precious, sunny day memories and visions of his pooches playing and entertaining the special needs children. Tonight, his pups were far away from those enjoyable days. The worried writer drained his now-cold coffee and decided to readjust his focus on how sweet the upcoming summer would be for them. "I refuse to let two cruel criminals ruin our lives. Instead, I'll ruin theirs."

Scooter felt ineffective, and his worry overloaded his already aching heart and stoked his emotional pain. Each time he paced past the wall clock, his eyes glanced at it, and his tension increased. He had no doubt Gabby was experiencing even more fear by not knowing what lay ahead. Scooter bent over the kitchen sink and splashed his face with cold water in an effort to clear his head. As he massaged his tight face, Flash's familiar howl sounded from the deck.

Scooter snatched open the door. "Hey, buddy!" He knelt and hugged the trembling beagle. "Good news?" Scooter asked, noticing the quickly swishing tail.

I found them! Let's go, Scoot. I found them!

Scooter released a satisfying sigh. "Easy, boy. Take a breath and relax. You've completed the most important step."

Flash moved over to his water bowl. He slurped for thirty seconds and then turned toward Scooter, beads of water dripping from his chin. *They aren't far from here.*

"Good!" Scooter looked at the clock. "It's two-thirty. I'll bet you found them on the other road."

Yep. I searched the beach road and turned at the 'S' turn and came back on Sandpiper. The vehicle isn't a car or truck, it's like they bring the children down here in. But it's dirty and stinks and doesn't have windows on the sides.

Scooter nodded. "That's called a van. And I'm not surprised it's in bad shape, considering the trash they left in the other cottage. How did you find them, Flash?"

The drops of oil on the road were really far apart. So I decided it was quicker to check every vehicle. Flash pawed his nose and sneezed. *I was getting real tired of smelling, but I finally found them. There was a puddle of oil under the van, and when I sniffed around the doors, Gabby's musk smell was strong, like the odor in the closet. It's them, Scooter! We've got them.*

Scooter stood. "Did you smell the human scent going into the cottage?"

They parked in a different place from the cottage they're in. I tracked them across the yards, and found out where they are. Let's go! I know you'll get Gabby back.

"We will get her back. Let me get a coat and some tools." Scooter hustled around and slipped into his black insulated coat, black wool cap, and dark gloves. He shoved a flashlight, hunting knife, and screwdriver in the pocket. "I've got a nylon rope downstairs in the storage shed. Those weasels will find themselves tied up like Gabby, except in an even more uncomfortable position."

Hurry, Scoot.

"We've got time. They're not going anywhere. Besides, I'm not going to barge in and get Gabby. No, I need a good plan to give them a surprise they'll never forget. They probably have a gun, too. We don't want anyone to get hurt...well, like shot...but there will be pain...but not for us."

I want to bite them.

"I understand. But you've done your job, Flash. Now it's my turn. Let's go south by way of the beach and then cut over to Sandpiper. You let me know where. Okay?"

Flash bounced up and down. *Yeah. I know where cause I marked it, Scoot-toot.*

Scooter chuckled. "That'll work fine. Let's go get our Gabby."

Without a doubt, Flash knew exactly where to go. Scooter followed, confident and proud of his beagle's determined focus. Other than Flash giving directions, they walked in silence. Beneath a dim street light, Scooter checked his watch to find it was only three-forty-five. With almost three hours before daylight, they should be able to find a suitable lookout location, check out where and how to enter the cottage, and plan the rescue. *It won't be long now, Gabby.*

When they reached the west side of Sandpiper Road, Scooter pulled up behind the trunk of a large pine tree. "Flash, do we go left or right?"

Flash raised his nose high in the chilly air. After a few sniffs, he pointed his paw to the left. *You'll see the dirty van on the other side of the road.*

"Let's stay in the yards behind the trees and shrubs."

They crossed four or five front yards, and Scooter spotted what looked like a tenement on wheels three cottages ahead, parked across the street in front of an old-style, one-story cottage. The rusted, dented van leaned to one side due to low air in the right front tire.

See it, Scoot?

"Yep. Now, in which cottage are they hiding out?"

The third one down from the van. Flash pointed with his front paw.

When the cottage's wooden nameplate, mounted to the front deck railing, came into view, Scooter smiled. 'Lucky Beach Break'. "Now it's *our* lucky break, but it won't be for you animal abusers," he whispered.

When they stepped into the expensively landscaped yard of a large vacant cottage across the street and in-between the dilapidated, crap-brown van and the 'Lucky Beach Break', Scooter duck-walked into a slatted area on the south side large enough to park a car. A huge clump of Pampas grass on the corner made this a perfect hiding place beneath the second floor. "Follow me, Flash," he whispered, keeping one eye on their target cottage.

We wait here, Scoot?

"Yeah. I've got a clear view of their cottage. They'll have to walk in front of us to reach their van. If we remain still and quiet, they won't have a clue we're here. When the time is right, I'll make my move. If I remember correctly, most of these old-style cottages have a stairway and deck on the back, like mine. That will be my best entrance, depending on their actions."

Flash settled beside Scooter's leg and stretched out. *I'm going to rest. Wake me if something happens.*

"Good idea. We've got a while. I'm hoping they go out and get coffee. We'll see."

In the early morning, three days before a new year, Sandbridge Beach remained graveyard quiet. A couple of cars slipped past the man and his dog, heading north. As the sky slowly swallowed the darkness to clear the way for dawn, Scooter checked his watch. "Six-thirty." He looked over at Flash, still asleep. "Poor guy's pooped." He directed his focus to the cottage across the street. Remembering the photo, he knew Gabby was inside, hungry and scared, lying in filth. Another rush of red-hot anger filled him, growing to the point of needing release. But Scooter understood only patience and careful planning would produce positive results, not anger. He leaned his head back against the sturdy piling and closed his eyes.

A gruff voice snapped Scooter out of a light doze and Flash from a deep sleep. Scooter rubbed his eyes, blinked, and focused on a fat, sloppy-looking, furry-faced man standing on the corner of the top deck. "You want doughnuts?" The reply came from an unseen, squeaky-voiced female. "Yeah! Six chocolate and six jelly-filled." The man responded, "Then I need more money. I only got enough for coffee and your cigarettes." He held out his hand.

Scooter felt adrenaline shoot through his veins as his breathing increased. *Showtime!* He eased his hand over and rubbed Flash's head. "Be very quiet," he whispered. Flash nodded.

Suddenly, a tall, thin woman with frizzy, bright red hair appeared on the deck and shoved what appeared to be several bills toward the man. "Don't forget my change."

"Will you quit worrying 'bout money, Melody? In a couple days, we'll be walkin' on easy street. When I get back, that rich mutt owner gets another call. This time, you should burn the dog's nose with a cigarette so he'll hear her whimper. That'll let him know we're serious."

"Just go get my doughnuts and smokes," blared the woman, taking another long drag from the cigarette hanging from her mouth. "This waitin' around is getting to me." She turned and stomped into the cottage.

Scooter felt his pulsing desire for action as the man bounced down the steps and crossed the yard, heading for the trashy van. *You'll be on easy street real soon, scumbag. Yep, three hots and a cot and living in a cage with a bunch of common men just like you.* The man reached the van, snatched open the driver's door, and climbed inside. After several attempts to start the wreck on wheels, the weak battery finally got it started. *Thank you, God.* White smoke billowed from the exhaust pipe each time the man punched the accelerator. Once the engine warmed, the man backed out onto the road, shifted into 'Drive', and rattled past Scooter and Flash, leaving a trail of swirling smoke. "That white smoke is the oil burning, Flash."

It smells worse than the oil on the road. Are we going in to get Gabby now?

Scooter arranged the coil of rope over his shoulder, moved his hunting knife from his coat pocket to his hip pocket, and took off his gloves. "The man's gone up to the corner market. He'll probably be gone ten or fifteen minutes. So here's what we're going to do." Scooter explained Flash's role in getting the woman out on the deck. "I'll come up from the back deck, rush her inside, and then restrain her. I'll whistle for you to come in. After I've tied her up, we'll free Gabby."

Flash's eyes twinkled as if he were about to get a treat. ***Got it, Scoot. I'm ready, not scared.***

"I know, because heroes don't get scared. With your expertise, we've almost wrapped up this ordeal. Now, once you see me disappear around behind the cottage, go do your thing." Scooter rubbed the pup's head. "See you inside."

CHAPTER 41

Scooter sprinted across the street, moved tight along the southern side of 'Lucky Beach Break', and stopped beside the far corner. He looked back to find Flash in position beside the Pampas grass, set to take off. The morning sun cast its orange glow across the eastern sky. *Time to get Gabby.* Scooter waved to Flash, then slipped behind the cottage. *Do your thing, little hero.*

The silence of the area suddenly erupted with a long, deep howl. Chills covered Scooter's arms. No sooner than the eerie bay ended, a series of loud barks exploded. *Good work, Flash. Let it rip.* When Flash released a high-pitched wail, Scooter heard the woman scream from inside the cottage. "What is that?!" Scooter chuckled. *Come out and see, you witch.*

At this point, Scooter knew Flash would be running around in the driveway acting like a wild dog. He readied himself when he heard the door squeak open, knowing the woman was now on the deck. Then she confirmed it. "Get out of here, you mutt! I'll take a stick to ya! Go away!"

That was Scooter's cue to climb the back stairs. He took two steps at a time. When he reached the north side of the deck, he paused and eased his head around the corner. *There she is.* The woman stood at the corner of the deck, looking down, and waving her boney arms. Her long, unruly red hair quivered, trying to keep up with the frantic shaking of her head. "I said, get out! I'm getting my stick!" She turned and stomped through the door. Scooter made his long-awaited move. In a flash, he stormed into the cottage. The woman turned upon seeing him enter. Their eyes locked. Scooter slowly pulled out his shiny, eight-inch knife, and calmly said, "Put down the broom. Sit in the chair." He nodded to a wooden kitchen chair. "Now!" he yelled.

The woman's eyes filled with anger. Her breathing increased as she adjusted her grip on the broom. "Who are you? What do you want? I ain't got no money."

"I'm not here to rob you. Now sit down before I knock you down!" Scooter took a step forward. "This is no game, lady! Now!" He jumped forward. Fear replaced her anger. She stumbled back, lost her footing, and fell. Before she managed to get her feet beneath her, Scooter flipped her on her stomach and jammed his knee into her back, pinning her down. He returned the knife to its leather sheath and let loose a loud wolf whistle. The woman wiggled and moaned while Scooter wrapped her hands and feet with the rope, formed a knot, and tightened it. He helped her stand, then dropped her into a chair just as Flash bounded through the open door.

He yipped once. "Go find Gabby, boy." Scooter wrapped another piece of rope around the woman's upper body and the back of the chair and tied it off.

Once the woman was firmly secured to the chair, Scooter leaned it back and dragged her into the kitchen, out of sight. He removed the duct tape from his coat pocket and ripped off a piece. As he leaned over to cover her mouth, she said, "You're the owner of the black dog!"

Scooter slapped the tape over her thin, lipstick-smeared lips. "Bingo." He turned and hustled down the hallway and stopped at the first room on his left. Flash was pawing at the door. *She's in here. I smell her.*

With trembling hands and a wildly beating heart, Scooter snatched open the closet door and dropped to his knees. His eyes blurred with hot tears of both anger and joy at the scene before him. "Gabby, we're here, girl." Her tail wagged slowly as he unbuckled the leather muzzle that held her jaws closed. After throwing it against the wall, he eased his arms under her, pulling her tight against his pulsing chest, and carried her from the urine and poop-filled closet. Gabby remained quiet, but her distant brown eyes spoke volumes. *You're safe now, Gabby.*

Scooter gently laid her on the carpet and carefully sliced the rope from her front and back legs with his razor-sharp knife. "Flash, you stay in here with her while I take care of the man. He'll be back any minute. Okay?"

Yeah. Nobody will ever hurt you again, Gabby. Flash laid his head on her shoulder. Scooter paused and took in the scene, noticing both pups' eyes were glassy. "I'll be back in a bit." Scooter picked up his knife and pulled the bedroom door shut when he walked out.

Once again, Scooter focused on the job at hand and moved quickly into the kitchen to check on the woman. She looked at him with red-rimmed eyes. An icy hatred flowed from her as if blaming him for detouring her from a life on 'easy street'. Scooter remained silent, choosing not to waste his time condemning her behavior. The law would clearly explain the depth of her sins and then provide a just punishment.

The noisy racket of a non-tuned, under-performing engine captured Scooter's attention. He peeked through the kitchen window in time to see the loser of the demolition derby rattle past. "Now the real fun begins," he whispered, turning and shooting a wink at the woman. "Your man is going to learn how pleasurable it is to be abused." He leaned down, inches from the wide-eyed woman. "And if I weren't a gentleman, I'd have delivered the pain you deserve, too."

Scooter arranged his pieces of rope, knife, and duct tape out of sight but within easy reach. Back in front of the window, he inhaled deep breaths through his nose and exhaled from his mouth in an effort to calm himself before the grand finale. *You'll never forget this day, scumbag.*

The heavy-set man walked slowly across the yard, balancing two large coffees on a box of doughnuts. "This will be too easy. Oh, well." *He'll probably need someone to open the door for him.* Scooter smiled. *As a southern gentleman, it'll be a pleasure to assist him.*

Scooter positioned himself against the wall beside the door. Clunky steps sounded as the man climbed the steps and crossed the deck. Then there was silence. Scooter figured the dummy was wondering how to open the door with no hands. *Be patient, he'll ask for help.*

Suddenly a knock, low on the door, invaded the quiet. "Hey! Open the door! My hands are full." Scooter took a deep breath and waited. *Does he really want me to open it for him?*

Several loud kicks preceded, "Open the door, Melody!"

Scooter corralled the pent-up anger and fear that had multiplied since these creeps had stolen Gabby and treated her like garbage. In a smooth, quick move, he appeared in front of the glass door wearing a broad, tight-lipped grin and gazed at the man with clear, focused eyes. In less than a split second, Scooter snatched open the door. His lean, muscular body filled the threshold while the man slowly processed who this doorman was. Scooter cocked his right leg at the knee, paused, and then shot his foot straight up into the box of doughnuts and hot coffee, sending them directly into the scraggly face of the astonished man. Before the man screamed or uttered a word, Scooter grabbed him by his worn, flannel shirt and jerked him inside. The man's nearly bald head snapped sideways as Scooter heaved him across the room like a rag doll. As the dingy striped sofa broke his fall, Scooter was there, waiting. By now, the cruel man had finally put two and two together and didn't like the sum. "What —?"

Scooter cut his statement short with a powerful right to the furry jaw. The sound of cracking teeth and crunching bones filled the room. Scooter watched two bloodshot eyes roll back into the man's head for a second, then reappear, blink, and refocus. "Take her!"

Scooter knelt in front of the cowering man covered in hot coffee, chocolate, and jelly. Bright red blood oozed from the corners of his mouth. Scooter sneered and slowly slipped his hunting knife from behind his back and held it inches from the man's flabby neck. "Didn't you say you would 'gut' my dog if I didn't pay you?" The man's eyes instantly grew large as saucers. He remained quiet. Scooter lightly touched him under his chin with the point of the cold knife. "Isn't that what you said, you bag of crap?" The man managed to produce a half-nod.

With a quick flick of his hand, Scooter flipped the knife to its dull edge and jammed it length-wise below the man's right ear lobe. In another lightning-fast move, he then pulled the dull edge all the way across the man's pudgy neck and laughed as he placed his hand on the man's head, holding it firm. "Now you're bleeding like the hog you are! They say you never feel a razor slice you open. Did you feel it?" Scooter shook his head and continued to laugh, watching the man's eyes attempting to look down at his chest to see if he was bleeding. "Since you were going to do this to my dog…I thought it would be fine for you, too." Suddenly a nasty odor filled the space between them. "Well, it looks like you are experiencing exactly the same 'stuff' you made my dog lie in." Scooter slipped his hand behind the man's hefty neck and jerked him forward off the sofa and shoved him face-down on the floor. Scooter rammed his knee into the man's lower back and tied his feet and hands together. "You wait right here, Stinky. I shall return with more fun and games."

Scooter entered the kitchen and stopped in front of the woman. "You should quit smoking and use your cigarette money to buy diapers for your man." Scooter chuckled when he heard the woman mumbling behind the duct tape while he filled a bowl with cool water for Gabby. He hurried into the bedroom and found his pups in the same position he'd left them. "How's she doing, Flash?"

The little beagle looked at him with the most pitiful eyes Scooter had ever seen. *She's not moving or talking. All she does is stare at me.*

Scooter cringed and ignored his pain. He dipped his fingers in the water and touched them to Gabby's very warm nose. "Here, girl. Drink some water. Everything's all right now, Gabby. The bad people are tied up, and I'm going to call the police in a few minutes. They will take them to jail. Try to drink some water." Her only response was an empty gaze into his eyes. Scooter swallowed and blinked back tears.

Suddenly, Flash was up and out of the room. Before Scooter could react, he heard a growl, followed by the man's loud screams. Scooter rushed into the room and found Flash with a head-shaking grip on the man's calf. Blood covered the beagle's tan and white muzzle. "Flash! No, boy! Don't! I've already handled him." Scooter stroked the pup until he calmed and released his grip. "He'll get what's coming to him. Now, go back with Gabby and try to get her to drink some water. She's dehydrated." Flash turned and disappeared.

Scooter looked at the whimpering man and shook his head. "You better be thankful I'm nowhere near as common as you. Because if I were, since nobody knows we're here, I really would cut you and your wench's throats and leave you here until spring when someone would find your rotted, worthless bodies. But I was raised better than that, you coward."

Scooter walked to the phone and called the Virginia Beach Police. He gave the dispatcher the address and a quick explanation about the dog-napping for ransom and informed her that the culprits were now comfortably detained. He thanked her, slowly returned the receiver to the cradle, and returned to the bedroom with his hurting, furry companions as tears trickled down his face.

CHAPTER 42

Gabby remained glassy-eyed, totally silent, and breathing faintly. Scooter ran his hands gently over her dirty, ratty fur and felt her protruding rib cage. These cold-hearted, selfish humans probably neglected to feed her, figuring a few days was no big deal. The addition of Gabby's fears, trembling, and hours spent in darkness sped up the weight loss. Scooter felt more helpless now than at any time during this entire ordeal because Gabby's condition and recovery fell way outside his abilities. "Well, I'm taking you out of this bedroom and clean you up, Gabby. I know how much you like to be clean and shiny," he whispered as he slipped his hands under her lifeless body and lifted her. In the small den area, he gently placed her on the shag carpet. "Sit with her, Flash. I'm going to get some warm soapy water and a washcloth."

Okay.

Scooter entered the main room and walked over to the prone man on the floor. He issued a full kick to the criminal's gut. "Roll over! You're going where you belong." The man groaned. After another gut kick, the man rolled. Scooter grabbed him under his arms and worked him to his feet. Scooter dragged him into the bedroom and shoved him into the closet where Gabby had been held. The man hit the back wall and fell to the floor with a spongy plop. "Enjoy."

Scooter hustled back into the kitchen and untied the boney woman from the chair. He put her light body under his arm like a sack of corn. "You two lovers should spend time together in the bedroom before the cops haul you to jail. You don't have to thank me for my kindness." When they approached the open closet, the woman spotted her man lying length-wise in the narrow space. She began wiggling and groaning as Scooter tossed her like a stick of firewood on top of the man. "Ignore the putrid smell, ma'am. It's your man's fragrance blended with my pooch's poop and urine. You both are responsible for that." Scooter slammed the door.

For ten minutes, Scooter gently bathed Gabby with warm soapy water and removed as much dirt and odor as he could. But he failed to clear her emotional pain and return her to reality. Flash watched in silence. After rinsing out the filthy water and refilling the bucket, Scooter rinsed her. During the whole process, Gabby never made a sound or moved a muscle. While Scooter dried her with a fluffy towel, his tears fell onto her pitch-black fur. "We'll get you back, Baboo."

Scooter and I will take care of you, Gabby. We love you.

The trio's quiet reverence was suddenly invaded by the shrillness of an approaching siren. Scooter sighed and pushed to his feet. "Stay with Gabby, little buddy. I'm going to meet the police. When they're finished with us, we'll all go home." *I hope they'll let me go home.*
Maybe Gabby will wake up when we get her home.
"That will surely help." Scooter walked from the den and into a chilly, sunshine-filled morning and leaned against the deck rail. "I hope we get an understanding officer."

The siren's volume increased to an ear-splitting level until a white Ford Bronco whipped into the driveway and shut down. Scooter whispered, "Thank God," after reading Virginia Beach Police K-9 Unit on the passenger door. "Must be a true dog lover," he said, removing his black wool cap from his head and running his fingers through matted hair.

After the officer finished speaking into the radio, he slipped from the vehicle and opened the rear door. Out hopped a beautiful black and tan German shepherd, who sat and waited while the officer hooked a leash to his navy halter. Then the pair cautiously walked up the steps and onto the deck. Scooter forced a smile onto his tense face. "At least we got a man and dog team." Scooter extended his hand. "I'm Dooley Bissell, but I prefer to be called Scooter. Nice to meet you."

After they shook hands, the middle-aged, stocky officer nodded. "I'm Sergeant Webb, but please call me Larry." He looked down to his partner. "And this is my companion and fellow officer, Corporal Razor. So, I understand you've apprehended a couple of dognappers out for money, right? I'm assuming it was your dog that was nabbed."

Scooter took a deep breath and shared information about the ordeal, including the ransom note and phone calls, adding how his beagle tracked them here. Scooter withheld Flash's expertise concerning the oil. Instead, he attributed the tracking to Flash picking up the humans' and Gabby's scents. "We're fortunate Sandbridge is mostly vacant this time of the year. And, as I'm sure you know, beagles are excellent trackers." *I hope that's enough info for now.*

Sgt. Webb slowly nodded and kept his eyes locked on Scooter's. "You look familiar."

Scooter swallowed in surprise. "I do? I've never been in any trouble with the law, unless you count a few surfing violations."

Webb chuckled and fingered his bushy, brown moustache. "If you count that, then I've got a record, too. Oh, I got it! A few days ago I saw you on television." He reached down and rubbed Razor's head. "My partner enjoyed seeing a couple of his own on the tube. Right, Razor?" The majestic shepherd yipped once. Scooter's stomach tightened. *Naw, couldn't be. He's just a smart dog.*

"Right," replied Scooter. "I think hearing about the Disney movie prompted these two low-class individuals to try and cash in on Gabby's success. They're inside waiting for you, Larry."

Webb nodded. "My dispatcher said you have them detained. Did either one sustain any injuries while you were detaining them?"

Scooter shoved his hands into his coat pockets. "Ah, the man's jaw might be dislocated, and he probably should see a dentist. His female companion is fine."

"Have they made any comments concerning the situation?"

"No. In my opinion, they're a few fries short of a Happy Meal." Scooter hoped a funny would slow the increasing interrogation.

Webb snapped his fingers and Razor hopped to his feet. "Let's check on your dog's condition first, since you have these scumbags secured."

Scooter smiled and pointed toward the door. "Gabby's alive, but she's really out of it, Larry."

A frown dropped the corners of Webb's mouth. The men followed Razor into the cottage, showing Scooter that's how this team works. Webb said, "Gabby has been through a major emotional trauma. How long was she held captive?"

"Two days."

"I see. Where is she?" Larry asked, pausing to scan the main room. His eyes fell on the upturned kitchen chair and length of nylon rope lying on the floor. "Looks like you came prepared." A smile replaced the frown. "And never attempt to rescue a pooch without your trusty knife."

Scooter's hand automatically reached to his back pocket and touched his knife. "And I wasn't even a Boy Scout."

Webb chuckled. "But I'll bet you know how to tie a knot."

"Taught by Uncle Sam," Scooter replied. "Army."

Webb snapped to attention. "Air Force."

Scooter led the way, Razor close beside him, down a short hallway to the den where Scooter had placed Gabby. He nodded toward the listless mixed black lab stretched out on the carpet. Flash lay next to her. Razor remained neutral, as if there were no dogs present. *Wonder if they taught him not to do the musk thing?*

Webb said, "Stay." Razor stopped and dropped to his haunches. Sgt. Webb slowly knelt on one knee and arranged his holster and nightstick. He whispered something to a curious Flash. Scooter said, "Flash, Larry is a good guy. He's here to help Gabby and take the bad guys to jail."

Flash yipped once and sniffed Webb's outstretched hand. "Nice to meet you, Flash. I hear you tracked the two criminals. Good for you, boy." Flash looked at Scooter and wagged his tail.

Webb leaned close and looked into Gabby's empty, brown eyes. Very slowly, he held up one finger, several inches in front of her eyes, moving it slowly from side to side. "Can you see this, Gabby?" No response. Webb stroked her beneath the chin. "Can you feel that?" Nothing. Then, he gently lifted her front leg and moved the paw back and forth. "Does that hurt?" He placed her leg down and moved his hand lightly, as if her fur were precious china, down her side, pausing on the protruding rib cage. He bowed his head. Scooter was unable hear his words, but he guessed this dog lover was saying a prayer.

Webb released a deep sigh. "Where are these two individuals, Scooter? It's time I introduced myself and Razor to them. Razor, come."

Scooter felt a rush of satisfaction race up his spine. "Follow me, Larry. I thought it only fair to hold them in the same closet they locked Gabby in. Hope I haven't broken some obscure law."

"Don't know of any."

They entered the bedroom behind Razor, his ears perked and nose twitching. Scooter stepped forward and put his hand on the metal knob. "Get ready for a horrible smell, Larry. They had Gabby tied up and lying in her poop and pee." He fought to keep from smiling, but failed. "And you'll soon see the man isn't housebroken."

Larry chuckled. "Don't worry. Where he's headed, they'll break him in right quick." He placed his hand on his pistol. "Okay."

Scooter opened the door and stepped back. As rays of morning sunshine invaded the closet's darkness, Scooter saw the man and woman remained stretched out on the floor, side by side. Both quickly turned their heads to shield the brightness. "Sergeant Webb, these are the two heartless rats who broke into two cottages, stole my dog, and abused her...all to extort money from me, and threatened to kill her if I didn't comply."

Webb shook his head and stared down at the culprits. "Sure looks like these two have experienced the fast-acting kind of karma. To obtain money, they steal a dog, lock her in a closet, and allow her to lie in her bodily functions. On top of that, they don't feed her or provide her adequate water, and they probably don't see anything wrong with their behavior." He looked down at Razor and back to the cowering criminals. He leaned toward the bound criminals and yelled, "Because to them...it was only a stupid dog!" Webb straightened up. "Well, thanks to this brave young man, you're both about to harvest a load of what you've planted." Webb chuckled. "And the good news is...your harvest will be long-lasting." Webb backed up a couple of steps and wiped his hand across his reddening face. "If it were up to me, your jail cell would have no toilet, but that probably wouldn't bother Mr. Stinky. And you'd only get enough stale bread and dirty water to stay alive...for many, many years." Webb turned, lost his sarcastic smile, and took a deep breath. In a surprising move, he kicked the door shut. "Let's go fill out the official report, Scooter, and then I'll call the wagon to haul this ignorant riff-raff away from decent animals and people and lock them up with their own kind. And I'll get pictures of this room to help our prosecutor put them away for a long time." He stormed from the room with Razor leading the way. Scooter followed, pleased with Larry's idea of punishment for animal abusers.

Webb and Scooter entered the den where Gabby was still motionless. Little Flash remained beside his companion. Larry said, "Scooter, I've trained and been around dogs for most of my life. In my opinion, Gabby's suffering from a light form of shock. This is not the first time I've seen a dog that's experienced a trauma of this type." He leaned over and stroked Flash's back. "Nature allows an animal to 'drop out'. In other words, Gabby realized her predicament was very bad. She was being mistreated, physically and emotionally, and separated from those who love and care for her. That fear was more than she could handle, so she checked out. I believe once she's back in her surroundings with you and Flash, she'll slowly return to the Gabby you know. I'm sure she can hear you, so keep talking to her." He gave Flash a scratch on the head and stood, giving Scooter a heartfelt smile.

Scooter needed to hear the positive outlook from this man who clearly knew and loved animals, and even trusted one with his life if duty put him in harm's way. "How long could it take, Larry?"

Larry placed his hand on Scooter's shoulder. "Emotionally, anywhere from a day to a week. But if she doesn't eat or drink within twelve hours, take her to your vet. Rest and the return to familiar surroundings with you and Flash will probably do wonders."

"Thank you, Larry. I'll keep a very close eye on her."

"Before I leave, I'll give you my home phone number. Feel free to call me if you have questions or need any help. I'll do whatever I can."

Scooter followed Larry and Razor back into the main room. "Where's the phone, Scooter? Before I get started on the arrest paperwork, I need to make a couple of phone calls, and one is very important. We need our top-notch prosecutor, Barb Hays, to handle this case. Talk about getting the maximum penalty for animal abusers? Barb is batting a thousand. As a successful vet, she became disgusted from treating so many abused animals; she returned to school and became an attorney. Barb usually handles our toughest cases, but her passion is getting convictions and nailing people like those two in the closet."

Scooter said, "She sounds perfect for this case. Nowadays there are too many slimy defense attorneys using loopholes to get trash set free." Scooter pointed to the kitchen counter. "There's the phone. I'll be with Flash and Gabby."

After Flash returned from visiting his math class, Scooter said, "The policeman said Gabby will be okay."

I hope so. Seeing her like this hurts.

"I understand, buddy. But at least we've got her back and can help her." He hugged the floppy-eared pup. "I want to say this so Gabby can hear it, too. I've finally found a perfect nickname for you."

Really? Flash's tail began to swish from side to side.

"Remember we said a nickname was special?"

Yeah.

"You have to earn it, right?"

Yeah.

"Well, you've certainly earned yours, Flash. From now on, your nickname will be 'Hero' because during this horrible situation, you have clearly been a brave hero." Scooter felt hot tears sting his eyes as he pulled Flash close. "You're our Hero."

Flash laid his head against Scooter's chest. *I like it, Scoot, but I didn't want to get a nickname this way. Gabby could have been hurt even worse, or...*Flash bowed his head.

"I know. Life doesn't always give us what we want. But our talented team overcomes and moves forward."

In the silence of the moment, one word was heard: *Hero.* Both of them looked down at Gabby, then back at each other. *Scooter, she said my nickname.*

Tears pooled in Scooter's eyes. "I heard her." He bowed his head and said a silent prayer. "She's slowly coming back. She heard us."

She likes my nickname.

"Yes, she does. And wait until we tell her the whole story of how you earned it."

I'll stay with her while you go talk to the nice policeman.

Scooter gave Gabby a gentle stroke on the head. To Flash, he whispered, "Thank you, Hero. Come get me if she says anything else."

I'll keep talking to her, Scoot.

"Good. She's listening."

When Scooter entered the kitchen, Larry was hanging up the phone. The desire to tell him about Gabby's one word was strong, but Scooter felt that nugget of information might cause Larry to wonder if Scooter had also bailed on reality. So instead, he said, "I think Gabby is slowly returning to us, but maybe it's just me."

Larry nodded. "Pet lovers have very unique ways of communicating with their pets. I'd put money on Gabby coming back stronger than ever." He chuckled. "But betting is against the law." The new friends laughed and exchanged a high-five.

CHAPTER 43

The small cottage on stilts had never felt more comfortable to Scooter as he plopped on the sofa beside Gabby, who remained curled up on a blanket. Sadly, she was still out of it. Flash, like a statue, sat at his feet. They had returned from the 'hostage cottage' an hour earlier, and Scooter had prepared a comfy place for Gabby, following Larry's suggestion to keep her in the midst of familiar surroundings. Her favorite aromas came from the nearby kitchen, and the small main room was the center of activity. Overwhelmed by the entire ordeal, little Flash had worked out his frustrations and worries with tiny whines and continuous pacing, but not speaking. From time to time, he would approach Gabby, sniff her snoot, and then back up and stare for several seconds. Then he would resume pacing around the room.

Scooter pulled his thoughts together and called Darla Kay to inform her about the terrifying events. He chose to leave out his not-so-nice treatment of the culprits. As Darla Kay listened, there was no denying her breaking heart; however, she was relieved Gabby was home and resting. Scooter said they should still get together the following night for New Year's Eve, explaining Larry's recommendation to get Gabby back into a familiar routine. Darla Kay agreed. "I'll see you tomorrow around six o'clock."

Flash finally settled down, and within minutes was asleep on the floor beside the sofa where Gabby rested. Scooter gently stroked his distressed pooch and whispered happy stories they had shared, hoping the memories would help her slip back into a safe reality. After an hour of blinking back tears and growing heartache from his recollection of those special times, sleep overtook Scooter.

At first Scooter thought the distant yip was from Flash. He opened his eyes and looked down and found Flash's nose inches from Gabby's muzzle, staring at her and slowly wagging his tail. Scooter asked, "Was that Gabby's yip?"

Yeah. I heard three of them. Maybe she's dreaming.

Gently, Scooter placed his hand on Gabby's shoulder and leaned over. "Baboo, we're back home now, girl. How about some cheese toast?"

That's one of her favorites.

Scooter nodded. "Maybe I'll fix a few pieces for us, and she'll get a whiff of it. Sure can't hurt. She needs to eat soon, or I'll take her to the vet. She must be hungry."

Good idea. We're all starving.

Flash remained with Gabby while Scooter prepared the cheese toast and slipped it into the oven. He brought a glass of cold water to the sofa and fingered a few drips to her nose and under her lip. "Here's some water, girl. Are you thirsty?" They waited in silence. No movement. "I'm fixing your favorite, cheese toast." Scooter took a deep breath, feeling even more helpless as he looked into her blank eyes.

The oven's buzzer signaled the toast was ready. Scooter hustled over and put the three slices on a paper plate. After it cooled enough to eat, he broke a piece off. "Here, Flash. Have a piece of my delicious cheese toast," he said, mainly for Gabby's benefit.

Flash gently took it and in no time had devoured it. *Yeah, Scoot-toot, that's good cheese toast. I want another piece.* Flash yipped twice.

"Glad you like it, Flash. Here's another big piece." After Flash took it, Scooter peeled off a sliver of melted cheese and held it close to Gabby's nose. "Here, Gabby. I know you love cheese." No reply or movement. So he touched it lightly to her nose, hoping its texture would prompt a response. "Lick your nose and you'll taste it." After thirty seconds and no reaction to words or smell, Scooter sighed and closed his eyes.

We'll try again later. She's probably real tired.

Scooter looked at the sad beagle sitting at his feet. "You're right. I'll break off a piece and leave it beside her." Scooter put a hunk on the sofa. "I'm going to take a shower. Come get me if there's any change."

I will. Flash hopped up on the sofa and cuddled close to Gabby. *Maybe she'll feel my heart beating.*

Scooter nodded. "Good idea."

The hot shower did little to relax Scooter's tense muscles. It did, however, provide a perfect place to dump his fears and tears. Scooter bowed his head beneath the pulsing water. "Please, God, bring Gabby back to us. She didn't deserve to be mistreated and deprived of food and water, and only You know what else. She's been through some bad times, but she always tries to help others, so please help her. She's one of your creations. Amen." After pulling himself together, Scooter stepped from the shower and dressed.

Entering the main room, Scooter found his pups in the same position, except now Flash's head rested on Gabby's hind quarters, and he was sound asleep. *Now that's a scene I'll never forget.*

Scooter decided that if Gabby showed no change by daybreak, he would call the vet, explain the situation, and then follow his suggestions. Scooter knew moving her to another strange location would be confusing and uncomfortable, but as Larry had said, she needed fluids to prevent dehydration. He moved in front of the glass doors and gazed into the cold, gloomy darkness. Glancing at the kitchen clock, he mumbled, "It's already five-thirty. Where has this afternoon of misery gone?"

Scooter heated up a can of chicken and rice soup, again hoping the aroma would tickle Gabby's nose. Flash got a cup of Puppy Chow, and they ate in silence, both looking back and forth from their food to Gabby. When they finished, Scooter took the bowl containing a couple of spoonfuls of soup over to the sofa and fingered several drops under Gabby's top lip. "Girl, I know you love chicken soup." After waiting for thirty seconds, and seeing no movement, he returned to the kitchen. "Flash, go tend to your business while I get my pillows and blanket. I'm sleeping out here tonight. I hate to move her; she seems comfortable."

Flash hopped up. *Okay, Scoot. I'll sleep here, too. Maybe your snoring will wake Gabby up.* The beagle yipped.

Once the lights were out and they were snuggled down, Scooter thanked Flash for his help in finding Gabby and for keeping a positive attitude.

You've always told me how tough Gabby is. She's going to get well. I feel it. 'Night, Scoot.

"You're right, partner. Sleep well, cause tomorrow's a new day, and the following day begins a brand new year. As long as you and Gabby are with me, it's going to be a great one, too." Scooter closed his eyes and gently slipped his toes under Gabby's warm body. *And what will the year be like if Gabby isn't sharing it with us?*

CHAPTER 44

Scooter woke every hour, re-situated himself on the cramped couch, and gave Gabby a gentle rub. After several minutes, he would drift away into another bout of restless slumber filled with confusing snippets of dreams.

Scooter snatched open the closet door, instantly overwhelmed by a wave of stench mixed with Gabby's eerie moans and whines. Barely able to see, Scooter blinked his eyes and spotted Gabby stretched out in huge piles of poop with silver chains around her legs. Fear and anger invaded his thoughts. "Oh, my. I'll get you out, Baboo," he cried out. He squatted down and reached out, but was unable, for some unknown reason, to reach past the threshold. *Scoot?* "I'm trying to reach you, Gabby." Using every ounce of strength he possessed, Scooter again attempted to shove his hands through some invisible wall to reach his suffering pup, but he was still unable to touch her. *Scooter?* Suddenly Flash appeared beside him, wagging his tail. "Hey, partner." ***Scooter? What's the matter? Can't you hear Gabby?*** "I'm trying to get her, Flash…I can't." *Please, Scooter. Scooter?* Again, Scooter forcefully leaned into the closet, but his fingertips remained inches from Gabby's soiled fur. "Crawl toward me, Gabby." *Scooter?* Suddenly the heartbreaking scene became foggy around the edges, then slowly disappeared. "No! Gabby! Come back, girl," Scooter screamed.

The sunshine-filled summer day was one Scooter had never experienced. It was perfect in every way. Scooter watched Gabby riding huge, crystal clear waves all the way up onto soft, shimmering golden sand. He waved. "Good one, girl!" *Look, Scooter. Look at me!* "I see you, showoff." Scooter blinked his eyes and looked to his right. Flash was paddling over another swell at least ten feet high. "Be careful, Flash. You've never been out that far." ***Scooter! Look at Gabby.*** "I know…I see her." *Scooter? I'm thirsty.* ***Scooter…please stop snoring and listen.*** "Keep paddling, Flash. The waves will bring you in." ***Wake up, Scoot!*** All of a sudden, a dark cloud shielded the brilliant sun, turning the beach into a moonless night. Scooter yelled, "Come in, pooches! It's dark! We gotta go to the cottage!" ***We're in the cottage, Scoot.***

Scooter found himself falling and flailing his arms as a piercing scream emerged from his pounding chest. His eyes opened wide, fueled with fear. His head sprung up from the damp pillow to find Flash inches from his face. ***Scooter...Gabby's awake!***

Bolting his sweaty, trembling body to an upright position, Scooter blinked his sleep-filled eyes and reached toward Gabby. When his fingers touched her soft fur, he mumbled, "Is she awake, Flash?"

Scooter, I'm thirsty.

See, Gabby's awake. She's thirsty and hungry, Scoot. Flash barked twice.

Scooter reached over and turned on the lamp. After a couple of blinding seconds, his eyes adjusted. He moved up beside Gabby, inches from her face, and saw her blinking her eyes. *It's bright in here, Scooter.* Tears of joy streamed down Scooter's cheeks as he hugged Gabby with one arm and Flash with the other. "She's back with us, Flash. God heard my prayer." Gabby's ice-cold nose nuzzled Scooter's neck. *I'm back.*

Scooter hopped up. "Let me get you some water, Baboo. I'm so excited you're awake, my head is spinning." He stumbled into the kitchen and filled a bowl with water. Glancing at the wall clock, he was stunned to see it was two o'clock in the morning. "Wow, I thought I was dreaming when I heard you and Flash calling my name." He returned with her water and held the bowl as she slowly lapped for the next twenty seconds.

Gabby ate the cheese toast, too.

For the first time in two days, Scooter released a loud belly-laugh. "Yeah, our Gabby is back! And we're as happy as frogs on a lily pad!"

The toast was cold, Scoot.

"Thank you for pointing that out, Gabby."

We knew you'd come back to us, Gabby. You're a tough pooch.

Scooter took a deep breath and absorbed the joyful scene. He realized Gabby was not back a hundred percent because she missed several excellent chances to zing him with one of her typical snappy comebacks. He decided to keep conversation slow and simple until she was fully re-oriented. The pressing task at hand was to get Puppy Chow and fresh water into her system. For the final day of the year, their agenda would consist of her recuperation. Scooter took a deep breath and whispered, "We all need to regroup and recharge."

Scoot?

"Yeah, Baboo?"

Can I have some Puppy Chow?

Scooter laid his head on her flank and whispered, "You sure can." He chuckled. "You requesting Puppy Chow is a first. You must really be hungry."

I'm starving.

Me, too, Scoot.

Scooter stood. "This beach writer will be pleased and honored to serve his two wonderful canines. I'm very thankful to have you both with me." He swallowed the growing lump and headed into the kitchen.

Sometimes Scoot can be so sweet, Flash.

Yeah. I like living here with you both. And I'm glad you're back, Baboo.

Hey, you called me Baboo.

Do you mind?

Heck no! In fact, somewhere in the back of my mind, I remember saying the word 'hero'. What was that about?

Flash remained quiet. Scooter picked up their bowls of Puppy Chow and set one down on the couch in front of Gabby and the other on the floor beside Flash. "I'll tell you, Gabby. Remember when Flash came here and I told him about my nickname for you?"

In between chewing her food, Gabby mumbled, *Yeah.*

"Well, we said nicknames should be earned, right?"

Right.

"Well, I never figured Flash would earn his nickname by helping me get you out of a dangerous situation, but little Flash performed like a true hero. If not for him, I'm not sure what would've happened. Your rescue certainly would not have gone as quickly or as smoothly. So I vote that his nickname is now 'Hero'. What'cha think, Baboo?"

Gabby swallowed, thinking about what had happened to her over the past couple of days, and looked down at Flash. *Flash, you are a hero. And for more reasons than finding me. Remember, you helped Scooter catch the muggers.* She reached a paw out and tapped Flash's head. *Hero. Yeah, I like it; it rolls off my tongue nicely. Hero. Flash is our Hero.*

I'm glad to have a nickname, but I only did what I had to do. I don't feel like a hero.

"Okay, Hero, we agree you are one, and that's the name of that tune."

Right. Gabby finished her half-cup of food and licked up more water. *Scoot?*

"Yes, ma'am?"

Will you help me go down to math class, please?

Scooter nodded. "I'd be honored to escort you both downstairs. And when you return, we'll hit the sack. It's still early, and we all need a big dose of good sleep."

As the happy trio moved slowly toward the sliding door, Gabby said to Flash, *I think Scooter would make a good servant. We could get used to that, right?*

Flash yipped twice.

While Scooter waited for his pooches, he looked over to the ocean. "Life's real good…again."

CHAPTER 45

The final day of 1995 began with an orange sherbet sunrise popping from the glassy Atlantic. Positive vibes filled the trio's small cottage. As Scooter enjoyed a steaming mug of coffee, he prepared a bowl of Puppy Chow for each hungry pup and delivered them into the bedroom. "Wake up, sleepyheads. Your breakfast is served. How're you feeling this morning, Gabby?" Scooter asked.

Gabby looked up. *Wow, you really did serve us breakfast in the room. Thank you. I'm feeling better than ever, Scooter, except for the day you adopted me from the shelter.* She resumed lapping the cool water.

Scooter welcomed the smile forming on his face. "I promised I would on a special occasion, and I can't think of a better occasion. So, how are you, Flash?"

The little beagle scratched his floppy ear with a hind paw. ***I agree with Gabby. I'm fine because we're all together again, and none of us was hurt. And my best day ever was when you and Gabby found me. Thank you for breakfast.***

Their heartfelt remarks told Scooter that what might seem a loving and kind thing to do for the caring people who adopted unwanted and abused pets was so much more to the recipients. "And I agree with both of you." Scooter held his mug high. "Cheers!"

What are we going to do today?

Scooter took a sip of his coffee. "Something brand new and long overdue."

Both pups moved in front of Scooter, their tails wagging. *Is it fun?*

"I think so. It will make you feel and smell real good."

Flash yipped. ***Not another bath in tomato juice.***

Scooter chuckled. "No. But you're right about the bath part. Let's go." Scooter clapped his hands and headed for the bedroom. When both pups followed without a comment, Scooter was totally surprised. He ran warm water into the tub and asked who wanted to be first.

How about Flash? I'm so glad to be back, I didn't want to mention it, but he stinks. I don't think the tomato juice worked.

I don't, either. When I curl up tight, I can smell the nasty odor on me. Yeah, I'll go first.

Gabby raised her front paw. *Scoot, would you please put clean water in the tub after Flash's bath?*

Scooter shut off the water and nodded. "Good idea, Baboo. The little wipe-down I gave you when you were found didn't do much. We certainly wouldn't want to add skunk stench to your fragrance, would we?"

No, we wouldn't. I'm not sure which smell is worse. Now, get on with this little treat.

One hour later, the bath session was complete. Scooter hugged two clean-smelling pups. "Now, you fragrant little furry ones, go take a nap while I shower. Afterwards, I need to make a few phone calls."

Gabby led the way into the main room, telling Flash she had a funny story about one of the movie scenes she was in. *You'll enjoy it. And it might help when they film you.*

Scooter placed the receiver down and leaned back in the chair. "Well, everything's still on schedule for our book-signing tour that begins in Florida on the fourth of January. And if Gabby feels up to it, she flies back to California on the third. Then, Flash and I will fly out there on the twenty-third for Flash's scenes." He clapped his hands and called them over. "The best news...after the final filming, we all fly back here together."

Both pups yipped twice. *Scooter, the movie stuff's been fun, and I've learned a lot, but I'll be so happy to be back here enjoying 'our' beach and entertaining the special children. I've sure missed being with you both.*

And I've had fun times on our book tour, but Gabby's right. We have more fun when we're all together.

Scooter hugged them tight. "I think you're both reading my mind. You're saying everything I'm thinking."

That's why we make a good team, Scoot-toot.

Bingo, little Hero.

"Now, I'm going to call Larry, the nice policeman, and give him the good news about Gabby being back with us and feeling better. Why don't you go do your math, and then we'll relax and listen to stories from our movie star." Scooter stepped over and opened the sliding door, receiving a face full of chilly breeze as the pooches filed out. "Hurry back."

Scooter detailed Gabby's return, and Larry was thrilled. "Scooter, that's great! What you should do now is give her a pressure rub. In other words, have her lie down and run your hands over her. Gently work her leg joints and see if she jerks or yips. If so, she's either sore or maybe has a slight sprain. You said she's walking normally and acting okay, but she might be favoring a sore spot. If you don't notice anything, and she's eating and having regular bowel movements, I'd say she's fine."

"Thank you, Larry. Your expertise has been an immense help. And I also appreciate your calm head during the investigation. It sure made everything easier on me."

"You're more than welcome, Scooter. If I'm down Sandbridge, don't be alarmed if Razor and I stop in for a quick visit."

"Our door is always open to the both of you."

"Oh, I almost forgot. Our skilled prosecutor, Barb Hays, got the case and had a sit-down with those two low-lifes. After she carefully detailed all of the charges they faced and the severe penalties she would demand from the court, both weasels pled guilty. So, no trial. And they will spend three to four years in jail. They both had records, and the man was on probation for three B&E convictions. They will also spend five years on probation, along with three-hundred hours of community service cleaning cages and runs at the area SPCAs and the Norfolk Animal Care Center in Norfolk."

"Whoopee! Serves them right. You tell Barb we all say 'thank you' for taking this heartless crime seriously."

"I'll do that, Scooter. I've got to run. Give the pooches a treat and a hug from us. See you soon."

Scooter was hanging up the phone when Gabby barked. He hopped up and opened the door. After giving them the good news about the dognappers, they both received a treat. "Time to relax. We're entertaining Darla Kay for supper tonight."

They both yipped and curled up on the rug. Scooter knelt beside Gabby and started the inspection suggested by Larry. *What are you doing?*

"Making sure you don't have any sprains or pains. We don't want to miss something with your physical health. You can't return to California expected to perform if you're not a hundred percent."

Well, hurry up. I feel just fine, Dr. Scooter.

Once the rubdown was complete, Scooter announced that Gabby was sound and showing no signs of injury. Gabby's reply was she could have told him that without him pressing on her and moving her legs around like pipe cleaners.

Like you said, Scoot, Gabby is one tough pooch.

"That she is. And so are you, dude."

Scooter stretched out on the sofa and released a satisfying sigh. One of his favorite songs by the Temptations came to mind. The words clearly described the trio's growing excitement for the upcoming months. He sang, "Like a snowball rolling down the side of a snow-covered hill…it's growing and growing."

Scoot, stick to putting words on paper…not singing them.

Scooter chuckled. "We're going to have a great year!"
I like your singing, Scooter.
"Thank you, Hero."

CHAPTER 46

-January 23, 1996-

Early Tuesday morning, beneath a cloud-filled sky, Scooter and Flash climbed the steps to the fancy Gulfstream 5 and were welcomed by Captain Brian Blow and Lt. Jim Wilson. "We fly many happy folks, but you two rate at the top," said Brian, shaking Scooter's hand. Jim followed suit and added, "Good to see you both again."

Flash yipped as Scooter replied, "We've been looking forward to going back to California and getting this movie finished. It's nice to have our good friends flying this beautiful plane again. And thank you for taking care of Gabby on her solo flights. She's made me proud."

"I'd say she's done well getting used to flying," said Wilson. "Still doesn't eat much, but she gets plenty of sleep."

Captain Blow said, "We've got a tailwind today, so we'll make good time. Let's get into the air, shall we?"

"We're ready, buddy." Scooter and Flash entered the top-of-the-line decorated galley and settled on the comfortable leather sofa. "You ready to go see Gabby?" Flash nuzzled Scooter's arm and softly yipped. "So am I," said Scooter.

California sunshine maintained temperatures at a pleasant sixty-eight degrees as they stepped from the plane at Bob Hope Airport. "Another super flight, gentlemen," said Scooter, shaking hands with the kind pilots.

"Our pleasure, Scooter and Flash," said Blow. "We're scheduled to take you three back to the beach when your duties are finished."

"It'll be good to have you all together," added Wilson.

"Prepare to see a happy Gabby. She's been a mite homesick," replied Scooter. The men waved as man and pooch disappeared into the shiny black limo.

After checking into their original room at the Annabelle Hotel, Scooter showered and changed into shorts, a Polo shirt, and flip-flops. He called Jan to let her know they were in town. He asked if she received the tape of the TV show.

"Yes! Thank you for sending it. I had copies sent out to other stations. Oh, and everyone is really excited to see you and Flash. Your limo should be out front in thirty minutes to bring you here. Then we'll go to the coast where they're filming. Our weather has been perfect for the past three weeks, and we're on schedule. See you in a little while."

Scooter hung up and relayed the good news to Flash while he filled his bowl with Puppy Chow. "I don't know about you, pal, but I'm ready to see Gabby and watch how a real movie is made."

I'm ready to see Gabby, but I'm nervous about being in the movie.

"After everything we've been through, Flash, running and playing in the water will be as natural for you as sleeping. And, don't forget, you know how to surf, making you one talented water bug."

Yeah. I'd forgotten that.

"Whatever Mr. Zurl asks of you, give it your best, and I'll be mighty proud."

Okay. I feel better now.

Their limo parked in a reserved slot near the Santa Monica Pier. The driver opened the rear door. "We're here, guys. Enjoy this beautiful day."

Scooter stood on tip-toes and looked over to the barricaded area on the coast, stunned to see so many people zipping around with cameras, props, and other equipment. In the midst of the humans, Scooter spotted his black pooch sitting calmly beside Vennie and Bobbi. "There's our Gabby." Flash jumped up and down, yipping. Scooter picked him up and held him high. "See her?" Flash's tail whipped from side to side.

"Let's worm our way through the on-lookers and get inside the set, Scooter," said Jan, leading the way.

"We're right behind you."

As they neared the set, Scooter spotted Kevin Costner and Meg Ryan talking with a group of children. Some were in wheelchairs with balloon tires, while others stood, aided by aluminum crutches. Costner lifted a red kite, took off running, and let out string, sending the kite high into the cloudless sky. The children whooped and cheered. "Wow! It's like they've watched Darla Kay and me at Sandbridge," Scooter said.

Jan giggled. "That's the idea." She flashed her laminated ID card to a guard, and he unhooked the chain and stepped back as they entered. "Now, we need to be quiet until Wayne hollers 'cut'. They're filming a scene, and with this breeze, we wouldn't want our voices to interfere," she whispered. Scooter nodded.

They slipped up beside Gabby and her talented friends. Gabby looked at them and set her tail into motion, but remained quiet. Flash rubbed noses with her and plopped on his haunches. Scooter stood in awe, taking in the action. Suddenly, Zurl shouted 'Cut'." The actors and children automatically stopped what they were doing. "This is amazing, Jan."

Everyone greeted each other, and Scooter knelt beside Gabby and gave her a hug. "You're sure looking sharp, Baboo." Gabby yipped and placed her front paws on Scooter's leg. "I hope we get to see you acting."

Vennie said, "Next scene, Scooter." She pulled a brush from a hip pocket and started on Gabby's back. "She's been an excellent actress and a pleasure to share my home with. You're one lucky man."

"Yes, I am. And I'm glad you two got along. Knowing Gabby was with you eased my mind."

Wayne walked up wearing a dapper Australian straw hat, shorts, and a Mickey Mouse T-shirt. "Good to see you again, Scooter. I'm pleased you will get to see us shoot some scenes."

"I'm already overwhelmed to see the actors doing exactly what we do. It's eerie watching your own actions performed by others. I'm sure when Gabby and Flash do their thing, it will certainly blow my mind."

Wayne laughed. "Acting!" He leaned down and greeted Flash. "Hey, little buddy. We're going to shoot your scenes today, too." Flash yipped.

Bobbi said, "Come on, Gabby. We've got to go prepare for the next scene." She and Vennie led Gabby down to the water's edge. Scooter was amazed at how professional Gabby's actions were. *She's really into acting.*

"Scooter, let's walk down and talk to Kevin and Meg. I'd like them to meet Flash, since they'll be in his first two scenes," said Wayne.

Scooter nodded slowly, as if stuck in the middle of a dream. "Okay, Wayne."

The three walked up as Kevin and Meg sipped ice water and discussed something in actor lingo, which zoomed right over Scooter's head. Since Scooter had met Kevin at the dinner, Wayne introduced Scooter to the very cute Meg first. *Wow! No wonder Darla Kay was impressed with Disney's selection to play her.* "It's nice to meet you, Meg."

"Same here. You have one super puppy, Scooter. Gabby's a real treat to work with."

Kevin smiled. "That she is." He tugged at his colorful, Hawaiian-print surf baggies. "Something you'd wear?"

"Yeah, I like them. And I caught a glimpse of the last scene, and you have me and Darla Kay nailed to a 'T'."

Simultaneously, Meg and Kevin replied, "Thank you."

Kevin added, "Being good copycats is why they pay us the big bucks."

Wayne glanced at his gold Rolex, then pointed to Flash sitting at Scooter's feet. "This is Flash. He'll be in a couple of scenes with you two. I want him to just be himself and entertain the children."

Meg and Kevin knelt and greeted the little beagle.

Wayne loudly announced to everyone that they would begin shooting in five minutes. The actors and crew refocused as quickly as switching a TV channel. They stood and picked up their scripts, and the set crew began moving into position. Scooter smiled as he recalled hearing Paul and Ruthie first mention submitting a script to Disney. Now, here it was, being filmed. *I'm still dreaming.*

Scooter asked Wayne, "You mind if I walk down and check out the water for a minute?"

"No. Help yourself, but I must warn you, it's a mite chilly."

At the water's edge, Scooter kicked off his flip-flops and gazed across the blue Pacific. He casually stepped into the white water, instantly receiving a bolt of cold up his legs. "Gee, it's freezing," he moaned, quickly tip-toeing back onto dry sand, hoping no one saw him. "And Gabby's been going in, and today Flash will also enter this ice bath. Bless their little 'acting' hearts," he said, relishing the warmth of the sand.

Jan used 'insider influence' to provide them with two comfortable director chairs perfectly placed for a bird's eye view of the set. As if that weren't enough, she placed a copy of the script on his lap. "Now you can follow what's happening and see what's to come."

"Thank you, Jan." Scooter quietly scanned the pages, with no idea where the next scene was. Jan noticed his confusion and reached over and flipped several pages. "Here we are now. Gabby's going to fetch a Frisbee after the little blonde-haired girl in the wheelchair tosses it into the water."

Scooter felt another chill run up his back as he heard the word 'water'. "Don't tell anyone, but I wouldn't go in that water without a wetsuit."

"I don't blame you."

"But the pooches go."

"They're better suited for it, especially Gabby, because she's part lab. It might be a bit colder for Flash, but Wayne will not leave them out for long. If they blow a scene, he brings them in and Vennie or Bobbi warms them up before another take."

Scooter looked over to where Kevin stood talking to Wayne. "Does Kevin go out?"

"Yep. But he doesn't stay long, either. Meg lucks out because she's not required to go out. The difficult thing is, Kevin has to pretend like it's a summer day at Sandbridge. That's why…"

Scooter finished her statement, "…they make the big bucks." They both laughed as Wayne called for silence. Jan whispered, "Here we go."

For the next hour, Scooter sat mesmerized while Gabby entertained the children and the 'fake' Scooter and Darla Kay. Wayne gave everyone a ten-minute break and joined Jan, Scooter, and Flash. "The next three scenes will feature Flash," said Wayne, rubbing Flash's head. "You ready to do your thing?" Flash yipped, and Wayne looked up at Scooter, wide-eyed. "It's like he understood me."

Scooter smiled. "He's a smart pooch. Oh, I wanted to tell you that he has mastered riding a surfboard."

A grin tightened Wayne's lips. "Really?"

Scooter nodded. "Yep. I draped a towel over my longboard and set him on it. When a small swell approached, I gently pushed the board, and Flash rode in standing up. He loved it."

Jumping up, Wayne said, "I'll be right back." He trotted toward Kevin as he yelled out a request for a surfboard to the prop manager.

"Looks like Flash will be riding a wave on the big screen, Scooter," said Jan. Flash yipped twice, and she giggled.

Scooter rubbed the beagle's back. "You can do it. The waves are smaller today than the ones you rode in Sandbridge. And you know how to swim, too." Flash looked up into Scooter's eyes. "Give it your best, Hero."

Several minutes passed before Bobbi approached. "Okay, Flash, it's time to do your thing." She knelt beside the excited pup. "Gabby will be in the first scene with you. All you two have to do is walk down the beach toward Kevin and Meg, just like you do at Sandbridge." She stood. "Tell Scooter to watch you perform." Flash yipped. She smiled at Scooter and Jan. "They're naturals."

"Go get 'em, Flash."

Flash slowly walked toward the water's edge with Bobbi. Jan commented, "They're going to get footage of your pups relaxing. Then they have the option to use these scenes in other segments during the film by splicing them together."

Scooter shook his head. "I never knew so much went into the production of a movie. It's amazing."

For thirty minutes Scooter watched his pups stroll the coastline, run, and splash in the water for the children, making each one feel special. Then Vennie and Gabby walked up. Scooter stood and motioned for Vennie to sit in his chair. "Wayne's going to have Flash ride a wave. The children will go bonkers cheering for him." She gave Scooter a smile. "You're proud aren't you, Scooter?"

"That's putting it mildly, Vennie. I can't believe those two are my furry friends. This must be a dream, so please don't wake me."

As Wayne announced 'Action', everyone became silent and turned toward the beach. Costner pushed a classic Dewey Weber longboard, draped with a colorful striped towel with Flash sitting proudly on it, into the icy water.

As if the ocean knew it was being filmed, a glassy knee-high swell humped and rolled toward the shore. Kevin leaned toward Flash and said something, then focused on the swell. At precisely the correct moment, Kevin gently shoved the board and stepped back. The wave picked it and Flash up. Just like the brave beagle performed at Sandbridge, Flash balanced on all four paws and looked toward the beach. With his ears floating from the off-shore breeze, he rode straight in, as easy as walking. Kevin clapped and trotted through the icy water to congratulate Flash.

Scooter and the group watched the filming of several more scenes, some in the water and others on the warm coast with the children. Wayne called 'cut' for lunch. Vennie motioned to Flash, and Scooter's little surfing partner wormed his way through the crowd and joined the group, including a very proud Gabby. They nuzzled each other and yipped once.

Scooter and the pooches followed Vennie, Bobbi, and Jan up on the boardwalk to a hotdog stand. While they relaxed and enjoyed lunch at a table in the sunshine, Jan explained the shoot would resume back at the studio in an exact replica of Scooter's cottage. "The pictures you sent us were perfect, Scooter. You're going to be very surprised what our skilled people can do."

"I couldn't be any more surprised than I've already been. This entire production blows my mind."

Vennie laughed. "One night, we finished a long, trying shoot. It was late, so Gabby and I spent the night on the bed in the stage bedroom. Without having to be told, she hopped up on the foot of the bed, executed her three-turn spin, plopped down, and was asleep in less than thirty seconds."

Scooter shook his head. "Now that doesn't surprise me, Vennie. When she's not on the beach or eating, she loves to sleep." Gabby yipped.

The cottage's interior and exterior shoot went smoothly. Scooter sat in a chair, feeling like a peeping Tom, and observed the movements, dialogues, and goings-on in the perfect, life-like duplicate of his cottage. *These movie people miss nothing.*

At three o'clock, Wayne adjourned everyone for the day and called it a wrap. While gaffers and crew shut down cameras, lights, and mikes, Scooter congratulated Gabby and Flash. "You both are real pros. I'm a proud dude." Scooter looked up at Wayne. "What's scheduled for tomorrow?"

"Tom and I will spend the rest of today viewing all of the scenes featuring the pups. If there are no scenes that need to be re-shot, your talented canines are finished. Tomorrow morning, we'll meet with you and Jan at my office to discuss our remaining production schedule, and then I'd like your input concerning the premiere in Virginia Beach. If all goes as I expect, we'll be on the big screen by the middle of May." He shook Scooter's hand. "I must say, this has been one of the smoothest, most trouble-free movies I've ever directed. A lot of the credit goes to Gabby, and, of course, little Flash. Both of them are naturals, in my professional opinion. You should be proud, friend."

"I am, Wayne. And from the little I've seen of this entire endeavor, you and your team are the ultimate professionals."

Wayne nodded. "It takes all of us to pull off a first-class movie. Thank you." They shook hands, and Wayne took off to start the critical screening process.

Jan returned from calling the limo for their pick-up. "Scooter, depending on Wayne's needs after viewing the scenes, I'll schedule your flight for early tomorrow afternoon." She looked at both pooches. "I'm sure the three of you are ready to return to Sandbridge. Remember, waiting for the premiere is the hardest part."

Scooter shook her hand, as well as Vennie's and Bobbi's. "After we relax for a week, we've got plenty of things to keep us busy. But tonight, I'm going to treat my pooches to a nice supper in our room, and then we'll all have a good night's sleep. Do you know what time the meeting will be in the morning?"

"Ten o'clock."

"Sounds good. I really appreciate your superb hospitality and assistance, and especially the care and love you showed Gabby. You have made what could have been a nightmare away from home a pleasurable experience that we'll never forget." Scooter smiled and bowed to the ladies. "You all have an open invitation to visit us at Sandbridge anytime."

Jan giggled. "You sound like this is the last time you'll see the three of us."

Scooter looked at each of them curiously. "What are you saying? Are you planning a trip to the beach?"

Bobbie and Vennie nodded. Jan said, "You really didn't think you and these cuddly canines would attend the premiere all alone, did you?"

Scooter looked at the pups. "Did you hear that? The girls are coming to view the movie in Virginia Beach with us!" Both pooches yipped twice and put their tails into high gear. Scooter smiled from ear to ear. "You have made our day. I was wondering how we could get you to 'our' beach. That's great news!"

The limo pulled up. "See you in the morning, Jan. Thank you for everything."

CHAPTER 47

-May-

The days after they departed California passed quickly, like the waves rolling onto shore. Scooter's sequel to 'If Bullfrogs Had Wings' was nearing one-third completion of its first draft and unfolding to be even better than its predecessor. Flash and Gabby spent their 'agenda-free' days relaxing and running the coast. Gabby was back with her normal snappy personality, appearing to have left her dog-napping experience behind. With the premiere only two weeks away, Scooter had them planning their own guest list, which proved entertaining whenever he eavesdropped, but it revealed their compassionate hearts.

After closing the document titled 'Out of the Rough' Scooter joined his pooches on the deck, enjoying the warm evening. "I know you both are happy because summer has arrived at Sandbridge."

The water's warmed up, too, Scooter. I've decided to let you teach me how to surf.

Scooter settled into his favorite beach chair. "Well, I'd be honored, Gabby."

Flash said the towel would keep me from slipping off.

Scooter nodded and leaned back, locking his fingers behind his head. "This is going to be a fantastic summer. We have friends coming to Sandbridge for vacation, so we'll invite them over for cookouts and spend some time with them on the coast."

Who's coming to see us?

"Well, Gloria, Terry, Mikael, and Matt from Pennsylvania." Scooter looked at Flash. "Maybe they'll bring you a pet skunk." Gabby yipped.

I never want to see another skunk.

Gabby nudged Flash with her nose. *Or smell one, either! Okay, who else?*

"The veterinarian and his family from Salisbury, Maryland, who treated Flash comes here every year for a vacation. I gave him my phone number the day we picked Flash up."

I remember him! He was real nice to me.

So do I.

"Let's see." Scooter scratched his head. "Oh, yeah. Jason, Rebecca, and little Kay from New York."

Oh, goodie! Gabby jumped to her feet and danced around. *Little Kay's coming to see us and meet Flash. Now I'm really excited.*

"And Jan, Vennie, and Bobbi are coming to the premiere. I invited them to stay a couple of days with us, but they have to fly back the next morning. Maybe one day they'll come here for a vacation."

Gabby settled down beside Scooter's chair. *Aw, I wish they could stay with us. They were fun to hang out with.*

Is that everybody, Scoot?

"I think so. But it will be fun to see them again and return their kindness. Right?"

Right. That's what we always said we'd do, Scooter. We want to help those less fortunate and show our friends...what do you call it? I forgot.

"Hospitality."

Yeah, that's it.

Scooter leaned forward and smiled. "And don't forget, tomorrow morning Darla Kay brings the first group of children down to kick off the new season."

The pups yipped twice.

"Oh, this group is the same one that was our final group last fall. You remember? Little Emmy was scared of dogs until she met Flash, and, in no time, she was petting you both and throwing the Frisbee for you to fetch. And there was little Sammy who learned how to surf. His parents came and brought ice cream. All of the other children will also attend."

I remember. Emmy is my friend.

That's when Darla Kay lost her bracelet and Flash turned down a delicious piece of grilled chicken and stayed out all night to find it.

Scooter nodded.

I ate the chicken for breakfast, Gabby.

And you didn't save any for me.

Scooter stood and glanced at his watch. "How about we have grilled chicken tonight?"

The pups hopped to their feet and yipped.

"Okay. I'll give you Puppy Chow first and then share my chicken with you."

I'm real hungry, Scoot.

So am I.

"I know. That's why you're having doggie food first. I'd hate to hear my special pooches' stomachs rumbling tonight while we sleep." Scooter chuckled and headed inside.

Flash, the way he snores, he couldn't hear a train coming through the room.

The little beagle yipped and followed Scooter inside.

While the pups were eating, Scooter prepared the chicken breast with Italian dressing and salt and pepper, then fired up the grill. "When you're finished, go on down and tend to business."

Yeah, that'll make more room for your delicious chicken.

"Always thinking how to get plenty of good stuff, aren't you?"

When Flash was almost finished, he looked over at Gabby and saw her closely watching Scooter's preparations in the kitchen. ***I'm going to walk down the beach a little farther before doing my math. Okay, Scoot?***

"Sure. Don't go far."

I won't. The beagle waited until neither of them was watching and quickly filled his mouth with the remaining nuggets. Satisfied with his mouthful of food, he turned and hurried out the open sliding door in silence. Gabby followed.

Beside the cottage, Gabby trotted over the sand dune into a clump of sea oats. Flash hustled about halfway down toward the water and then broke into a sprint to his right.

Scooter flipped the chicken breast and closed the grill. When Gabby returned and plopped on the deck, she found Scooter relaxing in his chair. "I think little Flash is getting in shape for swimming and surfing. For the last week, he's been taking a walk every morning and evening after he eats."

I don't have a clue what he's doing. I get my exercise playing on the beach.

"Well, it won't hurt him, and I'm happy he feels comfortable strolling down there."

I'll bet he's sniffing out wild animals.

"Now's the time to do it. In a few weeks, tourists will be here, and the beach will be crowded."

Fifteen minutes later, a winded Flash bounded up the stairs. He quickly stretched out in front of Scooter.

I like tourists. They always make over me.

"I know about you and the tourists, Baboo. You love showing off and being pampered."

Remember the first day I came to Sandbridge? I ran down the beach and everyone came over and greeted me.

"I remember. But I also told you not to go snooping around their blankets. Not everybody takes kindly to strange dogs. So you both remember that this year."

I will.

So will I, Scoot. Now, when will my chicken be ready? I'm hungry.

Scooter chuckled. "Why am I not surprised? It will only be a few more minutes. Hey, Flash, how was your walk?"

Fine. I walked some and ran some. It's good exercise. The beagle turned, faced the ocean, and sighed.

After they enjoyed a tummy-filling supper, they turned in for a restful sleep in preparation for the following day on the beach with Darla Kay and the children.

Dawn arrived escorted by a light shower, but by eight o'clock, the clouds had vanished over the horizon, allowing an early summer sun to warm the day. Scooter filled the pups' bowls with Puppy Chow while his cheese toast broiled in the oven. "Today's the big day, gang! The children come visit the beach."

Gabby quickly devoured her breakfast and plopped down, waiting for Flash. After five minutes she said, *I've been waiting for this day, Scooter. Now I'm out of here. It'll be lunchtime before Mr. Slowpoke finishes. I want to be ready for the children.*

Without commenting, Flash continued his regimented eating technique, watching Scooter out of the corner of his eye. When Scooter disappeared into his bedroom, Flash quickly filled his mouth with the remaining nuggets and pranced out the sliding door.

At ten o'clock, the yellow van rolled into the driveway. Darla Kay tooted the horn. Scooter set up the last beach chairs and ran to greet his visitors. Gabby and Flash stood beside Darla Kay, wagging their tails in anticipation of the children that would spill from the van. Scooter greeted Darla Kay with a gentle hug and shook hands with her assistants. "Welcome to Sandbridge, you bunch of beach bums." The van failed to contain the childrens' loud claps and cheers.

Once everyone was settled on the coastline, Scooter made his way around, speaking to all of the children. Flash steadily retrieved the red Frisbee tossed into the water by Emmy. She exploded with giggles each time the beagle gently placed the plastic disc on her leg. "Thank you, Flash. I've missed you this winter." Flash yipped. Emmy fired off another toss. When Flash returned, dripping with salt water, the little girl said, "I told my parents about how you made my fear of dogs go away. I asked if we could get a puppy, but they said our yard wasn't big enough, and it wouldn't be fair to keep a doggie in a small yard. But they said I could have a kitten. I'm so excited, Flash. In the next couple of weeks, we're going to the shelter to adopt one." She reached down and rubbed Flash's head. "And guess what? I want a girl kitten. I'm going to name her Princess, because I'll treat her like one." Flash swished his tail from side to side. He softly yipped three times as he recalled his deceased sister.

Scooter assisted Sammy and his foam surfboard into the water. Within five minutes, the boy was standing and riding waves. His classmates encouraged him with enthusiasm. "Mr. Scooter, I think surfing is the coolest," the little guy said, waiting for the next swell.

"Sure is. And you have great balance, too. I've now entered you into my surfing Hall of Fame."

The boy's eyes widened as he smiled broadly. "Wow! I'm so glad you taught me how to surf. I couldn't wait to come back."

"We've been looking forward to seeing all of you again. Okay, one more wave before lunch, big guy. And here it comes. Show me how it's done."

Sammy lay down, paddled, and waited until the wave picked him up. Slowly, but confidently, he struggled onto his feet and rode in like a pro. As he came to a stop in the shallow water, he raised his hands. "Cowabunga, dudes!"

Scooter and Sammy gathered the board and readied to walk up to the beach camp for Scooter's famous PB&J sandwiches, Sammy whispered, "Mr. Scooter, I hate to tell you this, but I won't be back any more this summer." The boy dropped his head and swished a foot in the white water.

Scooter stopped and put the board down on the damp sand. "Why, Sammy?"

"I need an operation on my back. The doctor said it will ease my pain, but I'll have to stay in the bed for three months."

Sammy's reply hit Scooter like an 18-wheeler. He placed an arm around the boy's shoulders and felt him trembling in a brave attempt to hold back tears. "I'm sorry to hear that. But if surgery will help, it's best to get it over with now." Scooter gently turned the boy around to face the ocean while swallowing the lump in his own throat. "This much I do know, Sammy. You see those waves?"

"Yes, sir."

"They will still be here when you come back. We'll get the board out, and you'll be riding again in no time." He squeezed the boy's shoulder. "Surfing is like riding a bike...you never forget."

Sammy looked up into Scooter's moist eyes. "I'll remember that, Mr. Scooter. I've had lots of surgeries, and I hate having to stay in the bed. There's nothing much to do."

Scooter took a deep breath, trying to picture what that would be like. His response came quick, and directly from his heart. "Do you like to read?"

"Yes, sir."

"Great. I have a proposition for you, Sammy. You up for it?"

"About reading?"

With everything Scooter's novel had accomplished, he suddenly realized there might be something else it could achieve. Just maybe it could help a young fellow feel worthwhile in the midst of difficult circumstances and possibly lead him down a path that would benefit his future. If nothing else, Sammy would realize Scooter had confidence in his abilities, no matter what he was facing physically. "Yeah, you could say it involves reading, but more." Scooter knelt in the sand, and Sammy did likewise. Scooter shared a few stories about his writing career, its ups and downs, and, of course, its challenges. "When it comes to overcoming adversity, Sammy, you're miles ahead of me. But, honestly, I could use your help."

The boy raked his fingers through the wet sand and looked at Scooter. "You need my help? On what?"

"Well, since my first novel is about two boys a couple of years older than you, I'd like you to read my novel and tell me what you think. Good or bad, I want the truth from your viewpoint. Please do not tell me 'it's good' just because we're surf buddies. That's not what I need to hear."

"So, if I don't like it…you want me to tell you that?"

Scooter nodded. "Exactly."

"Why? Wouldn't that make you feel bad?"

A small smile tightened Scooter's lips. "Yeah, it probably would, but it would also help me become a better writer."

Sammy shrugged his shoulders and nodded.

"But, along with that, I want your suggestions on the new novel I'm just now starting. See, this one is called a sequel, which means the story and characters follow my first one. It's set two years later than the first, and the two main characters are dealing with a different set of circumstances and new obstacles in growing up and making decisions."

Sammy nodded. "I've heard my mother talking about sequels to novels she reads."

"Good. If you would be willing to read my first novel to get an idea of the story and my writing style, then whenever I complete several chapters of the sequel, I'll have Miss Williams get them to you. As you read them, I would appreciate comments and suggestions from your point of view as a young person." Scooter smiled. "At any time, if you get sick of my story, you can quit. We'll still be friends. Remember, not every reader enjoys every book."

As the information Scooter delivered sunk in, Sammy smiled. "Wow! Yes, I'd like to do that. So, I'll read your first one, and then help you on the second one, right?"

Scooter extended his hand, and they shook. "You are correct, partner. And I'm serious about you telling me exactly what you think. So you'll help me?"

"You bet I will!"

Two happy and encouraged guys returned to the group. Scooter and Sammy handed out the sandwiches, chips, and cups of lemonade. Darla Kay assisted the children and couldn't miss the smile etched on Scooter's face. She slipped up beside him. "You're in a fine mood today. I'd say you and the pups are glad to kick off the summer with us."

Scooter took her hand and looked into her eyes. "I'd say you're right. And I have realized that, just when you think you're doing all you can for those who need it, another opportunity arises."

"I'm not sure exactly what you're talking about, but my guess is it has something to do with the children or at least one of them."

Scooter looked at her with puzzled eyes.

Darla Kay smiled. "Because I feel it." She sipped her lemonade. "And that confirms you have the gift."

Scooter turned, faced the ocean, and ran his fingers through wind-blown hair. "I don't know what it's called, dear, but I'm thankful to have it."

After lunch, the cheerful but pooped children gladly received their new T-shirts and thanked Scooter, Gabby, and Flash with hugs, high-fives, and applause. As they all made the trek back to the van, Scooter absorbed the sights and sounds, locking them into his collection of priceless memories. When they reached the cottage, he went upstairs and grabbed a copy of 'If Bullfrogs Had Wings' from a large box. As he signed it for Sammy, tears filled his eyes. He put down the pen and whispered a prayer for Sammy, his family, and a successful surgery. Standing to leave, he glanced back to the box of his novels. "If my story could entertain or maybe even encourage one young person to have a go at writing, then from today on, all of our special needs children will not only receive a trip to 'beach camp' and a T-shirt, but also a copy of my novel." He swiped a couple of tears from his cheeks, sat down, and signed a book for each child and their dedicated teachers.

Scooter handed out copies of his heartwarming story of two teenage best friends in West Virginia overcoming the trials of growing up. The smiles he received from every person filled him with the most rewarding feeling he had ever experienced. In silence, Gabby and Flash looked on. When the final book was passed out, both pooches yipped. The crowd cheered, loaded into the van, and pulled out with waves coming from every window.

Scooter knelt beside his two furry friends. "You both helped make today very special. We do make a great team."

I enjoyed doing the movie, Scoot. But having fun with the children is better.

Flash placed his head on Scooter's chest. *I agree with Gabby. Miss Celie said one day I would make people happy. I didn't understand then, but today little Emmy said I helped her to not be afraid of dogs.* He looked up at Scooter. *All I did was be nice to her last year.*

Scooter took a deep breath of salt air and thought about Sammy and the other children. "I think that's all we have to do. Maybe, at times, people try too hard. Kindness is better received when it comes naturally."

This is going to be a funtastic summer, Scoot-toot.

"Where did you come up with that word, Baboo?"

Gabby sat up. *Heard it on the set one day and thought it was neat.*

Scooter stood and brushed sand from his knees. "After I bring up our stuff, let's relax a while and then take a stroll. For supper we're having steak and baked potatoes. Is that okay with my pooches?"

Gabby bounced like a rubber ball and yipped.

Flash wagged his tail and barked.

"I'll take your replies as a 'yes'." As Scooter walked down to load up his cart, he whistled a happy tune. *Life is a story and every day we write a page.*

CHAPTER 48

The Sandbridge trio relaxed on the sofa early on Friday morning, watching Kaycee McCoy's TV show Sunshine & Rainbows. Her final segment was dedicated to announcing the premiere of Disney's movie 'Gabby...All About Me'. "You saw these two talented pups, Gabby and Flash, on this program last year. Now you can see them on the big screen tomorrow night at Strawbridge Regal Movie Theatre. That's right! This delightful movie is recommended for all ages, especially if you like dogs, children, and the beach...and who doesn't?" Kaycee giggled. "According to my sources, if you are there by seven thirty, you'll see the pups and Scooter in person when they arrive. Also, two well-known actors who star in the movie will be on hand." The attractive host shot the camera her natural smile and leaned forward. "Can you say Kevin Costner and Meg Ryan?" Kaycee leaned back and clapped her hands. "I look forward to seeing all of you tomorrow night. Have a great day, and keep smilin'..." Kaycee waved as the screen switched to the colorful logo, and the instrumental 'It's A Beautiful Morning' played.

Scooter cheered and stroked his pups' heads. "Well, I don't know about you, but I'm excited."

I'm nervous, Scooter.

I'm not. No, sirree! We're going to have a great time.

"You'll be fine, Flash. All of your friends will be there."

Yeah! All of our friends from California, and most of our children and their parents and teachers are coming. Oh, and Miss Darla Kay, too. Gabby looked at Scooter. *I see you grinning, Scoot-toot. I told you way back she had a crush on you.*

And the policeman who helped us with you, Gabby, he's coming. He was friendly, and I liked his partner, Corporal Razor.

"Yes, Flash. His name's Larry Webb, but he said he couldn't bring Razor. Don't worry, they'll stop by one day this summer to visit us. Now, let's get serious for a minute."

Gabby looked at Flash. *Uh-oh, here come the rules for tomorrow night, Flash.*

Scooter shook his head. "No rules. You both know how to behave in public...and remain silent. Anyway, I want you to know that I'm very, very proud of you. When we were working on the guest list for the premiere, the first people you wanted to invite was our children and their parents. That only confirmed to me just how compassionate you both are." Scooter took a deep breath. "I'm sure each child was thrilled when their teachers informed them of the invitation. The night will not only be exciting for us, but for them, too."

Scooter, you remember we decided a long time ago to share and help others, right?

Scooter nodded.

I've heard the children talking to each other down here, and a lot of them say they don't have many fun things to do, you know, because of their health problems. So, we include them in our happy times, because that's sharing.

Gabby's heartfelt words touched Scooter's heart. "I couldn't have said it any better, Gabby. You know when we share, we all have a better time." He swiped a tear from his cheek. "My best two days on this earth were when I met each of you."

Flash sat up. **Scooter, I have a question.**

Scooter cleared his throat. "Okay, little buddy."

Well, if you'll give me permission, I can do something to help someone.

"That's great. Sure, I'd never stop you from helping others. What do you want to do?"

The little beagle looked at Gabby and then back to Scooter. **Can I show you? It's easier.**

Scooter's curiosity was piqued. It had taken Flash a while to fit in with the two of them because of his shy personality. Now he was comfortable with who he was, his unique personality was blooming daily, and his heart was packed with bravery and compassion. "Help yourself."

I'll be back in a few minutes. You and Gabby wait here.

"Take your time. We'll be here when you return."

Flash threw his tail into swish mode, turned, and trotted on stubby legs toward the open sliding door. *I'll be right back!*

Where's he going, Scoot?

Standing, Scooter said, "You've got me, girl. I need a glass of ice water. I'm sure whatever it is, it will be interesting."

He has been acting a little strange for the past week, Scooter. Have you noticed?

"Not really. You're the one with the knack for picking up those things."

Gabby joined Scooter in the kitchen. *Yeah. I guess it's another of my many talents.*

Scooter drained the water. "I won't argue with that."

Before Gabby had time to put together one of her snappy comebacks, they heard Flash's steps on the deck stairs. *Here he comes.*

Flash and a scraggly-looking black kitten with four white paws slowly entered the cottage. Scooter and Gabby's eyes opened wide, and their mouths quickly followed suit. Flash settled on the tile floor and the kitten sat and leaned against him, looking from Gabby to Scooter with beautiful golden eyes.

She's been living alone under a cottage, Scooter. I've been feeding her with some of my food. Her name's going to be Princess, like my sister.

Gabby eased down to her stomach and slowly moved toward the trembling kitten. *Hey, little one. I'm Gabby.*

"She's precious, Flash," whispered Scooter. "I'll bet you smelled her, right?"

Yeah. She needs a bath, Scoot.

"She wasn't scared of you, you know, because you're a dog?"

I did what Gabby did for me and brought her food, cause she was real hungry. After a while we became friends. And today Emmy said her parents would let her have a kitten, and she was going to name it Princess. Flash nudged the little black ball of fur. *And I hoped we could take Princess tomorrow night and give her to Emmy. That way, we're helping both Emmy and Princess. Right, Scooter?*

"You are something, Flash. Yes, we'll do that and help them both," Scooter said, as his eyes blurred again. He knelt down beside the cute kitten. "Welcome, Princess. It's nice to meet you, sweetie."

The golden-eyed kitten slowly stared at each of them for several seconds, and then her tiny tail began to wag. Scooter held his breath, but the next sound heard in the small beach cottage was a crisp, clear 'Meow'.

Scooter smiled larger than a Sandbridge sunrise. Gabby quietly yipped. Flash did likewise. Scooter whispered, "Never thought a simple 'meow' would sound so sweet."

FROM THE AUTHOR

Thank you for sharing your time to read my story. I hope you've enjoyed Flash and Gabby's adventures and actions. Of course, Scooter always has a great time with them.

If you are so inclined, I would certainly appreciate a review on Amazon from you. If not, I'm still smilin'…and say thank you!

Check out my other novels and short story compilations on my website: **LeeCarey-author.com**

MYSTERY/CRIME

'The Thin Line'

'Dawn's Death'

'Justice in Hollowell County'

YOUNG ADULT/BABY BOOMER

'If Bullfrogs Had Wings'

'Out of the Rough'

PET NOVELS

'Gabby…All About Me'

'Flash…the Humble Hero'

'Pets in Paradise'

SHORT STORY COMPILATIONS

'Beach Shorts'

'If You Dance…You Will Pay the Fiddler'

Keep smilin'…

Made in the USA
Charleston, SC
02 July 2013